LAUGHING IN A FOREIGN LANGUAGE

Published on the occasion of the exhibition
Laughing in a Foreign Language, The Hayward,
London, UK, 25 January – 13 April 2008

Exhibition curated by Mami Kataoka
Exhibition organised by Mami Kataoka
and Charu Vallabhbhai

Art Publisher: Caroline Wetherilt
Publishing Co-ordinator: Charlotte Troy
and Giselle Osborne
Sales Manager: Deborah Power
Additional editorial assistance by Helen Luckett
Translators: Alfred Birnbaum, Robin Thompson
Catalogue and typeface design by A2/SW/HK
Printed in the UK by BAS Printers

Cover: Julian Rosefeldt, *Clown*, 2005
(cat. 63, production stills, details)

Published by Hayward Publishing,
Southbank Centre, Belvedere Road,
London, SE1 8XX, UK,
www.southbankcentre.co.uk

ISBN 978 1 85332 266 2

Distributed in North America, Central
America and South America through D.A.P. /
Distributed Art Publishers, 155 Sixth Avenue,
2nd Floor, New York, N.Y. 10013,
tel: +212 627 1999, fax: +212 627 9484,
www.artbook.com.

Distributed outside North and South America
by Cornerhouse Publications,
70 Oxford Street, Manchester M1 5NH,
tel. +44 (0)161 200 1503; fax. +44 (0)161 200 1504,
www.cornerhouse.org/books

LAUGHING IN A FOREIGN LANGUAGE

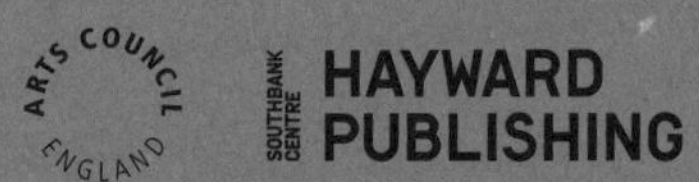

CONTENTS

6 / PREFACE
RALPH RUGOFF

9 / LAUGHING IN A FOREIGN LANGUAGE
MAMI KATAOKA

17 / LAUGHING AT FOREIGNERS: A PECULIAR DEFENCE OF ETHNIC HUMOUR
SIMON CRITCHLEY

25 / ARTISTS
HELEN LUCKETT

145 / LIST OF WORKS

150 / LIST OF COMPARATIVE ILLUSTRATIONS

PREFACE

RALPH RUGOFF

Contemporary art is getting funnier. Far from being a trivial matter, this suggests a significant change in the cultural landscape. Wit has always had a place in the history of art, of course, but primarily through caricature and visual punning and playfulness. 'Serious' artists, though, traditionally dealt with 'serious' subjects. But as *Laughing in a Foreign Language* reveals, an increasing number of artists from across the globe are making humour a crucial and indispensable part of their work.

Humour's expanding role in contemporary art is a result of many factors, but perhaps above all it represents a kind of allergic reaction to the legacies of modernism. In contrast to the heroic rhetoric of modern art, much contemporary work reflects a general attitude of scepticism. Many artists today share a pervasive doubt about all forms of authority as well as our most cherished myths and beliefs, including our preconceptions about art and artists. In the hands of these artists, humour can be a means of deflating and puncturing our self-importance. At the same time they have upended our notions of what makes art 'serious' – or, to put it another way, what makes it merit our close attention.

Laughing in a Foreign Language, both this catalogue and the accompanying exhibition, surveys a broad range of art from around the world. Set within a contemporary context of globalisation, much of this art examines the follies, failures and incongruities that arise from acts of mistranslation and cross-cultural misunderstanding. Some of it is intended to make us laugh. Almost all of it, however, aims to make us think about laughter and its role in an era of global communication. It prompts us to re-examine what we find funny and why, to speculate on the degree to which humour is culturally specific and, on the other hand, the extent to which it can help us to understand the unfamiliar. At the same time, it raises similar questions about the nature of art as well.

With its global sweep and fresh insights into the culture of our times, *Laughing in a Foreign Language* epitomises The Hayward's commitment to presenting lively international art that probes and reflects upon the way we live now. Organised with great wit and intelligence by Mami Kataoka, The Hayward's International Curator, *Laughing in a Foreign Language* reminds us that humour's revelatory shocks can be applied to subjects like globalisation and cultural difference in ways that enhance, rather than diminish, our sense of their complexity. This terrain is explored both in this book's lead essay by Mami, and in the witty and insightful text by Simon Critchley and in texts on each of the artists by The Hayward's Exhibitions Interpretation Manager, Helen Luckett.

This exhibition would not have been possible without the generosity of the participating artists and lenders. We are also grateful for the support provided by the Finnish Institute London, the Japan Foundation, the Austrian-Cultural Forum London, and the Daiwa Anglo-Japanese Foundation. In addition, we are thankful for the assistance provided by the many galleries associated with the participating artists.

Numerous people at The Hayward and Southbank Centre have contributed in substantial ways to *Laughing in a Foreign Language*. While there are too many names to mention here, I would like to single out Assistant Exhibition Organiser Charu Vallabhbhai, who played a key role in all aspects of this project, and Operations Manager Ruth Pelopida, whose team ably oversaw the exhibition's complex installation.

RALPH RUGOFF
Director, The Hayward

LAUGHING IN A FOREIGN LANGUAGE

MAMI KATAOKA

As Charlie Chaplin is said to have remarked, 'Life is a tragedy when seen in close-up, but a comedy in long-shot.' Humour, in other words, depends on maintaining a certain distance. Our laughter emerges in the rifts that appear when one steps back from a situation or person, and the amount that we laugh is often a result of how far-removed we feel from the object of our humour.

The sense of removal intrinsic to comedy can be grounded in a subjective attitude towards the world, but it can also derive from exploring subjects that are unfamiliar. Confronted by a foreign culture, we may feel left out or alienated but at the same time we gain the distanced viewpoint that is so crucial to humour. As a Japanese curator working in London, I have had the opportunity to experience on a daily basis the cultural gaps that can make 'foreigners' look askance at their surroundings or to see them from a skewed perspective. At the same time, I have also witnessed the difficulties of translating humour from one culture to another, as much of what we find funny is linked to the shared history and memory of our given community or language group. Yet like many of the artists in *Laughing in a Foreign Language*, I have often found freedom and respite in humorous situations that, although sometimes hard to translate, can often be shared across the barriers of cultural difference.

My own experience in London, of course, is widely mirrored in today's globalised world where the diverse and the disparate meet head-to-head at a previously inconceivable pace. The artists in *Laughing in a Foreign Language*, who hail from around 20 different nations, delve into this territory of absurdities and contradictions. Often from the vantage point of marginal figures, they create works that expose the humour – sometimes dark, sometimes absurd – in the slips and misses that arise when one culture, language or set of customs is translated, transposed or even misplaced into another environment. In their work, the vocabulary of contemporary art becomes a means of transgressing the boundaries between foreign and native tongues, the self and the other, and the known and the unknown. The results are frequently funny in the traditional sense, but they are also often strange and poignant, revealing fundamental human truths and raising unsettling issues relating to identity, stereotyping, prejudice, immigration and enduring socio-economic divisions.

CLOSE ENCOUNTERS

The anxiety that comes with finding yourself in a new environment where you cannot speak the language is multifaceted. Beyond the frustration of not being able to communicate verbally, it is also fuelled by one's unfamiliarity with the locale, its social codes and mores, its unspoken rules and collective memories. These are all invisible factors that provoke a sense of alienation and of being cast adrift. One way of dealing with this isolating experience, however, is to make a clean break from egocentrism and laugh at oneself. Many of the artists in *Laughing in a Foreign Language* do just this, often using semi-autobiographical material to expose the humour and ridiculousness of their situations, but at the same time revealing the more serious side of their alienation and marginality.

Japanese artist Makoto Aida, for instance, vented his frustration at not speaking English in a photo-documented march he staged around Washington Square with fellow resident foreigners when he lived in New York in 2000. Carrying placards with the words 'Your pronunciation is wrong' and 'Don't speak fluently', Aida wasn't so much making a statement against the global primacy of the English language as absurdly transmuting his own inferiority complex towards English speakers into a cathartic outburst of laughter.

Similarly, Danish artist Peter Land presents photo works showing himself timidly standing on street corners in New York and Chicago holding suitcases with messages exposing and poking fun at his vulnerability as a foreigner. In New York, he is seen toting a suitcase inscribed 'Hi I'm new around here, so please don't rob me, mug me or kill me. Could you please direct me to a cheap hotel?'; and, in Chicago, the message on his suitcase declares, 'Hello – I don't speak your language very well, so please when you talk to me speak slowly and clearly and please don't use any slang, Thank You.' Land states that he attempts to put himself, 'in situations within the work where I'm removing myself from my socially provided feeling or idea of dignity, I try to negate my own identity to a degree where a revised or renewed self-perception may arrive.'[1] Land takes on an objective stance and another's viewpoint in order to try 'to reflect some basic conditions of my own existence and perhaps to fill some sort of apparent meaning into the meaningless.'[2]

Odd props also figure in Taiyo Kimura's *Typical Japanese-English* (2005) – the title coming from a snide comment the Japanese artist was dealt while residing in Germany. In this work, the viewer peers down through the collar of a shirt in a laundry basket to witness a strange sequence of gags screened on a tiny monitor, all metaphorically summing-up the embarrassment, feelings of inadequacy and surreal daily mishaps Kimura experienced abroad. In *Black Hole* (1995–2005), a teddy bear is buried under multiple headphones playing some 20 different radio stations, simulating the incessant babel of foreign languages – an idea that came to him in a dream.

English, in its capacity as a global language, can link people with different mother tongues and give them a way of communicating. However, as a result, the world has become very centred on the English language – an effect that puts non-English speakers at a disadvantage. But this relationship between majority and minority languages is sometimes inverted – for instance, when English speakers find themselves in an environment where their language is not dominant. The work of South African artist Candice Breitz plays on this inversion. She made a list of the 150 Japanese words she knew when visiting Japan for the first time in 2002 – a lexicon largely limited to electronics brands, pop culture icons, world-famous Japanese foods and other superficial images of Japan familiar to non-Japanese everywhere. She then asked five people in the guise of Japanese stereotypes, such as 'Japanese businessman' and 'kimono-clad lady', to use this fixed vocabulary and engage in puzzling impromptu conversations. The resulting video, *Aiwa To Zen*, makes no sense in Japanese, but bubbles with ridiculous ironies. While depicting a certain position within the international worlds of industry and economy, it reveals the shallowness and ignorance present within clichéd representations of other cultures.

EXAGGERATED STEREOTYPES, CLICHÉS AND IMITATION

Humour does not, of course, depend solely upon language; typically, in the case of shared social backgrounds, memories and histories, the laughs play off stereotypes. Many of the artists in *Laughing in a Foreign Language* explore the use of exaggerated and overused stereotypes and clichés in their work, straying far from reality into the realm of the ridiculous. As discussed, Candice Breitz's work *Aiwa To Zen* delves into this territory of exaggerated stereotypes. So too does the work of Kalup Linzy, with his depiction, soap opera-style, of a typical black American family in *Conversations wit de Churen* (2005–06). In Kutlug Ataman's video *Turkish Delight* (2006), the Turkish artist performs a belly dance that plays on a stereotypical image of his country. Other artists intentionally remove or displace stereotypes and clichés to create a conversation or situation so strained and pointless that the result is inevitably laughable.

Here, distances can be variously conceptualised as buffer areas or grey zones between the cultural, social or political majority centre and minority fringes. The post-colonialist theoretician Homi K. Bhabha discusses colonialist mimicry as it relates to cultural stereotypes and their periphery. He points out that acts of imitation occur in the form of the impulse to follow the centre and the resistance put up by colonialised minorities to the centres of culture and domination. But such acts of imitation possess a certain ambivalence as mimicry that is almost, but not exactly, the same.

Chinese-born, European-raised Jun Yang addresses complex identity issues in his semi-biographical video *Camouflage – LOOK like them – TALK like them* (2002/03). This video traces Yang's coaching of an illegal Chinese immigrant friend on how to act and look like a Westerner so as to pass in post-September 11 society where newspaper headlines warn 'All Citizens Under General Suspicion'. In the pictographic work *X-Guide* (2004), which acts as a pendant to *Camouflage*, basic instructions on how to act in Western society are presented visually in public service announcement format, accompanied by captions such as 'Don't be too noisy', 'Don't wear headscarf in public' and so on. Behind the humorous images and text, however, we get a keen sense of unspoken political-economic disparities.

Expanding on the situation of 'All Citizens Under General Suspicion', Barthélémy Toguo, a frequent traveller between Europe from Cameroon, lends an even more sobering note of reality to behavioural guidelines and dress codes. In his *Transit* series (1996–99), he uses photos of sculptural or symbolic objects together with anecdotal texts to present a journalistic account of his interrogations at various passport control checkpoints. In *Transit 1*, he tells the story of a set of solid wooden suitcases and the trouble that ensues when they cannot be opened by airport security.

Through humour and irony, several artists address the serious problems faced by immigrants living in the gaps created by globalisation and in the 'intermediate zones' between national borders. South Korean artist Gimhongsok, for instance, places life-size figures dressed in animal suits in a gallery space, on a plinth inscribed with the message: 'Here is the Sierra family from Mexico, performing in costumes from the Bremen Town Musicians. They currently reside in Korea and work in a shoes manufacturing factory as labourers. Despite their immigrant status as illegal aliens in Korea, they will be paid five dollars per day for being hired for this art exhibition eight hours a day.' While the text clearly sets forth the gap between the silly looking characters and a very real social issue, the veracity of the story is left unclear. At the same time, the faces and forms of the people supposedly present inside the animal suits are concealed – a masking device that heightens the sense of ambivalence and universality of the immigrants' plight.

Iranian-born artist Ghazel, who now resides in France, based her ongoing series of works *Wanted* on her first-hand experience of receiving a deportation order from the French authorities in 1997. In the first of these poster works, made in 1997, Ghazel identifies herself as a 30-ish Middle Eastern female artist without residency papers seeking a legal European resident husband. In later versions, having been granted a limited residency permit, she offers to marry an illegal male so that he can obtain residency. The absurdity of thinking of people solely in terms of their legal identity is suggested by the way in which the woman searches for a marriage partner with her face concealed under a chador.

A series of video clips entitled *Hip Hop* by Chinese artist Cao Fei also gives us an interesting insight into the idea of mimicry. In *Hip Hop: Guangzhou* (2003), ordinary citizens dance hip hop on the streets of Canton. Hip hop attained worldwide popularity in the 1990s, but here one old woman still dressed in a Cultural Revolution-era 'Mao suit' performs something that looks distinctly more like *tai chi chuan*.

THE CLOWN'S TWO FACES: THE AMBIVALENCE OF LAUGHTER

While clowns are symbolic embodiments of humour, they are also avatars of melancholy, an ambivalence that has made them a favourite motif for artists ranging from Pablo Picasso, Georges Rouault and Marc Chagall to Bruce Nauman and Cindy Sherman – not a few of whom have crafted clowning metaphors in their works. This ambivalence is very close to the multi-faceted approach to ambiguity in respect of other cultures that I have been discussing and to the dark undercurrents of self-deprecatory laughter. The clown motifs in the work of Julian Rosefeldt and Ugo Rondinone and the clown-like characters set within a social context as seen in the work of artists such as Azorro, Roi Vaara and Kutlug Ataman need to be viewed in this light.

By concealing their human faces, clowns become symbols for duality, for laughter and melancholy. In this way, they recall the masked characters of the sixteenth and seventeenth century *Commedia dell'arte* plays. Masks themselves are also used to conceal the essence and truth of things, but their physical presence stimulates more interest in the person who lies beneath. As we have seen, mask-like elements are evident in the animal suits present in the work of Gimhongsok and in the efforts in Ghazel's work to find a marriage partner based exclusively on legal identity.

German artist Julian Rosefeldt's *Clown* (2005) is a three-screen video work in which the circus entertainer wanders aimlessly in the Brazilian jungle. The French philosopher Henri Bergson, writing on the meaning of comedy in *Laughter: An Essay on the Meaning of the Comic* (1910), states that 'comic meaning [is] obtained when an absurd idea is inserted into some well-established phrasing.'[3] The humour in this work derives precisely from this absurdity, with the clown oddly out of context. Far from any show-business audience, the clown must trudge on and on in silence.

Ugo Rondinone from Switzerland has also created numerous video works and installations on clown themes.[4] In *ZERO* (2006), we see a worn-out pair of clown shoes strung from an oversized nail on the wall, hinting that the clown has 'hung up' his entertainer self to pursue other options. In the British curator David Thorpe's appraisal, 'Rondinone shares this somewhat bleak humour with his Swiss predecessors, artists Roman Signer and Fischli and Weiss. It is a humour that cannot really be described as funny, owing more to the tragic-comic than farce, and closer to Samuel Beckett's Lucky [in *Waiting for Godot*] or Bruce Nauman's clowns.'[5]

Kutlug Ataman, who plays a belly dancer in his video work *Turkish Delight*, calls into question not only the stereotypical notion of Turkish culture but also the idea of the artist as entertainer. Ataman states, 'I have long tried to establish that the Orientalist vision actually does exist in every culture, including Turkey, and I have jokingly asserted in the past that a lot of similar notions held in Turkey are Occidentalist. The deeper problem here is the question of the other.'[6] Even his comic struggles as a bare-bellied middle aged man trying to dance to music are calculated to create a distance in a humorous way, 'so that the assigned role is a restriction on me because of the sheer fact that I cannot really perform the role that is cast on me as an artist.'[7]

The street performances of Finnish artist Roi Vaara are more self-referential. They often show the artist in an unexpected context, dressed and behaving in an unusual manner – his performances recalling those of clowns or pantomime artists. By removing his performances from the museum or gallery context, his actions question the position of contemporary art in society. In his video work *Artist's Dilemma* (1997), Vaara lingers at a signpost on a frozen lake 50 kilometres from Helsinki puzzling which way to go, towards *Art* or towards *Life*. The stark contrast between the artist's dinner jacket and the icy expanse underscores the impossible gravity of the black-and-white dichotomy, as if to echo Bergson's dictum on the equivocal nature of the comic: 'It belongs neither altogether to art nor altogether to life.'[8] The absurdity of the artist in this intermediate setting, dressed appropriately for a formal function but hardly for sub-zero temperatures, is reminiscent of Rosefeldt's *Clown* – both have been transposed from their usual environment into isolating and confusing foreign territory.

Economic and industrial matters affecting art are such that people involved in the arts all over the world have the same behavioural patterns, and it is this effect of globalisation that serves as a ready target for the group of Polish artists known as Azorro. By examining the stereotypical behaviour of people in the art world from a seemingly objective and ironic stance, they play with the notion that people in the art world might appear as clowns or fools to the general public. In their work *We Like It A Lot* (2001), the artists emerge from a Warsaw gallery and start describing their impressions ('I like it a lot', etc) without ever referring to any specific work. *Portrait with a Curator* (2002) is the title of a work in which the artists sycophantically include opportunistic shots of curators and critics in the camera frame.

Jake and Dinos Chapman's *Dinos and Jake's Progress* (2007) is based on William Hogarth's celebrated eighteenth-century work *A Rake's Progress*. Laughter here results from a critical, satirical humour in which the Chapmans overthrow fixed attitudes and ideas as well as existing systems such as that of the art world itself. The work resonates with a spiritual rapport to the Hogarth work that spans the centuries. Hogarth's original *Rake's Progress* is a series that depicts the fall into ignominy of a prodigal son who squanders his father's legacy.

By drawing on top of this celebrated work and 'reworking and improving' it – creating 'masks' for the original characters – the Chapmans take an ironic view of the value of art, including the hubbub of the art market. The images seem to superimpose the present onto images of the eighteenth century, when life was similarly dominated by material riches. The faces of the characters drawn by Hogarth have been replaced by the faces of snowmen, animals and ogres, and perhaps reinforce the essence of these characters wallowing in greed and desire.

THE UNKNOWN AND THE UNKNOWABLE

The word 'foreign' covers a wide range of meanings from merely 'uncommon' to mysteries and concepts transcending human understanding. Curiosity is the human impulse to bridge the gap between the known and the 'foreign'. But when excessive curiosity gets the better of someone, their errant attempts to reach or understand the unknown can become grounds for humour and laughter.

Attempts to understand the 'foreign' when it relates to the animal kingdom can be fraught with even more absurdity and futility, as Finnish artist Janne Lehtinen attests to in his photographs. In his *Sacred Bird* series (1998–2004), Lehtinen photodocuments repeated low-tech attempts to achieve the dream of flight that has eluded mankind since ancient times, and which is illustrated in the Greek myth of Icarus. Yet the gap between his studious endeavour and the pathetic futility of the results is nothing less than hilarious. Likewise with UK artist Marcus Coates – who, as a pelt-girded shaman in *Journey to the Lower World* (2004), channels animal spirits to communicate with the unseen world to resolve community issues – the gap between earnest intensity and the dubiousness of the whole enterprise can only elicit uncomprehending laughter.

Israeli artist Guy Ben-Ner often transforms ordinary objects into something amazing through his striking handicraft skills. The process is shown in the form of video, in which the artist often enlists family members as performers. In *Wild Boy* (2004), for instance, he constructs a jungle in one room of their flat in which his 'savage' son is discovered then gradually taught human speech and behaviour via a storyline rich in gestures and visual language.

Japanese artist Shimabuku has frequently used non-human perspectives to shed new light on the commonplace world. In the series *Born as a Box* (2001–08), common everyday cardboard boxes are given sound system 'personalities' that proceed to tell their life story – 'I am happy to be born as a box' – in Italian, Japanese and Chinese. Austrian artist Martin Walde brings curiosity and scientific method to bear upon ordinary phenomena to create mystifying situations, often with interactive elements to spur viewer curiosity. In his ongoing project *The Key Spirit* (1997–2008), he scatters hundreds of ordinary house keys on the floor as if daring us to see which will open the door on a meowing cat. While wondering about the cat, we never know which key is the right one and where the door leads. And even if we find the right key, the story will continue.

Walde's psychological curiosity game directs us towards Danish-born London-based artists Nina Jan Beier and Marie Jan Lund's work. They examine behavioural patterns and psychology within the customary structures of society. In their *Play Me series* (2006–07), they give groups of people a set of perplexing instructions – 'Hide behind the trees', 'Stay underneath the surface', etc – then video the entire process to its conclusion.

TEXT, STORY AND VISUAL ABSURDITY

As we have seen, many of the works in *Laughing in a Foreign Language*, such as those by Makoto Aida, Ghazel and Peter Land, combine words and images. However, some of the artists go a step further – using text and narrative in a visual way to enhance the humour of their work. Needless to say, the more we seek to understand these works through words alone the less likely we are to 'laugh in a foreign language'.

Bulgarian artist Nedko Solakov's works are largely textual, touching upon everything from fairy tales to history and politics, though always undercut with critical insights. Solakov works directly on walls and sometimes on classical floral-printed wallpaper, his texts infiltrating everywhere, from the galleries of an exhibition space to the toilets, luring the viewer into his own private cosmos. His absurd use of architectural space can be seen by visitors in the site-specific text works he's produced for The Hayward exhibition, which can be found in unexpected locations around the gallery's staircase area.

While Solakov's handwriting has its own allure, British artist David Shrigley's freehand texts also have their own distinctive quirkiness and charm. They become part of his drawings together with hand-drawn images. Black humour is often evident, but the atmosphere of the clear, halting drawings created simply with a black pen has the effect of alleviating the trenchancy of the text. Shrigley employs a wide range of media, some of which, like sculpture, are not usually accompanied by words. But there is a situational humour in these works that is shared by his drawings on paper, which are also accompanied by words, creating a narrative in the viewer's mind.

Australian artist Matthew Griffin uses cut-out slogans together with live models to make impromptu installation 'presentations'. 'The whole idea of the movie pitch is to give the least amount of information possible and let the narrative be imagined, to take something and place it in an unusual situation: "die hard on water".'[9] As he himself describes his multi-media sources of inspiration, 'Most of my work comes from daydreams and jokes.'[10] Similarly, American artist Doug Fishbone culls images, mostly off the internet, edits them together using his own unequivocally 'democratic' remix strategies, then cleverly segues them onto his own frenetically paced voice tracks. His slideshows irreverently strip images from their original contexts to crisscross boundaries of satire, taboo and politically incorrect expression with unaffected charm, reconfirming Bergson's observation that 'nothing disarms us like laughter'.[11]

Los Angeles-based artists Harry Dodge and Stanya Kahn make films; typically Dodge works the camera while Kahn improvises unforgettable running monologues. In *Can't Swallow it, Can't Spit it Out* (2006), Kahn wears a Viking helmet with a green polka dot dress and wanders about the whole day with a bloody nose and a large wedge of Swiss cheese under her arm, angrily ranting against some unseen enemy or abstract threat. 'It's basically a portrait of civilian anxiety in a time of war. We tried to capture or translate the feedback loop of grief and paralysis that people are feeling.'[12] Theirs is a curious amalgam of stand-up comedy and soap opera staged at identifiable places around Los Angeles, a conceit that heightens the immediacy and appeal of the spoken word.

German performance artist and filmmaker John Bock's video work *Palms* (2007), the first film he has produced in the United States, also explores this kind of mad counterpoint, effortlessly stringing together unrelated scenes and dialogue as if in a dream. Words play an important role, but far more striking is the sheer degree of sensory overload – mysterious settings such as the interior of the Palms bar, inexplicable actions, intricate and excessive props, highly textured materials – elements that combine with allusions to modernist art, such as the houses of Richard Neutra and Rudolf Schindler, to elevate the work to a category all its own.

Likewise, in the Swiss artist Olaf Breuning's video work *Home2* (2007), the narrator talks directly to the camera while scenes jump between Ghana, Tokyo, Papua New Guinea and Switzerland, all 'exotic' locations glossed with a childlike innocence bordering on political incorrectness that is ultimately defused by the bizarrely-costumed characters. This same exacting balance between the photography and near-freehand sculptural objects also informs his installation work.

*

Contemporary art shows us a variety of viewpoints of the world in which we find ourselves. It often expands the domain of normality and established notions and questions our awareness and range of tolerance. This expanded domain overlaps with the area created by laughter as we have been considering it. But the humour and criticism evident in contemporary artworks often have no clear tagline and are not moral or educative in nature. The meaning lies in our attitude of seeking out the truth and the process whereby we interpret weird situations appearing before our very eyes. As Dinos Chapman tells us, 'I don't see any problem with being critical. To not be able to look beyond the initial layers of things and take them apart, to see what's really there – anyone who doesn't do that is kind of half-living.'[13]

The fluidity created by laughter has the effect of slightly unravelling complexly intertwining threads of reality and thus creating a new line of development. Laughter also opens up new circuits of communication that transcend joint experience, memory, cultures and traditions. It provides us with a means for advancing further in life no matter in what situation we find ourselves. Because human life, when seen from a distance, is a mere comedy.

1 Peter Land, 'Dear reader – some notes about my work', in http://www.nicolaiwallner.com/artists/peter/peter-text.html, 2000.

2 Ibid.

3 Henri Bergson, Chapter 2, 'Le comique de situation et le comique de mot', in *Le rire: Essai sur la signification du comique*, Les Presses universitaire de France, Paris, 1900.

4 Ugo Rondinone, *Where Do We Go from Here*, 1996.

5 David Thorp, 'Artist in the Landscape', in *ugo rondinone zero built a nest in my navel*, Whitechapel Gallery, London, 2006, p. 276.

6 Kutlug Ataman, interview, *Shooting Back*, Thyssen-Bornemisza Art Contemporary, Vienna, 2007, p. 116.

7 Ibid.

8 Henri Bergson, Chapter 3, 'Le comique de caractère', op. cit.

9 Matthew Griffin, *tema celeste*, no. 105, 2004, p. 84.

10 Ibid.

11 Henri Bergson, Chapter 3, 'Le comique de caractère', op.cit.

12 Harry Dodge and Stanya Kahn, 'On making comedy in a time of war', in *Modern Painters*, November 2006, p. 83.

13 Dinos Chapman interviewed by Matt Lippiatt, in *FLUX*, November/December 2005.

LAUGHING AT FOREIGNERS: A PECULIAR DEFENCE OF ETHNIC HUMOUR

SIMON CRITCHLEY

Jokes are like tiny anthropological essays, and humour is a form of critical social anthropology. Viewing the world awry, bringing us back to the everyday by estranging us from it, humour provides an oblique phenomenology of ordinary life, an indirect description and evocation of our life in the world.[1] It gives us an alien perspective on our daily practices and routines. It lets us view the world as if we had just landed from another planet.

The comedian is the anthropologist of our humdrum everyday lives. So is the comic artist. When we cast our eyes around at the extraordinary range of works gathered together in *Laughing in a Foreign Language*, what do we see? A series of Martian images of life on earth. Multiple eruptions of the strange, the grotesque, the perplexing and the delightfully peculiar. We see the foreign in the familiar and the familiar in the foreign, and their sudden and surprising conjunction makes us laugh out loud. By inserting the strange into the ordinary or by making the ordinary strange, the artists defeat our usual expectations and momentarily change the situations in which we find ourselves.

Any study of humour, also like anthropology, requires fieldwork and detailed contextualisation, and is only as good as its examples. And what makes humour both so fascinating and tricky to think and write about is the way in which the examples continually exceed the theoretical analysis one is able to give of them – they say more in saying less. And we certainly don't require a philosophical theory of humour in order to understand what is at stake in humour.

In my view, the lesson to be drawn from anthropology is the humility of a certain cultural relativism, as a strategy aimed at combating the intolerance and racism of Western ethnocentrism. Now, is the same true of humour? Your sense of humour may not be the same as mine – let's hope it isn't for both of our sakes, as mine is extremely filthy – but does the study of humour lead us to embrace cultural relativism, that big bad bogeyman of Western culture? Can we legislate for humour like philosopher kings, coming up with general laws about what is permitted and not permitted? We will see.

With the question of relativism, arguably the most intractable dilemma of humour can be broached: the universal *versus* the particular. Most studies of humour, jokes and the comic begin by claiming that humour is universal. Apparently, there have never been cultures without laughter, although the varieties and intensities of humour vary dramatically. However, to say that humour is universal is, of course, to say almost nothing, or very little. All cultures laugh, just as all cultures have a language and most of them seem to have some sort of religious practice usually involving a belief in a hidden metaphysical reality and an afterlife.

So what? The fact that all cultures laugh might be a formal universal truth, of the same order as admitting that all human beings eat, sleep and breathe, but it tells us nothing at the level of a concrete context, and that is where matters begin to get difficult, and interesting. Humour is local and a sense of humour is usually highly context-specific. How does one laugh in a foreign language? Anyone who has tried to render what they believe to be a hugely funny joke into a foreign language only to be met by polite incomprehension will have realised that humour is terribly difficult to translate, perhaps impossible (in fact, I did this with a French friend in New York last Sunday. As usual, it was a joke involving bears).

Although various forms of non-verbal humour can cross linguistic frontiers – witness the great success of the travelling comedic plays of the *Commedia dell'arte* throughout Europe in the sixteenth and seventeenth centuries and the enduring popularity of various forms of mime and silent comedy, such as Charlie Chaplin, Monsieur Hulot and Mr Bean – verbal humour is notoriously resistant to translation. The speed and brevity of wit can become tiresome and prolix in another tongue, and a joke explained is a joke killed. In 1921, Paul Valéry noted, 'Humour is untranslatable. If this was not the case, then the French would not use the word.'[2] But if Valéry is right and the French use humour because it is untranslatable, then might it not be the very untranslatability of humour that somehow compels us? Might not its attraction reside in the fact that it cannot be explained to others, and that humorous *savoir faire* always contains a certain *je ne sais quoi*?

Humour is a form of cultural insider-knowledge, and might, indeed, be said to function like a linguistic defence mechanism. Its seeming untranslatability might endow native speakers with a sense of their cultural distinctiveness or even superiority ('No one understands our jokes, because they are so stupid'). In this instance, having a common sense of humour is like sharing a secret code, often an obscene code. Indeed, is this not the experience of meeting a compatriot in an otherwise foreign environment, on vacation, at an art gallery or a public toilet or wherever, where the rapidity of one's intimacy is in proportion to both a common sense of humour and a common sense of humour's exclusivity? We wear our cultural distinctiveness like an insulation layer against the surrounding alien environment. It warms us when all else is cold and unfamiliar.

I argue in my book *On Humour* that laughter returns us to our physicality and animality. But it also returns us *to locality*, to what the Greeks would have called an *ethos*. It takes us back to the place we are from, whether that is the concreteness of a neighbourhood or the abstraction of a nation-state. The word *ethos* must here be understood in its ancient Greek sense, as both custom and place, but also as disposition and character. A sense of humour is often what connects us most strongly to a specific place and leads us to predicate certain characteristics of that place, assigning certain dispositions and customs to its inhabitants. The sweet melancholy of exile is often rooted in nostalgia for a lost sense of humour. As a voluntary exile from England, what I really miss is its humour, in particular absurd and extremely obscene humour, the effortless sense of the funny that one can share with another cultural insider.

There is a further link to be made here between *ethos* and *ethnos*, in the sense of a people, tribe, social group or, in the modern world, nation- state. In relation to humour, this is often vaguely expressed in two ways: firstly that 'foreigners' do not have a sense of humour; and, secondly, that they are funny. Such are the powerful basic ingredients of ethnic humour. Recall that George Orwell famously said that the British Empire was based on two fundamental beliefs: 'nothing ever changes', and 'foreigners are funny'. In ethnic humour, the *ethos* of a place is expressed by laughing at people who are not like us, and usually believed to be either excessively stupid or peculiarly canny or clever. The logic of ethnic humour is about the relation to the other, as either stupid or distrustfully clever.

In England, the Irish are traditionally described as stupid and the Scots as canny; in Canada, the Newfoundlanders and the Nova Scotians assume these roles; in Finland, the Karelians are deemed stupid and the Laihians clever; in India, the Sikhs and the Gujaratis occupy these places; in the US, it is Mexicans or blacks who are deemed stupid. It is unclear who Americans find funny, maybe Jews, maybe the English, maybe English Jews. The Jew is an outsider because they are seen as suspiciously canny, which is usually run together with being miserly and money-obsessed (this is also how the Scots are seen in English jokes). Either way, seen as stupid or clever, the belief is that 'they' are inferior to 'us' or at least somehow disadvantaged *because* 'they' are not like 'us'. Such is the menacing xenophobic flipside of a belief in the untranslatability and exclusivity of humour.

The facts of ethnic humour are all too well known: in the European context, with which I am more familiar, the French laugh at the Belgians, the Belgians laugh at the Dutch, and the Dutch laugh right back. The Danes laugh at the Swedes, the Swedes laugh at the Finns, and the Finns laugh right back. The Scots laugh at the English, and the English laugh at the Irish, and the Irish laugh right back. The Germans laugh at the Ostfrieslanders and everyone else laughs rather nervously at the Germans.

In relation to humour, the Germans are obviously a special case and much could be said about anti-German jokes, whose history stretches back at least 200 years; a case that was obviously not helped overmuch by the events of the last century. German humour is no laughing matter. Ted Cohen relates a splendidly objectionable joke: 'The thing about German food is that no matter how much you eat, an hour later you are hungry for power.'[3] This qualifies as what Cohen calls a 'meta-joke', where the condition for the joke is the fact that you already know the joke about Chinese food invariably leaving one hungry soon after eating. Therefore, this is not just a joke, but a joke about a joke, a sheer play upon the form of the joke. As a hypothesis, I would say that much of the fascinating visual humour in the works reproduced in this book consists of meta-jokes, of plays upon form that critically address our usual comic reactions, so that the laughter sticks in our throats.

In my view, the intimate connection between the ethnicity of humour and what we might call its 'ethicity' must be recognised and not simply sidestepped. Ethnic humour is very much what Thomas Hobbes saw as the laughter of superiority or sudden glory at our eminence and the other's stupidity. It is a curious fact that much humour, particularly when one thinks of Europe, is powerfully connected to perceived, but curiously outdated, national styles and national differences. There is something deeply anachronistic about much humour, and it refers nostalgically to a past whose place in the present is almost mythical, certainly fantastical. For good or ill, old Europe still has a robust fantasy life, but at least we are not killing each other just at the moment.

Although I have spent many happy hours thumbing its pages, it is always an open question how much etymological authority one should invest in the Oxford English Dictionary. If one consults the entry on 'humour', the OED states that the first recorded usage of the word to indicate something amusing or jocular occurred in 1682. This is obviously not to say that there was no humour prior to that date, but rather that the association of the word 'humour' with the comic and the jocular is an innovation that belongs to a specific time and place: the English language in the late seventeenth century.

Prior to the late seventeenth century, humour signified a mental disposition or temperament, as in Ben Jonson's play *Every Man in his Humour*, from 1598. The earlier meaning derived from the ancient Greek medical doctrine of the four humours or fluids that made up and regulated the body: blood, phlegm, bile and black bile *(melan-colia)*. It is this link between humour and melancholy that André Breton suggests in his notion of *humour noir*, a retrospective category a little like *film noir*. Breton coins the notion of *humour noir* in 1940[4] (a particularly *noir* moment in European history) to describe, or more properly to invent, a tradition that extends from Franz Kafka back to the eighteenth century. The first entries in Breton's *Anthology* are on Jonathan Swift and the Marquis de Sade.

Thus, the association of humour with the comic and jocular is specifically modern, and emerges in the period of the rise of the modern nation state, in particular the astonishing rise of Britain as a trading, colonising, slaving and warring nation after the establishment of constitutional monarchy in the so-called Glorious Revolution of 1689. This dating is confirmed if we turn to Shaftesbury's hugely influential treatise on humour from 1709: *Sensus communis. An essay on the freedom of wit and humour*. Shaftesbury, a pupil of John Locke, was the first theorist of humour. Shaftesbury saw humour as the expression of *sensus communis* – a shared, public sensibility or moral feeling rather than mere 'common sense'. He thought that humour was an essential ingredient in the life of a free society. In Shaftesbury's view, humour should be permitted in the discussion of religion because there can be no better test of a belief than to see if it can withstand mockery. What is perhaps not so funny is the fact that Shaftesbury was also a key figure in the establishment in the USA of colonies in the Carolinas. Together with Locke, Shaftesbury drafted the Fundamental Constitutions of the Carolinas in 1669, which was an excessively feudal and restrictive document for such champions of freedom.

The modernity of humour is something apparent in French accounts of the origin of the concept. Although the English word is originally a French borrowing, from the Anglo-Norman *humour* and the Old French *humor*, it is curious to note that French dictionaries claim that the modern sense of humour is an English borrowing. The *Dictionnaire de l'Académie Française* is quite adamant on this point. 'Humour', is a, 'Word borrowed from English. A form of irony, at once pleasant and serious, sentimental and satirical, that appears to belong particularly to the English spirit *(l'esprit anglais)*.'[5] With the dissenting voice of Voltaire, who thought that the English had stolen the notion of humour from the comedies of Pierre Corneille, French authors in the eighteenth century, and as late as Victor Hugo in 1862, refer to 'that English thing they call humour'.

One finds the same view in Denis Diderot's and Jean le Rond d'Alembert's *Encyclopédie*, in a fascinating short article that may have been written by Diderot himself, although the attribution is not certain. 'Diderot' writes:

> 'HUMOUR: The English use this word to designate an original, uncommon and singular pleasantry. Amongst the authors of that nation, no one possesses *humour*, or this original pleasantry, to a higher degree than Swift. By the force which he is able to give to his pleasantries, Swift brings about effects amongst his compatriots that one would never expect from the most serious and well-argued works, *ridiculum acri*, etc. Thus it is, in advising the English to eat little Irish children with their cauliflowers, Swift was able to hold back the English government which was otherwise ready to remove the last means of sustenance and commerce from the Irish people. This pamphlet has the title, "A Modest Proposal".'[6]

We should note the exemplary place of Swift in this French history as the '*plus haut point*' of English humour. This is something continued in Breton, who begins his anthology of *humour noir* with Swift's 'Modest Proposal'. Breton claims Swift as 'the true initiator' of *humour noir*, and as the inventor of 'ferocious and funereal pleasantry' *('la plaisanterie féroce et funèbre')*. Of course, the question of ethnicity returns once again here, for it is curious, indeed paradoxical, to define humour as something essential to *l'esprit anglais*, and then to give Swift as the highest example of English humour; Jonathan Swift was not exactly English. As Samuel Beckett replied when he was asked by an American journalist whether he was English: *'au contraire'*. The same reply might also apply to Jonathan Swift, Laurence Sterne, Oscar Wilde, James Joyce and many other Irish contraries to Englishness. But if Irishness is the contrary of Englishness, then it is important to point that it is an internal contradiction. Humour is a battlefield in the relation between what Richard Kearney rightly calls those national Siamese twins, England and Ireland, locked together in a suffocatingly close, often deathly embrace.

So, to return to my main theme, humour is what returns us to our locale, to a specific *ethos* that is often identified with a particular people possessing a shared set of customs and characteristics. A sense of humour is often what is felt to be best shared with people who are from the same place as us, and it is that aspect of social life that is perhaps the most difficult to explain to people from somewhere else. That is to say, humour puts one back in place in a way that is powerfully particular and recalcitrantly relative. This point is important because we should not, in my view, shy away from the relativistic nature of humour. When it comes to what makes us laugh, we must, as a teacher of mine put it many years ago, have the courage of our parochialism. As I have claimed, humour puts us back in place, whether the latter is our neighbourhood, region or nation.

Now it *can* do this triumphantly, and this is the basic feature of the overwhelming majority of ethnic humour. However, it *need not* put us back in place in this manner. It might equally put one back in one's place with the anxiety, difficulty and, indeed, *shame* of where one is from. Perhaps one laughs at jokes one would rather *not* laugh at. Humour can provide information about oneself that one would rather not have. It reminds one that one is a person that one would rather *not* be.

This phenomenon is probably most sharply revealed in the gap between what one found funny in the past and what one now finds funny. Episodes of *Monty Python* that had me innocently rolling on the floor in pre-pubescent mirth in the early 1970s, and which we – like so many others – laboriously tried to rehearse word-for-word during lunch breaks at school, now seem both curiously outdated, not that funny, and crammed full of rather worrying colonial and sexist assumptions. Equally, as a right-thinking leftist, I would rather not be reminded of national differences and national styles. Yet our sense of humour can often unconsciously pull us up short in front of ourselves, showing how prejudices that one would rather not hold can continue to have a grip on one's sense of who one is. There is an obscene kernel to our subjectivity that one simply denies and represses in po-faced humourlessness.

In this sense, one might say that the very relativity of humour can function as an (un)timely reminder of who one is, and the nature of what Martin Heidegger would call one's *thrownness*, of the fact that one finds oneself always cast away in a familiar and shared world. If humour returns us to our locale, then my point is that it can do this in an extremely uncomfortable way, precisely as if thrown into something I did not and would not choose. If humour tells us something about who we are, then it might remind us that we are perhaps not the people we would like to be. As such, the very relativity of humour might be said to contain an indirect appeal that this place stands in need of change, that history is, indeed, in Joyce's words, a nightmare from which we are all trying to awake. Beneath our easy laughter, it seems to me that the critical function of art is to remind us of this nightmare.

A similar point can also be made in Freudian terms. In *The Interpretation of Dreams*, Sigmund Freud makes a very perceptive remark about the relation between the comic and repression:

> 'Evidence, finally, of the increase in activity which becomes necessary when these primary modes of functioning are inhibited is to be found in the fact that we produce a *comic* effect, that is, a surplus of energy which has to be discharged in laughter, if we allow these modes of thinking to force their way through into consciousness.'[7]

The claim here is that I produce a surplus of energy in laughter to cope with my inhibition when repressed unconscious material threatens to force its way through into consciousness. For example, my tight-lipped refusal to laugh at an anti-semitic joke might well be a symptom of my repressed anti-semitism, or refusing to laugh at a Mexican gag might be a symptom of my quiet contempt for Mexicans. As Freud claims, jokes have a relation to the unconscious, they articulate and reveal a certain economy of psychical expenditure. In this sense, ethnic jokes can be interpreted as symptoms of societal repression, and they can function as a return of the repressed. As such, jokes can be read in terms of what or who a particular society is subordinating, scapegoating or denigrating. Grasping the nature of societal repression can itself be liberating, but only negatively. As Trevor Griffiths writes, 'A joke that feeds on ignorance starves its audience.'[8]

Looking at the works in *Laughing in a Foreign Language*, I don't think they starve their audience. On the contrary, at their best, they make any easy laughter stick in our throats. In this way, I think we approach the paradoxical core of the best humour: it is not funny. Rather, it is troubling, unsettling and disorientating. The joke that one thought was about the stupid or canny other ends up reflexively rebounding on oneself. In great humour, in my view, the joke is always on us. I think the best humour implicates its audience, it grabs hold of us and refuses to let go. Any laughter here sticks in our throats and we begin to choke.

I often sit in diners in New York and look at the yellowing, dog-eared poster about applying

‘The Heimlich Maneuver’ to a choking person. Named after its inventor, Henry Heimlich, the maneuver involves a powerful abdominal thrust that clears any obstruction to breathing. Now, as I’m sure many readers know, the German word *unheimlich* means something uncanny, not at home, strange or bizarre. At its best, art can produce an *unheimlich* maneuver. We begin to choke and there is no known cure. Funny, isn’t it?

1 See Simon Critchley, *On Humour*, Routledge, London and New York, 2002.
2 *Le Grand Robert de Langue Française*, vol. 15, Paris, 1985, p. 288.
3 *Jokes*, University of Chicago Press, Chicago, 1999, p. 21.
4 André Breton, *Anthology of Black Humor, (Anthologie de l’Humour Noir*, 1940), City Lights Books, San Francisco, 1997.
5 *Dictionnaire de l’Académie Française*, Huitième Edition, Hachette, Paris, 1935, p. 29.
6 *Encyclopédie*, Nouvelle impression en facsimile de la premiere edition de 1751–1780, vol. VIII, Fromann Verlag, Stuttgart-Bad Cannstatt, 1967, p. 353.
7 Sigmund Freud, *The Interpretation of Dreams*, Penguin, London, 1976, p. 766.
8 Trevor Griffiths, *Comedians*, Faber, London, 1976, p. 23.

MAKOTO AIDA
KUTLUG ATAMAN
AZORRO
GUY BEN-NER
JOHN BOCK
CANDICE BREITZ
OLAF BREUNING
CAO FEI
JAKE AND
DINOS CHAPMAN
MARCUS COATES
HARRY DODGE AND
STANYA KAHN
DOUG FISHBONE
GHAZEL
GIMHONGSOK
MATTHEW GRIFFIN
NINA JAN BEIER AND
MARIE JAN LUND
TAIYO KIMURA
PETER LAND
JANNE LEHTINEN
KALUP LINZY
YOSHUA OKON
UGO RONDINONE
JULIAN ROSEFELDT
SHIMABUKU
DAVID SHRIGLEY
NEDKO SOLAKOV
BARTHÉLÉMY TOGUO
ROI VAARA
MARTIN WALDE
JUN YANG

MAKOTO AIDA

Born in 1965, Niigata, Japan
Lives and works in Chiba, Japan

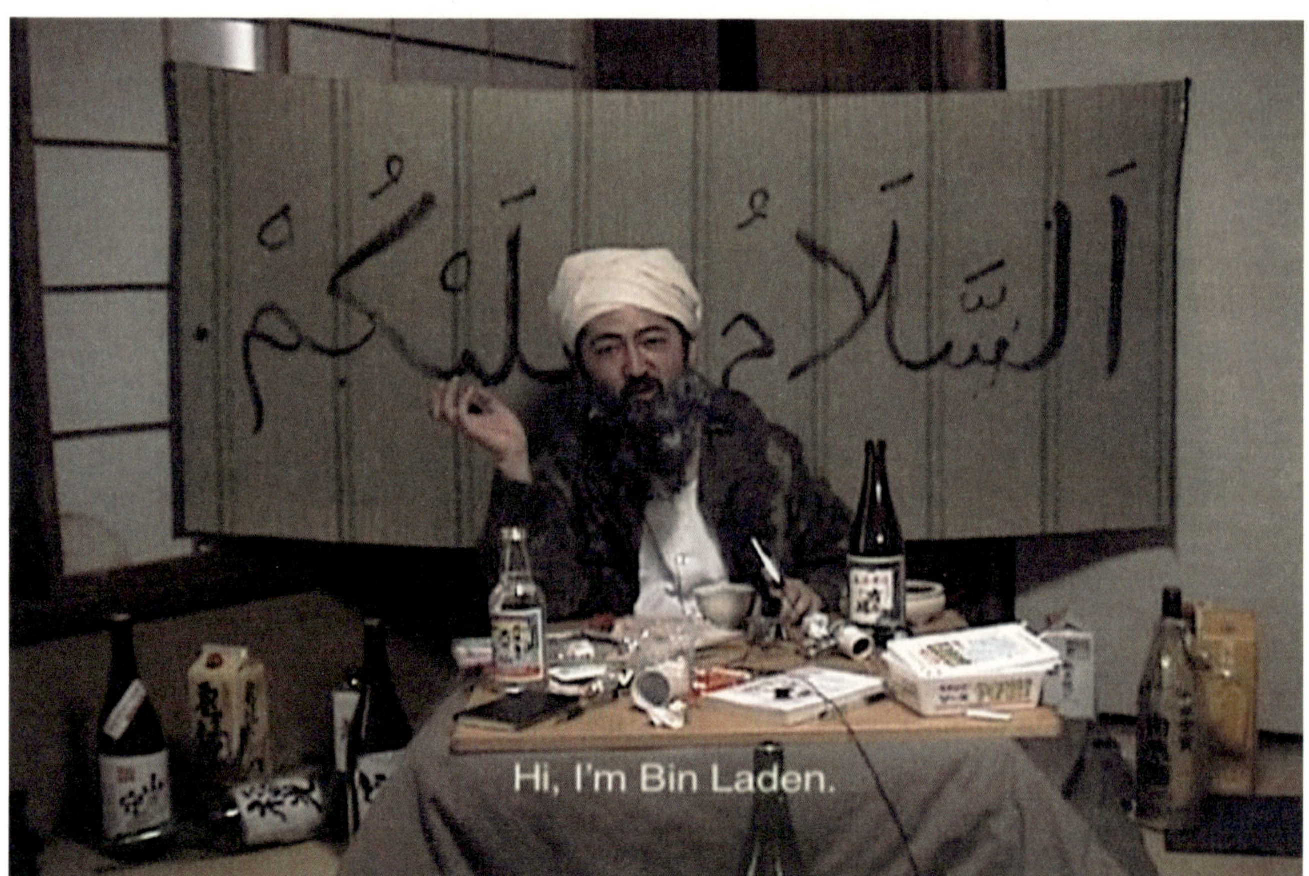

ABOVE AND RIGHT / 2 Makoto Aida, *The Video of a Man Calling Himself Bin Laden Staying in Japan*, 2005, stills

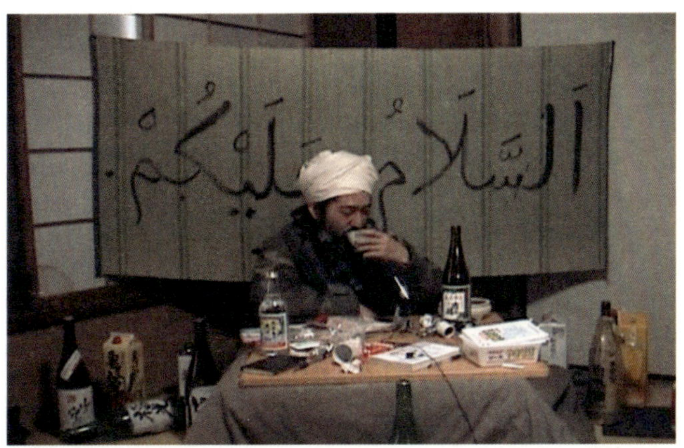

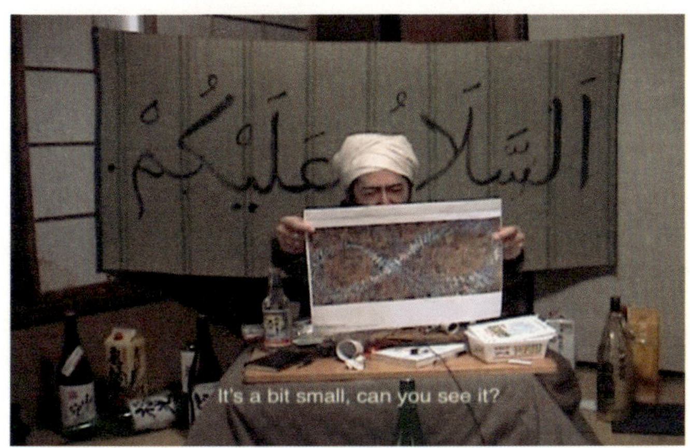

One of Japan's most eclectic artists, Makoto Aida's work includes manga, painting, video and installation. In *The Video of a Man Calling Himself Bin Laden Staying in Japan*, the elusive al-Qaeda leader is discovered not in some remote hideout in Afghanistan but enjoying life in Japan, declaring that thanks to the pleasures of Japanese life there will be 'no more terrorism for me' and revealing that 'drinking sake in the bath is awesome'. Made after Aida was told that he looked like Osama bin Laden, the video contains jokes within jokes, some of which are directed at Aida's own art. At one point, Bin Laden holds up a small reproduction of *A Picture of an Air Raid on New York City*, a vast folding screen that Aida painted in 1996 and that now appears horribly prophetic of the 9/11 terrorist attacks in 2001. 'I kinda like it,' Bin Laden remarks, adding that it was painted by the chap who is hiding him.

Your Pronunciation is Wrong!, a C-print made in 2000, documents a demonstration that Aida staged in New York, in which he and fellow foreigners voiced their frustration at not speaking English by carrying placards exhorting Americans to 'pronunce [sic] simply and shapely as Japanese do' and advocating the use of *katakana*, the simple Japanese syllabary used for the transcription of words from foreign languages.

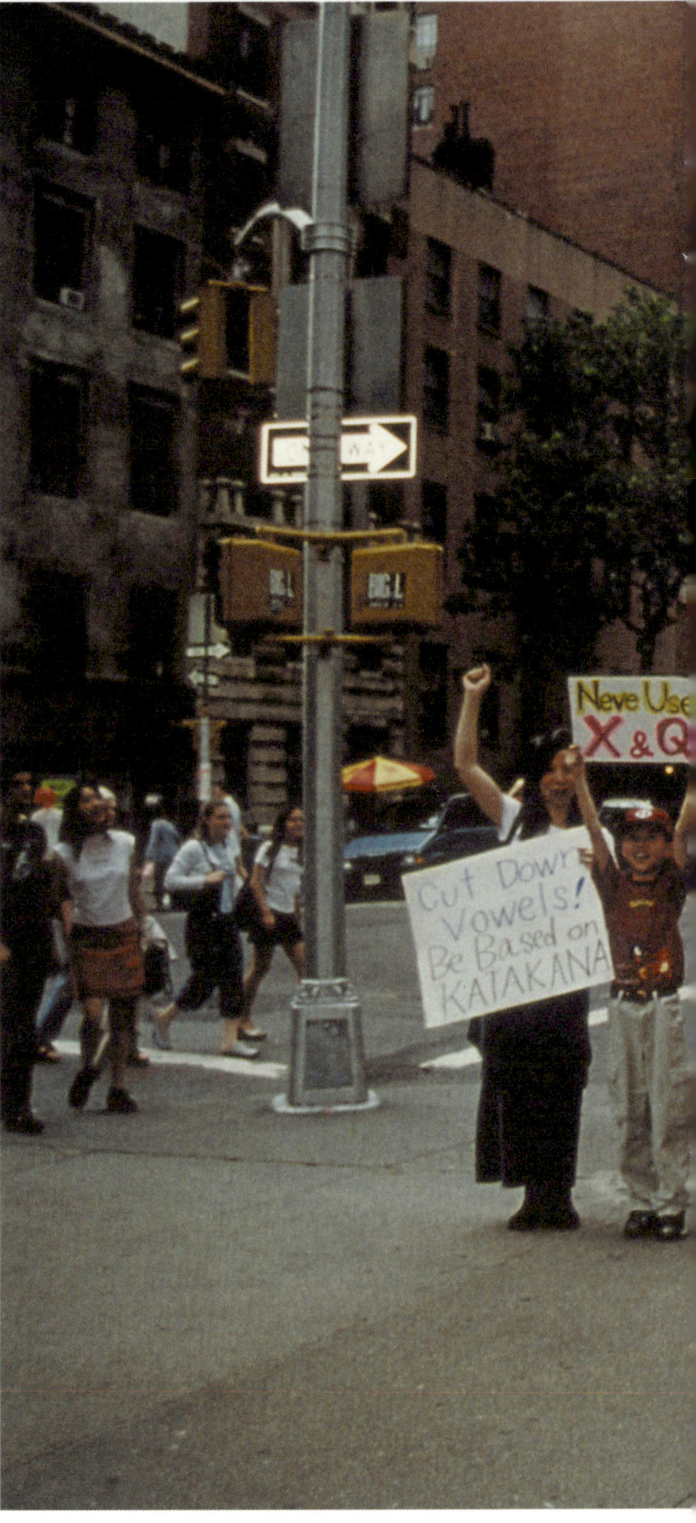

1 Makoto Aida, *Your Pronunciation is Wrong!*, 2000

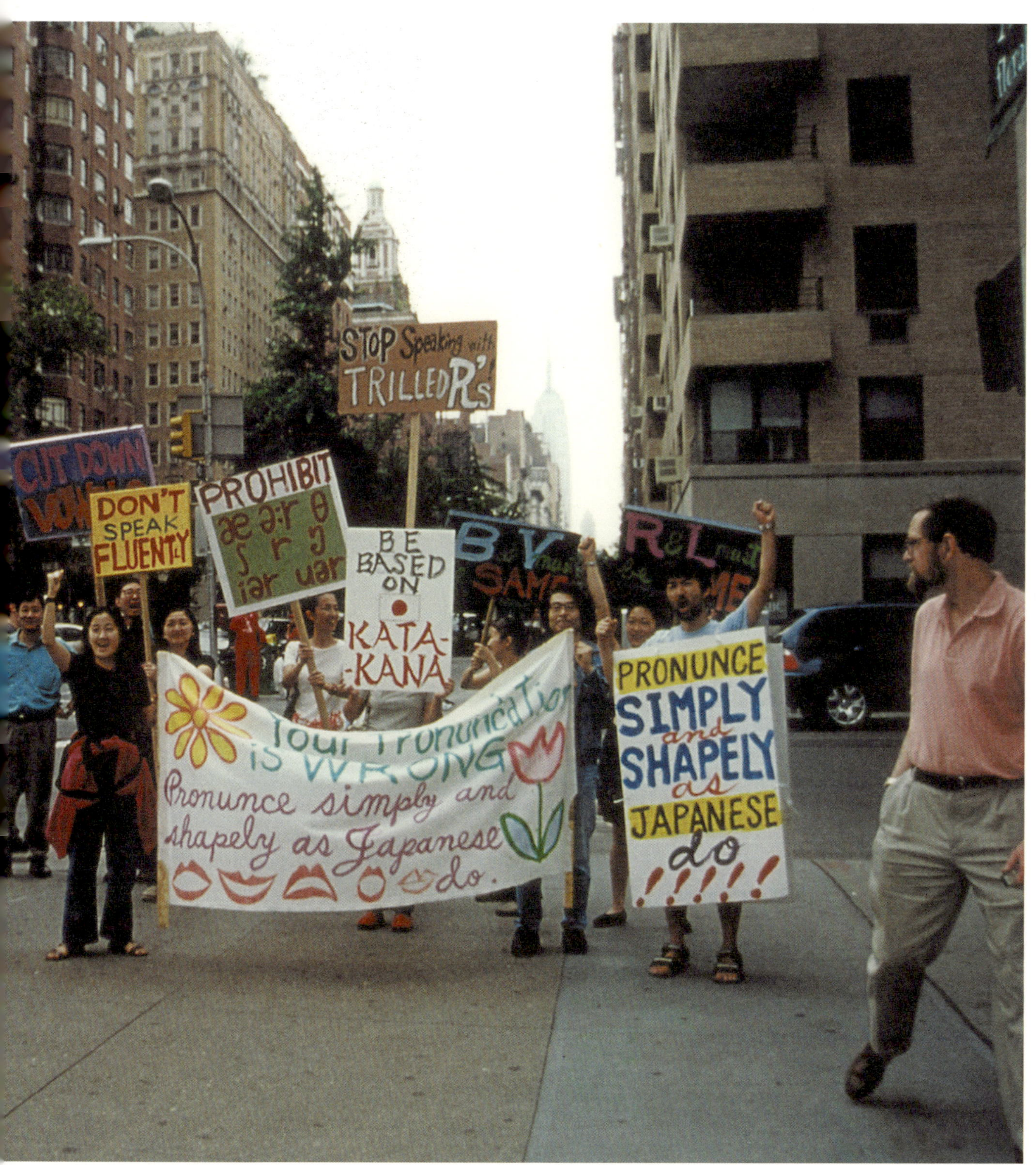
CUT DOWN
DON'T SPEAK FLUENTLY
PROHIBIT
æ ə:r θ ʃ r ʒ iər uər
STOP Speaking with TRILLED R's!
BE BASED ON KATA-KANA
Your Pronunciation is WRONG
Pronunce simply and shapely as Japanese do.
PRONUNCE SIMPLY and SHAPELY as JAPANESE do !!!!!

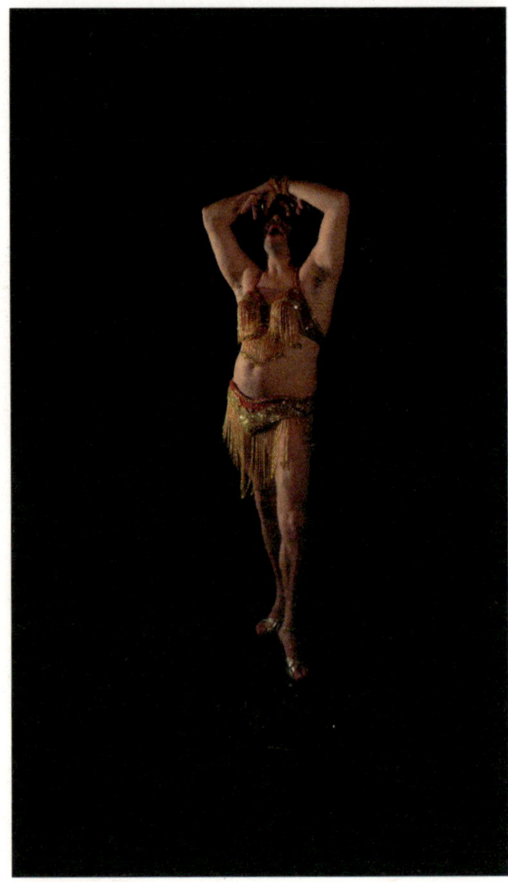

ABOVE AND RIGHT / 3 Kutlug Ataman, *Turkish Delight*, 2006, stills

KUTLUG ATAMAN

Born in 1961, Istanbul, Turkey
Lives and works in Buenos Aires, Argentina; London, UK; and Istanbul, Turkey

Kutlug Ataman makes films, videos and installation works. His work often hovers between fact and fiction and frequently involves multiple-screen projections in which disenfranchised and disempowered people are allowed to tell their own stories, which may or may not be true. 'I am pointing the camera at people who are refashioning their lives, but they also genuinely live them, so the viewer questions whether the piece is real or not,' he has said, and adds that, in the construction of an identity, 'reality is just one ingredient'. But in his single-screen video *Turkish Delight*, Ataman points the camera at himself, dressing as a traditional belly dancer with finger cymbals, scanty costume and high heels, and dancing to the music of a Turkish gypsy song while nonchalantly chewing gum.

Turkish belly dancing is celebrated for its expressiveness, energy and athleticism. In Ataman's burlesque version there is a conspicuous lack of allure; his performance is funny but also pathetic. As Ataman says, 'it's a performance and non-performance at the same time'. A semi-fictitious self-portrait, *Turkish Delight* not only portrays an artist who happens to be Turkish, but also looks askance at conventional ideas of Turkey and stereotypical ideas of the 'exotic'.

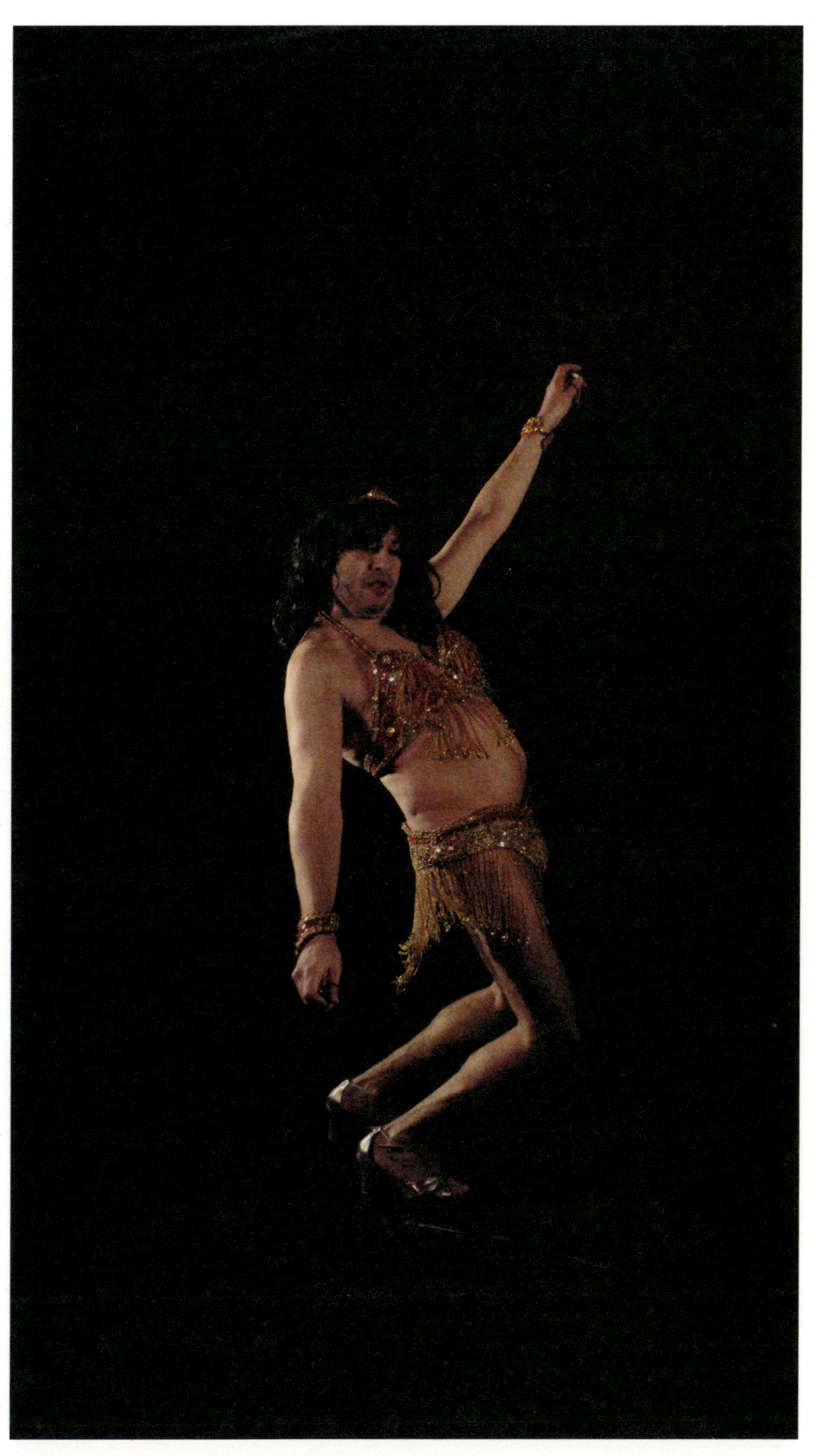

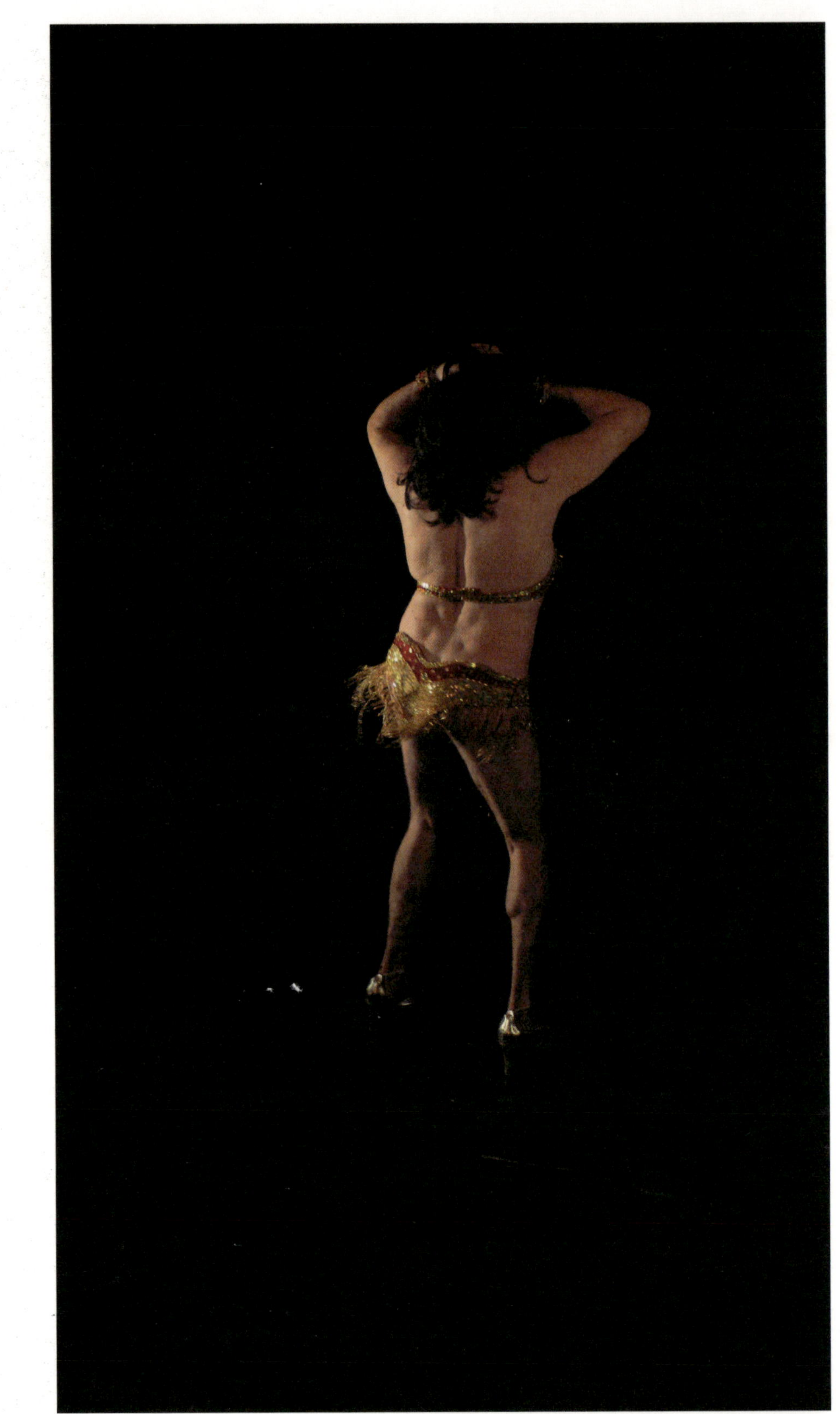

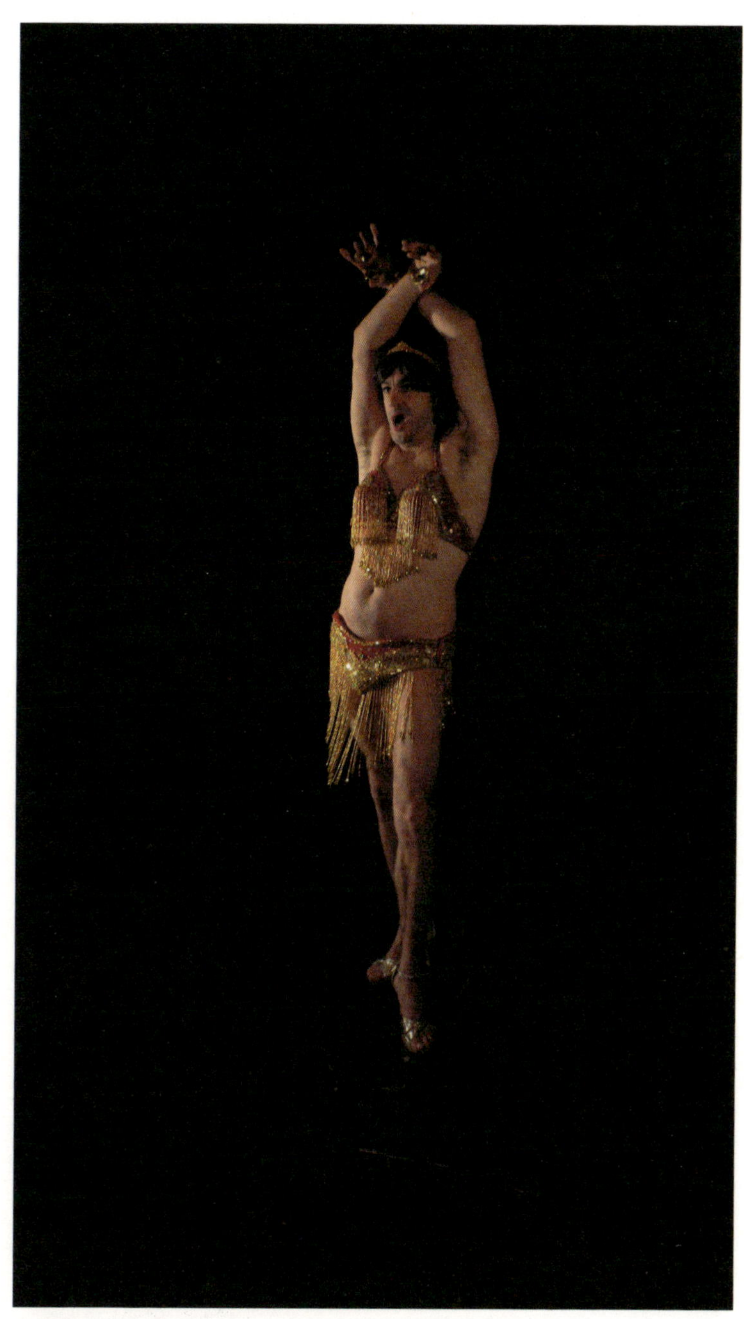

ABOVE AND LEFT / 3 Kutlug Ataman, *Turkish Delight*, 2006, stills

AZORRO

Group founded in 2001
The members are:
Oskar Dawicki (born in 1971)
Igor Krenz (born in 1959)
Wojciech Niedzielko (born in 1959)
Lukasz Skapski (born in 1958)
They live and work in Cracow and Warsaw

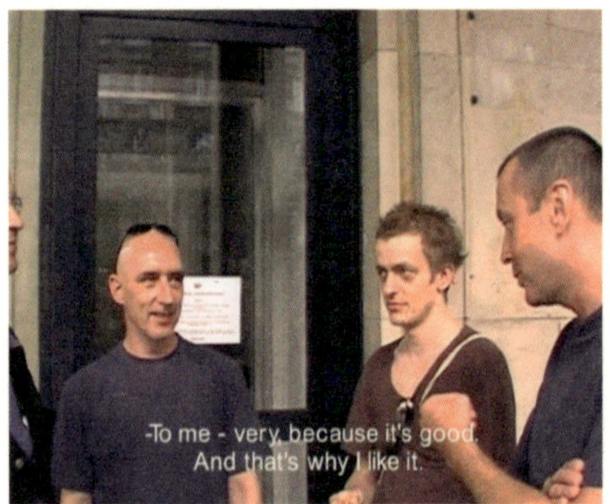

The four artists who collectively form the Polish Supergroup Azorro are each well-known for their own work in installation, performance, photography and video. Together they make films that take an ironic look at the world of contemporary art. Their focus is on Poland, which, since achieving democracy in 1990, has raced to catch up with the West.

In their first collaboration, *We Like It A Lot*, Azorro go on a tour of Warsaw's art galleries, offering us crucial insights into the discourse of art criticism. While we, the audience, do not get to see any contemporary art at all, they emerge from gallery after gallery exclaiming how much they liked what they saw. Nothing is described and the only phrases they use are variations on 'I like it' and 'very nice'. As one of them helpfully concludes, 'It's good. And that's why I like it.'

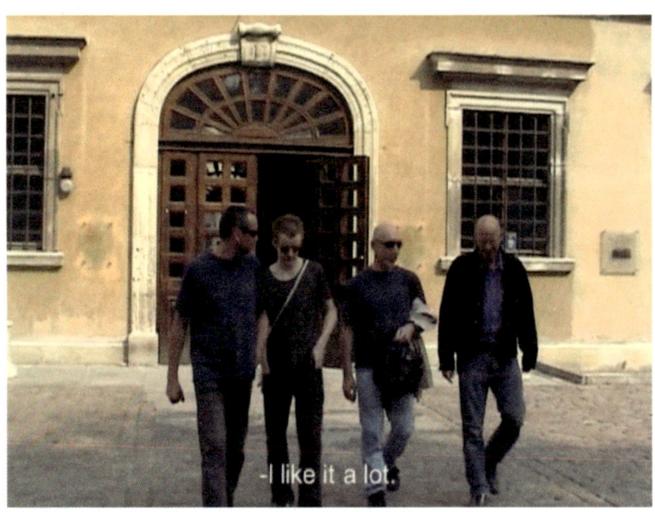

ABOVE / 4 Azorro, *We Like It A Lot*, 2001, stills

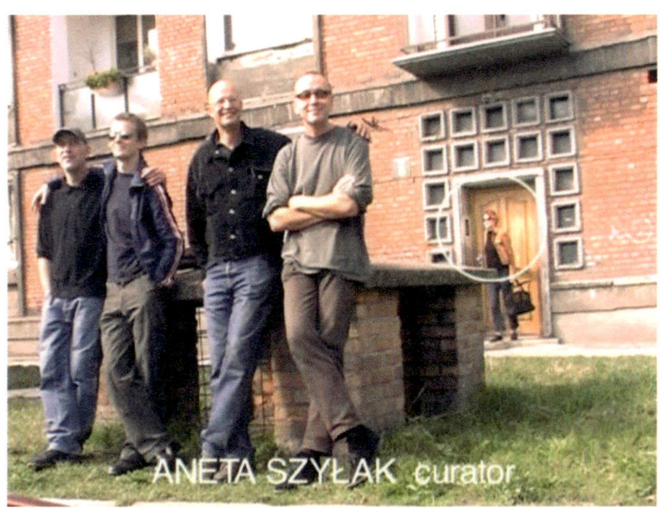

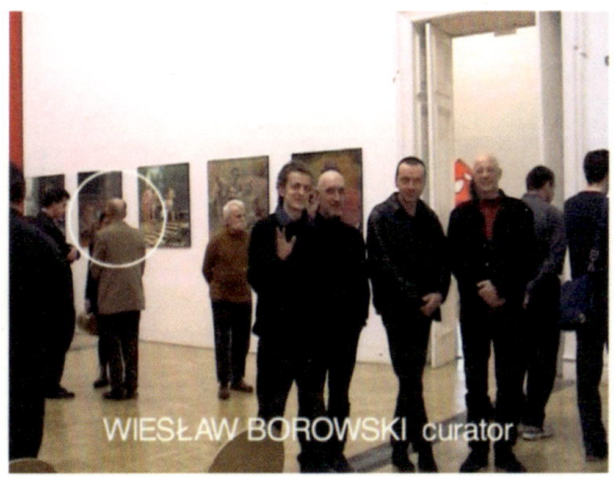

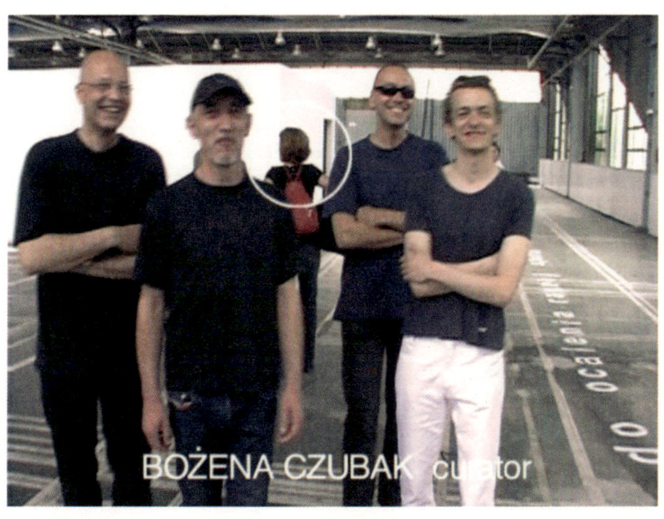

ABOVE AND RIGHT / 5 Azorro, *Portrait with a Curator*, 2002, stills

In *Portrait with a Curator*, Azorro attend a plethora of exhibition openings. On each occasion, they line up for a group portrait and smile at the camera, managing – by sheer good fortune – to capture a prominent Polish curator or art critic in the background of every shot, which they then freeze-frame, circle and identify. Pointing out that 'curators are important people and therefore it is good to get photographed with them,' Azorro add that 'they [the curators] will certainly notice it; these people are vain and have their complexes.' With charming optimism, Azorro add their personal email addresses to the film credits in order that these powerful people can contact them.

GUY BEN-NER

Born in 1969, Ramat Gan, Israel
Lives and works in Berlin, Germany

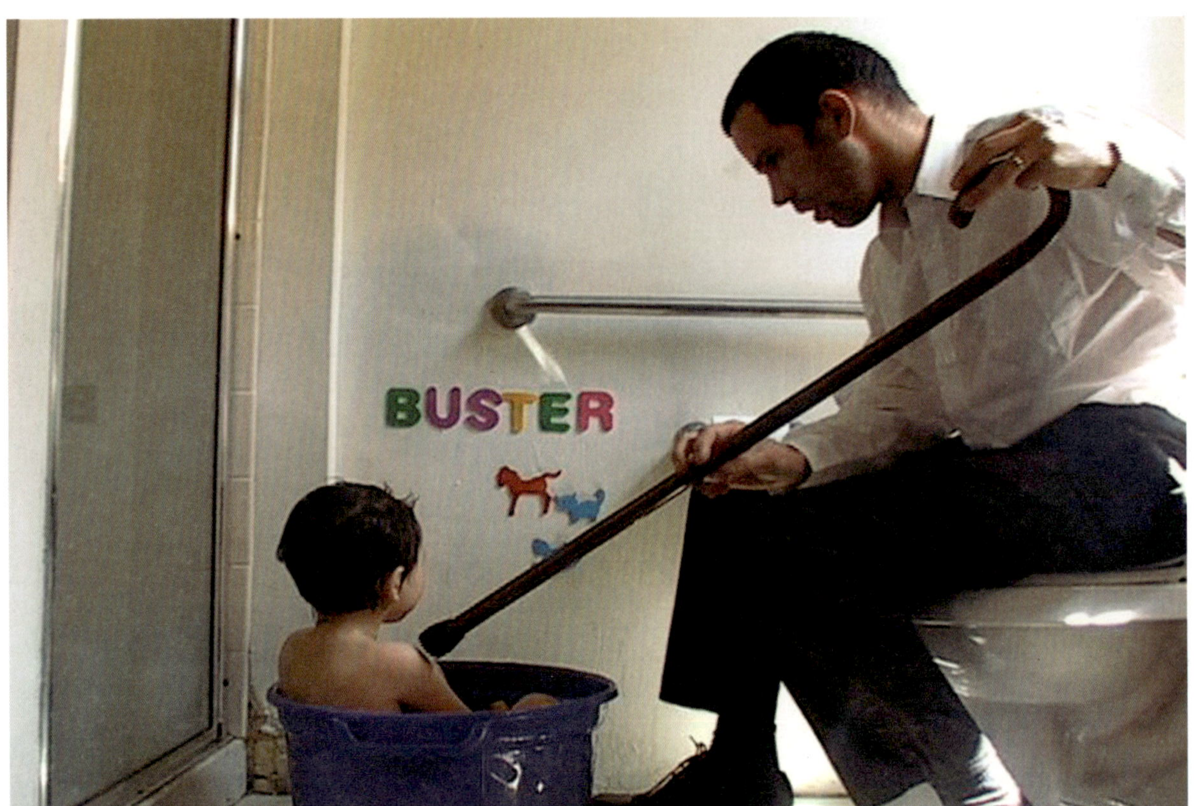

ABOVE AND RIGHT / 6 Guy Ben-Ner, *Wild Boy*, 2004, stills

Since 1996, Guy Ben-Ner has been making video works set in his own home and featuring himself and his family. In *Wild Boy*, Ben-Ner's son plays the role of a feral child who is captured in the wild by a teacher (Ben-Ner) who then attempts to dominate, tame and train the foundling. In Ben-Ner's words, *Wild Boy* is 'a story of power relations and the fantasy of bringing somebody up after one's own image ... *Wild Boy* is based on several case histories, some myths, some educational manuals and is referring to a wide range of movies, from old photos left of the vaudeville acts by father and son, Buster and Joe Keaton, through Truffaut's *Wild Child*, to *The Kid* by Chaplin.'

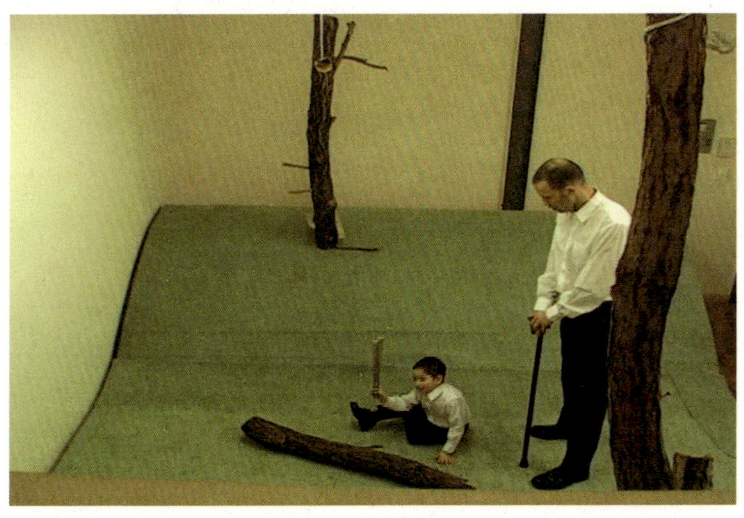

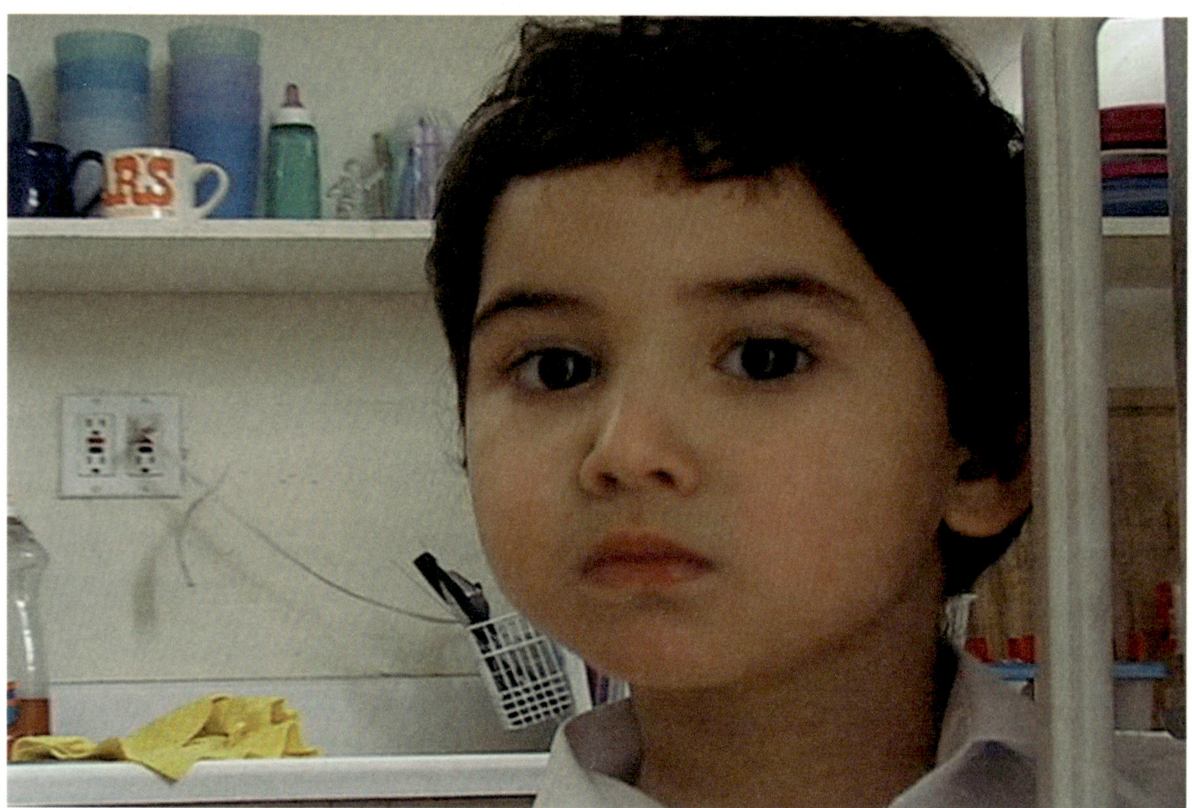

ABOVE AND RIGHT / 6 Guy Ben-Ner, *Wild Boy*, 2004, stills

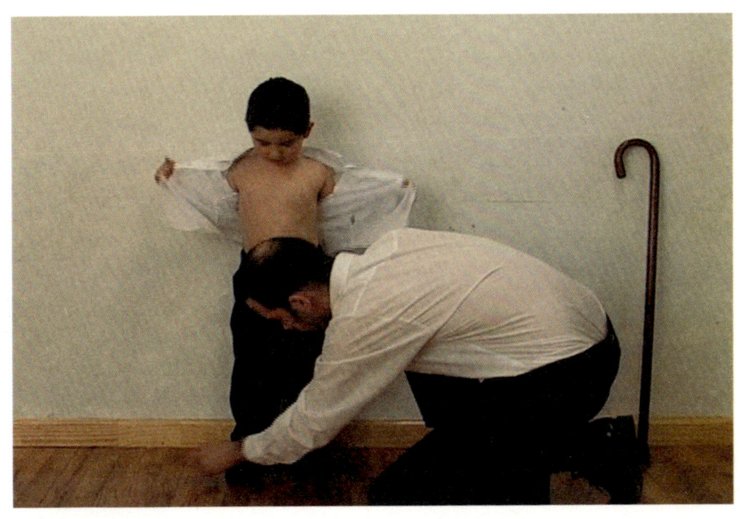

Transforming his apartment into a self-contained wilderness, landscaped with Astroturf and do-it-yourself contraptions, Ben-Ner makes sets and then improvises with the domestic objects that are already there. At one point he creates a sunrise by slowly opening the fridge door, and at another the refrigerator is turned into a backlit book. Child's play and make-believe are intertwined with references to 1970s performance and body art, as well as to the pioneers of silent film. The teacher names the wild boy 'Buster' and shortly afterwards Buster begins carrying a Charlie Chaplin-type walking stick and moving in sync with his master. Tribute is also paid to even earlier cinema; the teacher amazes the uncivilised child by creating a flipbook showing Lumière's *The Arrival of a Train at the Station* (1895), one of the first films ever projected, which allegedly caused its audience to stampede in terror.

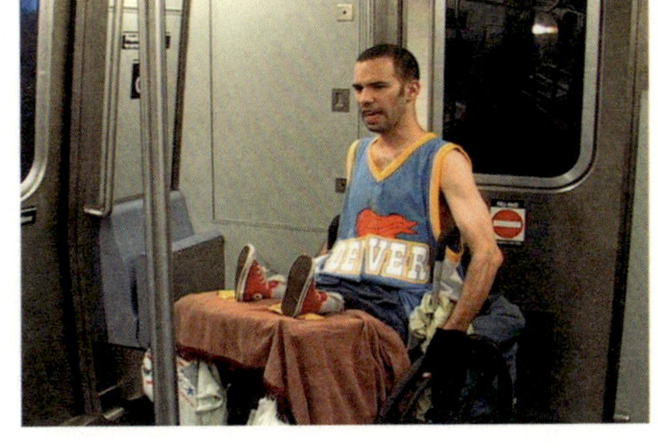

JOHN BOCK

Born in 1965, Itzehoe, near Gribbohm, Germany
Lives and works in Berlin, Germany

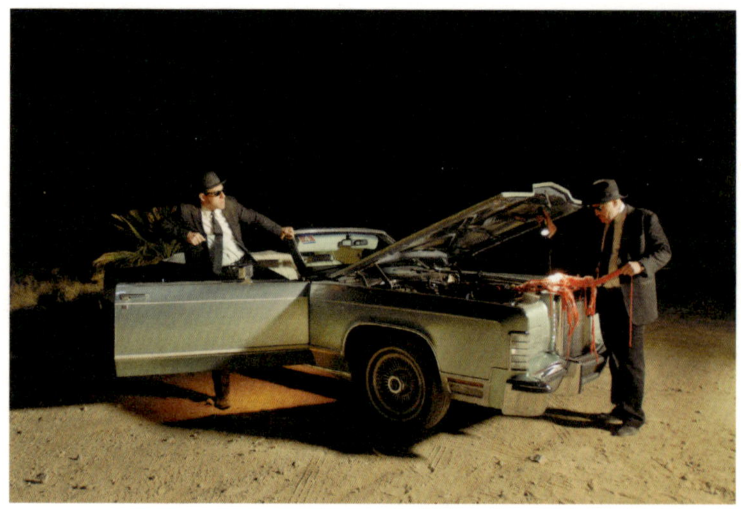

A performance artist, sculptor and filmmaker, John Bock creates bizarrely enigmatic worlds in which humour treads a fine line between the absurd and the grotesque. *Dandy*, made in 2006, was filmed in France at Chateau du Bosc, the family home of the painter Henri de Toulouse-Lautrec, and features spectacular costumes, extraordinary props and a manically convoluted storyline.

Palms, a macabre and anarchic hour-long video shot in the Californian desert, is a cross between a road movie and a gangster film. Two assassins, dressed like characters from Quentin Tarantino's *Reservoir Dogs*, fly in from Germany

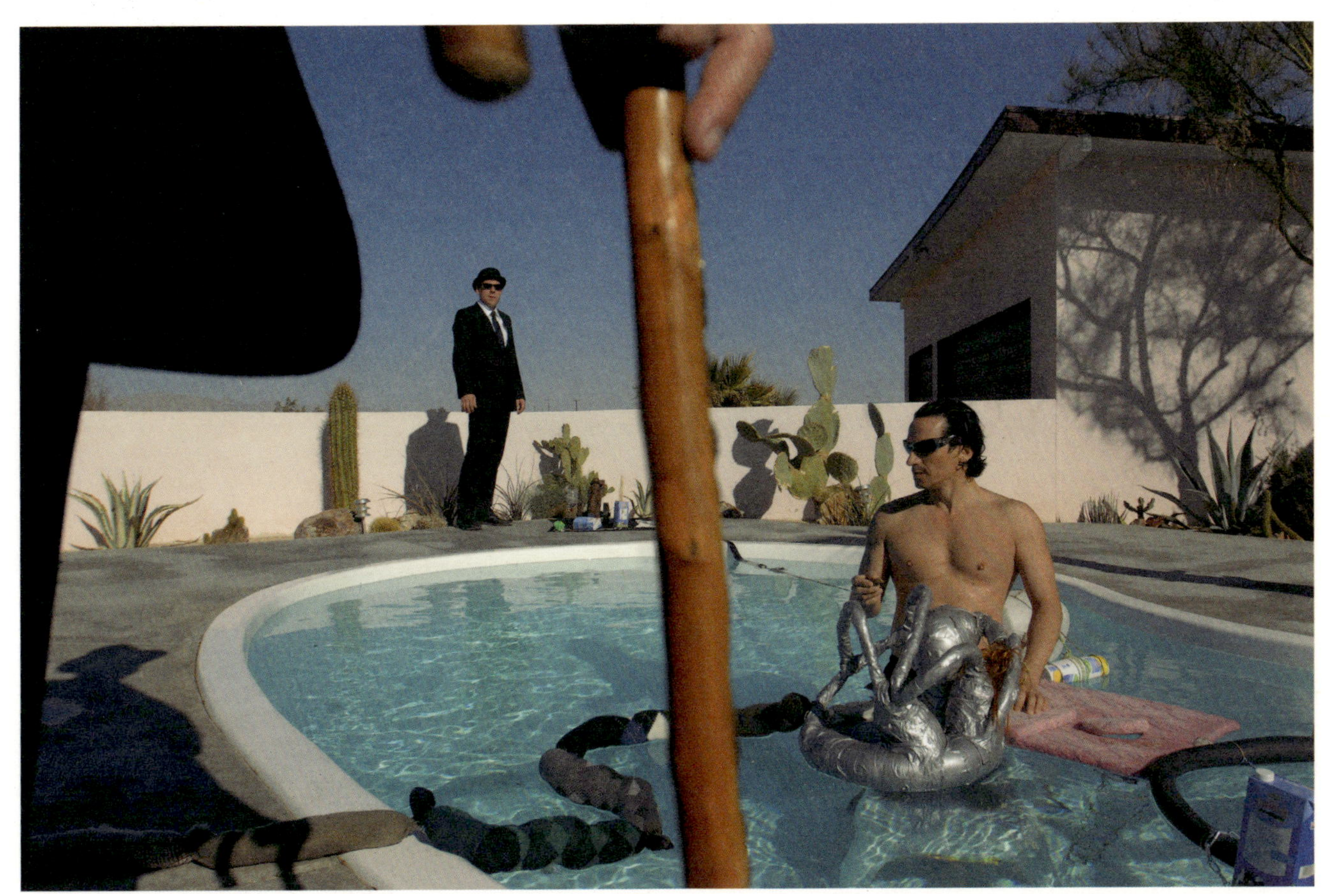

ABOVE AND LEFT / 7 John Bock, *Palms*, 2007, stills

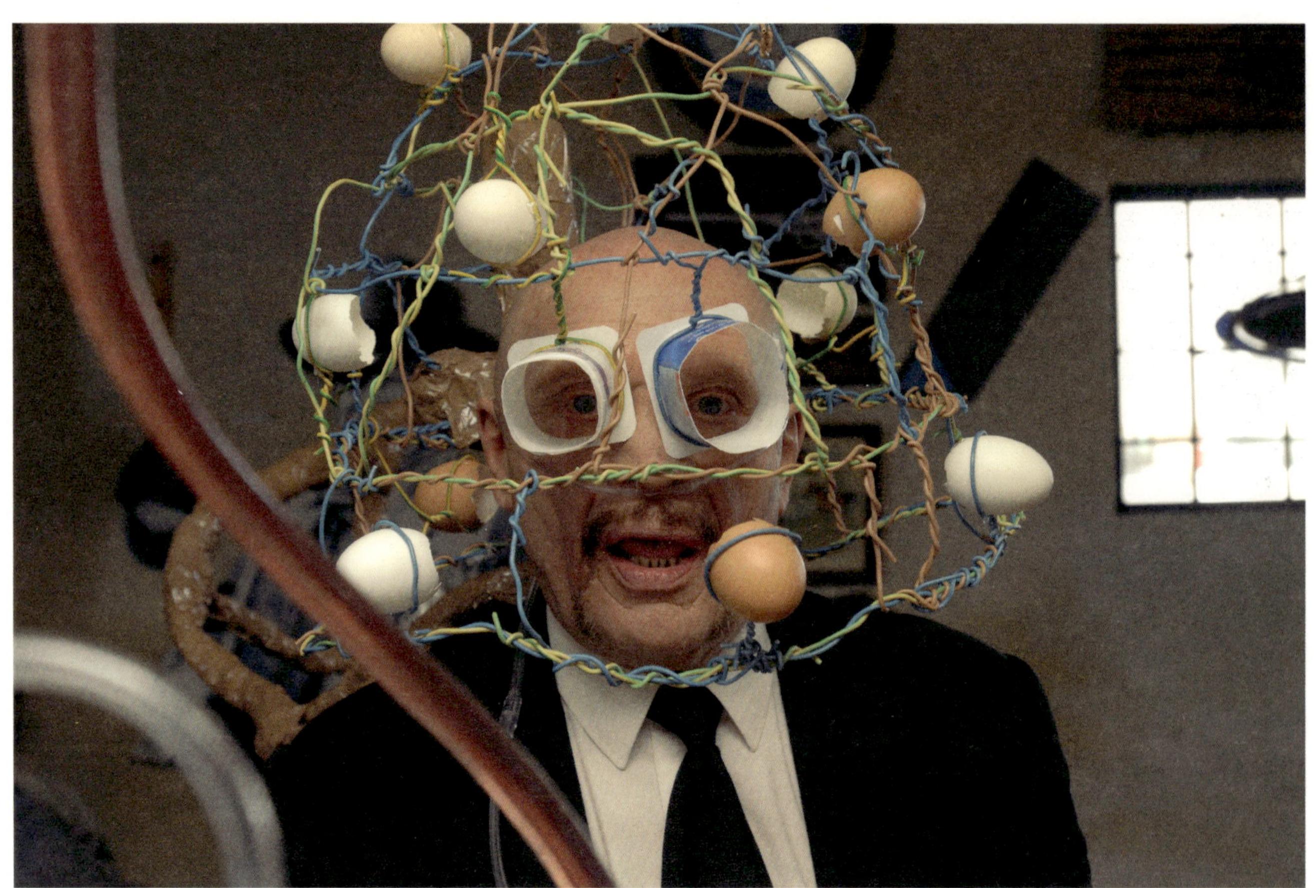

7 John Bock, *Palms*, 2007, still

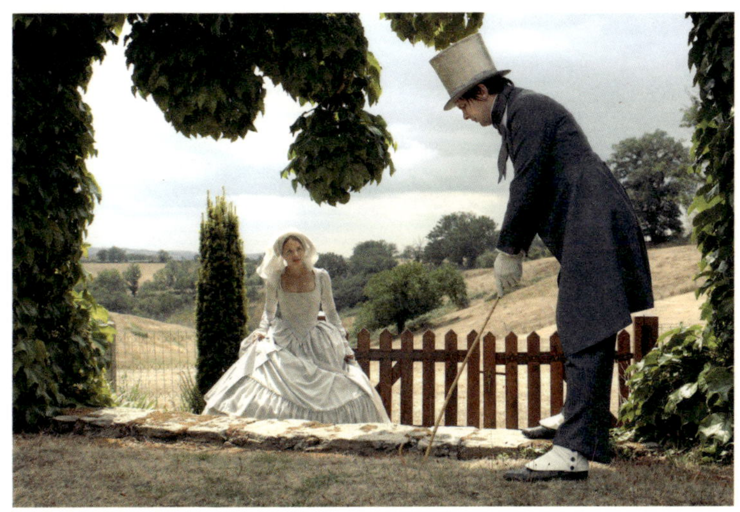

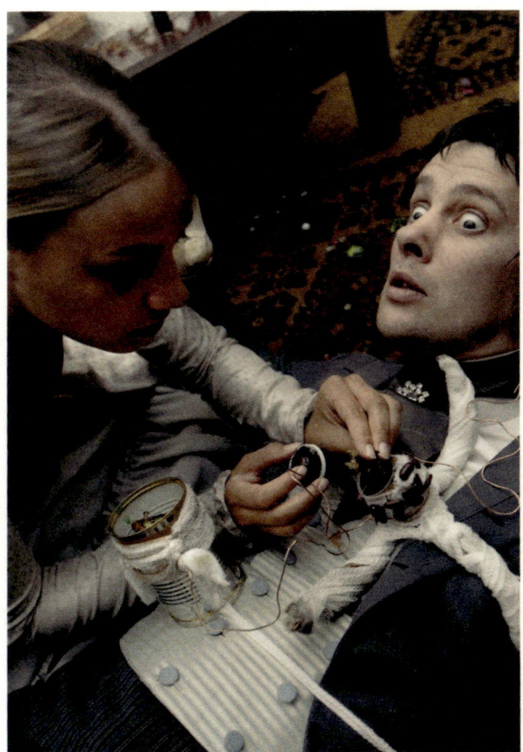

ABOVE John Bock, *Dandy*, 2006, stills

on a mission to kill a former member of their gang. During their odyssey they indulge in acts of gratuitous violence, killing the traitor's collaborators and destroying his art. The black humour embraces surreal and violent slapstick, pratfalls, stream-of-consciousness gobbledegook and 'in' jokes for those familiar with contemporary visual art and popular cult movies; David Lynch's unorthodox style of narrative filmmaking has particular resonance. The assassins' journey begins and ends at houses that are important examples of early modernist architecture. Weird constructions, amateur architectural models, arcane diagrams, milk cartons, cotton buds and earwax, and a multicoloured, many-tentacled creature are recurring motifs.

The video takes its title from a bar in Wonder Valley, which becomes the setting for the central part of the film and is owned by a band called The Sibleys, one of whom becomes a victim of the assassins.

CANDICE BREITZ

Born in 1972, Johannesburg, South Africa
Lives and works in Berlin, Germany

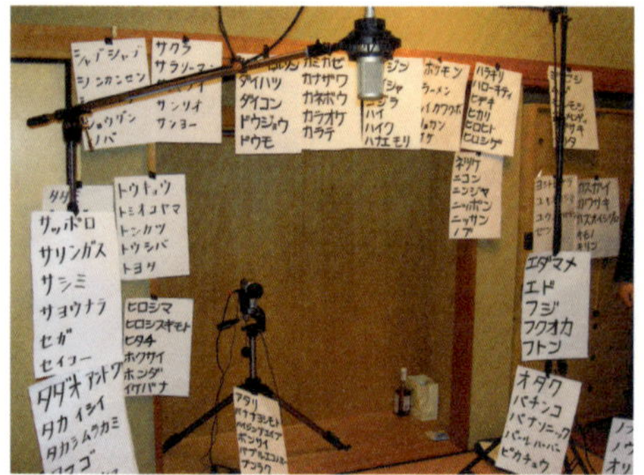

Candice Breitz, The Making of *Aiwa To Zen*, 2003 (see cat. 8)

In her photography and video installations, Candice Breitz uses aspects of popular culture and global consumerism as devices to expose the absurdity of how we construct meaning through stereotypes. The short film, *Aiwa To Zen*, made on Breitz's first trip to Japan, relies entirely on the small number of Japanese words that she knew in advance of her visit. 'The thin vocabulary of about 150 words that I managed to scrape together had to do almost exclusively with an exotic and imaginary Japan, or a consumable Japan ... with eating Japanese food, Japan at war, Japanese pop culture, the Japanese art and fashion worlds, and, overwhelmingly, with dozens of Japanese brand names,' she recalls.

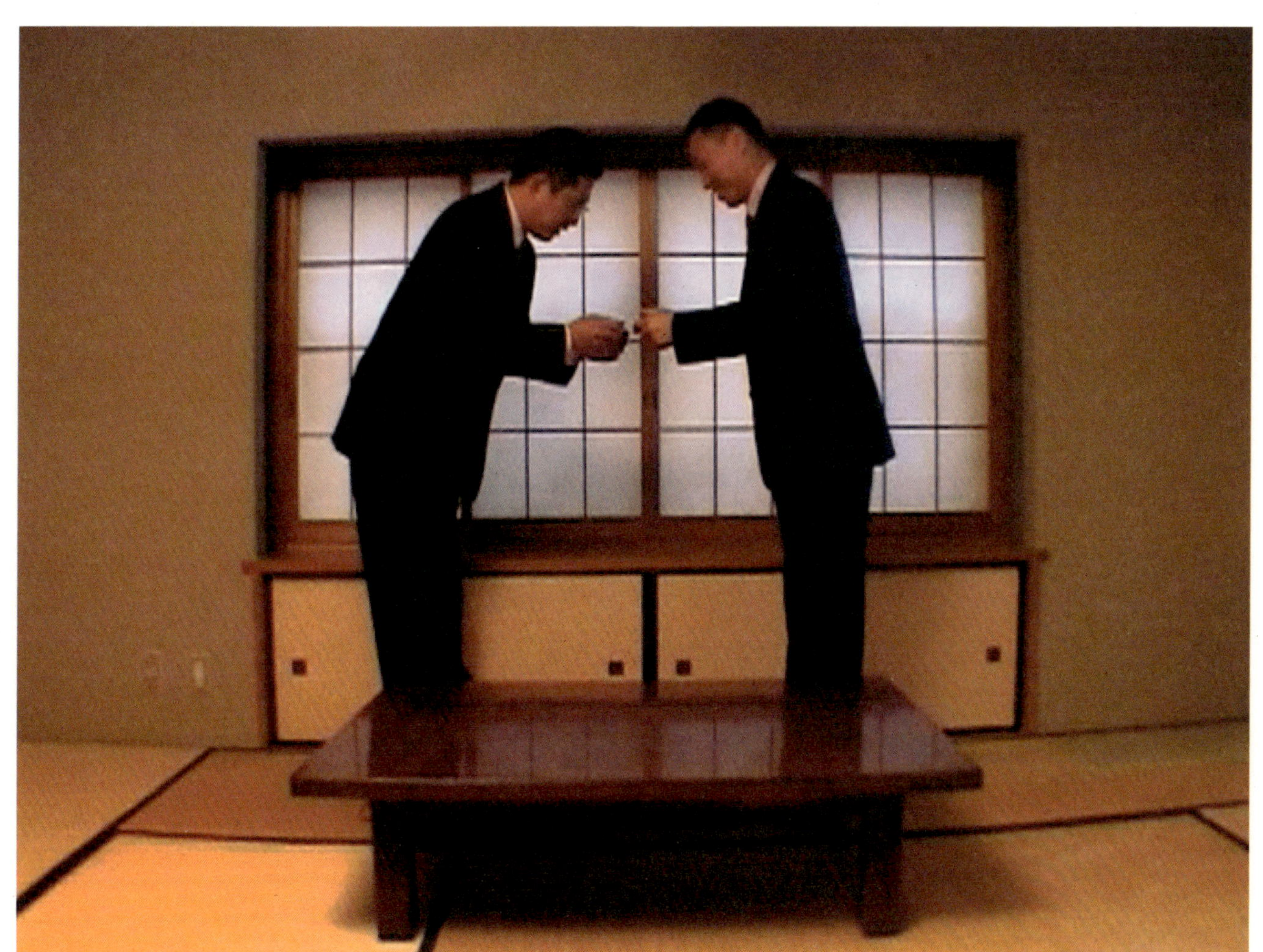

8 Candice Breitz, *Aiwa To Zen*, 2003, still

Using this bizarre lexicon as her script, Breitz constructs a story involving five characters: Wise Old Man, Bunny Chan, Salary Man, Kimono Lady and Super Salary Man, all of whom are played by Japanese-speakers. The narrative revolves around Super Salary Man's thwarted love for Kimono Lady.

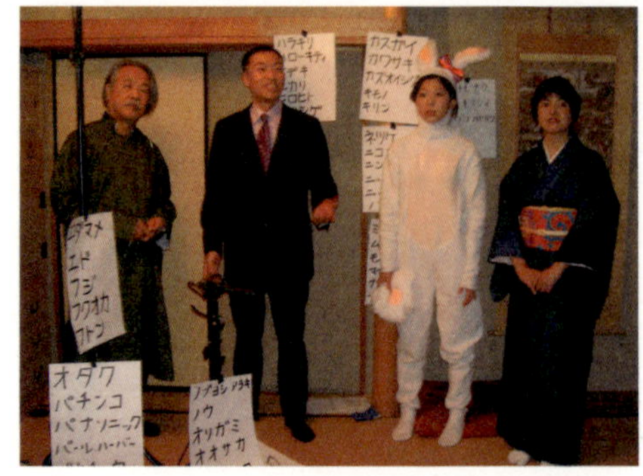

Candice Breitz, The Making of *Aiwa To Zen*, 2003 (see cat. 8)

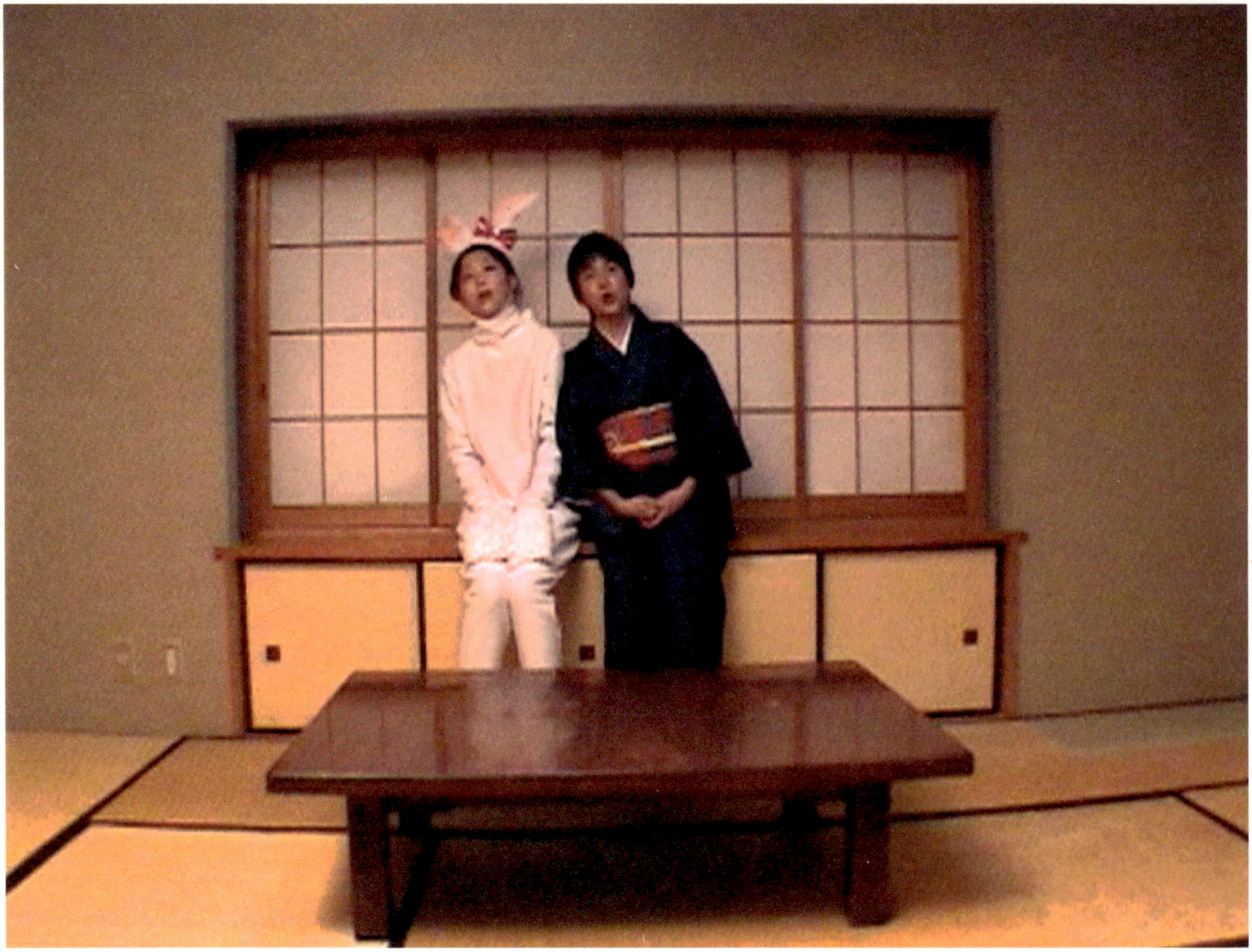

ABOVE AND RIGHT / 8 Candice Breitz, *Aiwa To Zen*, 2003, still

Feeling rejected by her and humiliated by the other characters, things come to a head when he whispers 'SUSHI!' and their response is 'SASHIMI!'. All hell breaks loose, and Salary Man muses: 'COMME DES GARÇONS DAIHATSU DOJO DOMO SAPPORO SASHIMI SAYONARA TOKYO TOMIO KOYAMA TONKATSU TOSHIBA TAKASHI MURAKAMI HARA KIRI HELLO KITTY SAPPORO SARIN GAS.' But in the end they all live happily ever after, singing 'SEGA! SEGA! SEGA! A-NIIIIIII-MEEEEEEE.'

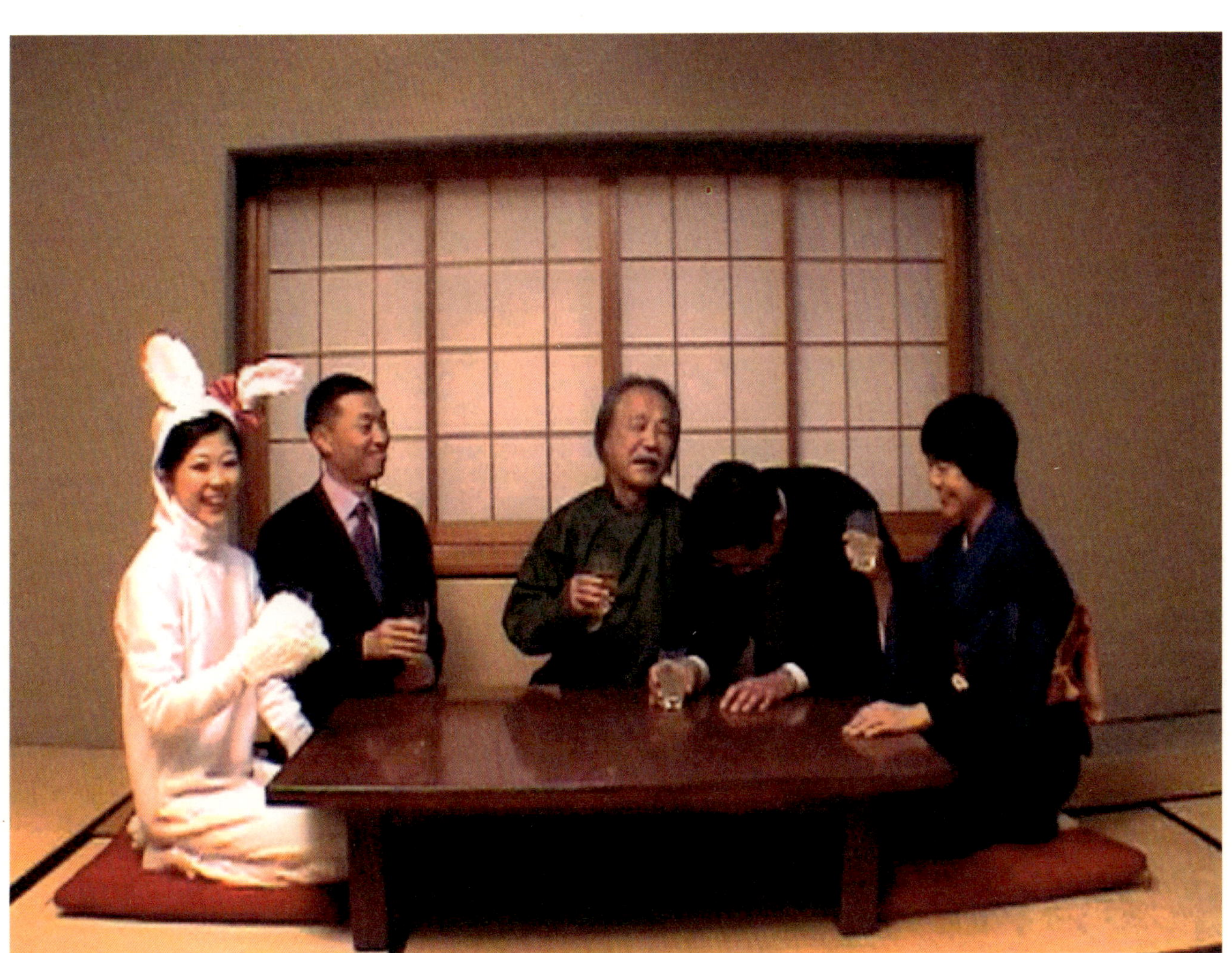

OLAF BREUNING

Born in 1970, Schaffhausen, Switzerland
Lives and works in New York, USA,
and Zurich, Switzerland

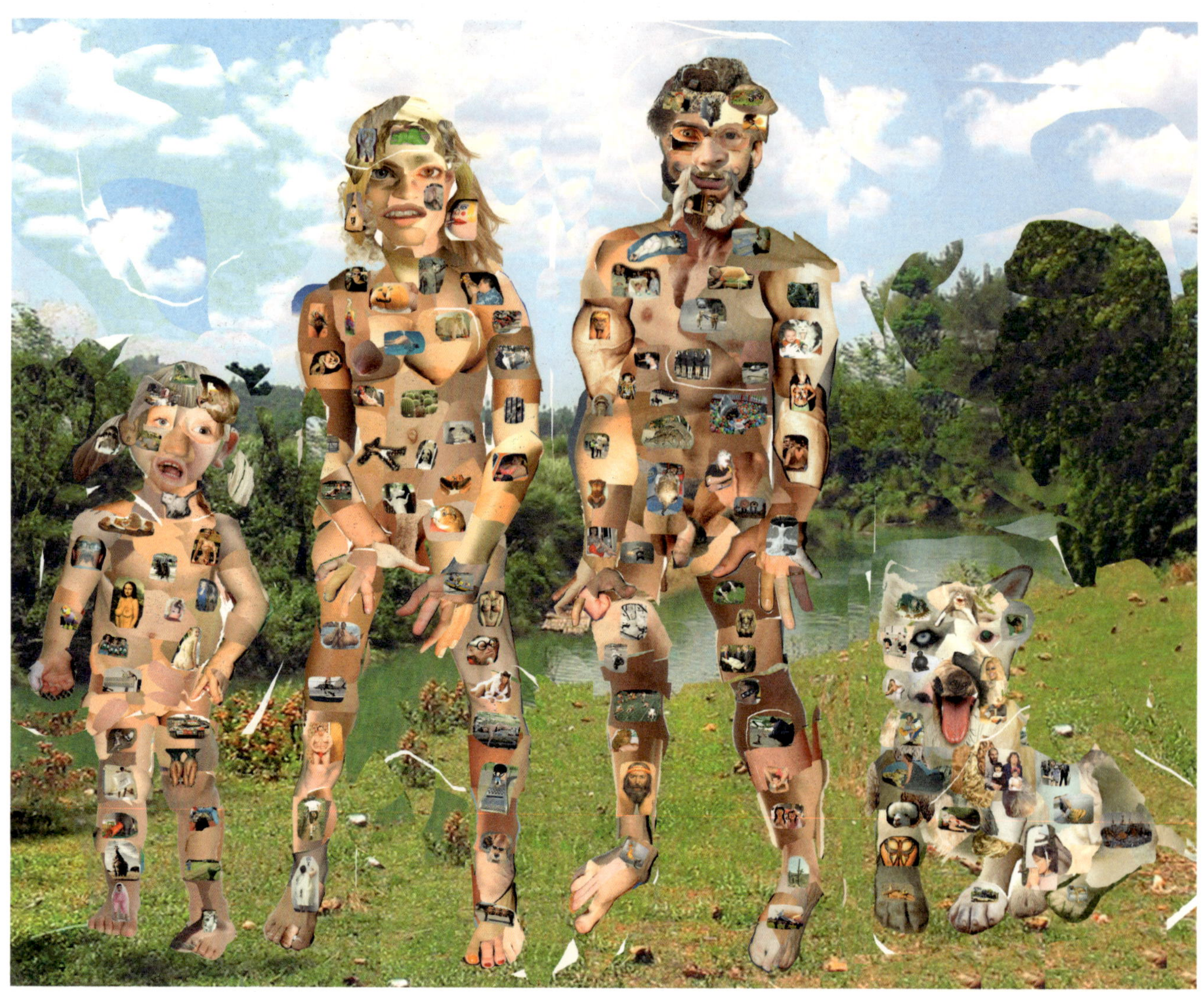

 Olaf Breuning, *collage family*, 2007

The only thing that is predictable about Olaf Breuning's videos, photographs and installations is their unpredictability. Their common denominator is a wildly irreverent sense of humour that demolishes at least two stereotypical views of the Swiss – that they are cold and serious and that they like things clean.

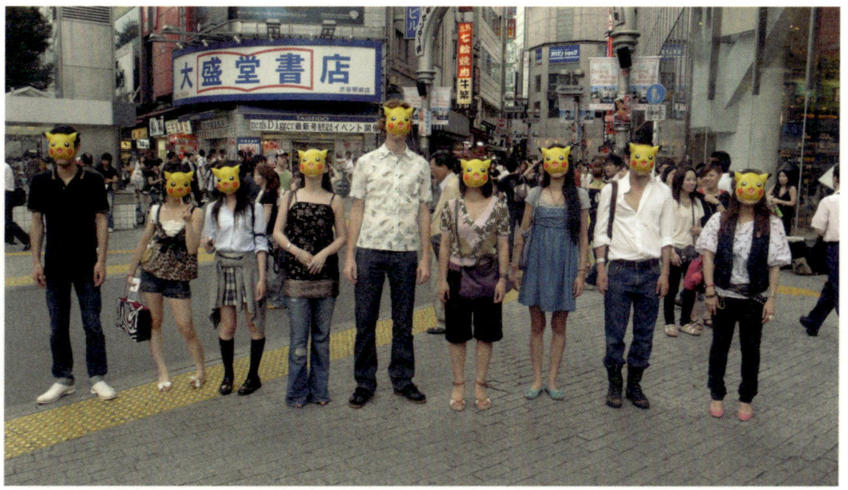

11 Olaf Breuning, *Home2*, 2007, still

Home2, a sequel to his lower-than-low budget two-screen video *Home* from 2003, is a single-screen 'home-made' travelogue filmed in Papua New Guinea, Japan, Ghana, and the Swiss alpine region of Appenzell. Talking direct to camera, an amiable but slightly unhinged dork whispers appallingly non-PC confidences while breaking all the rules of good tourist behaviour, making us complicit in his excruciating practical jokes. At one point, while handing out banknotes to kids on a rubbish dump in Ghana, he provokes a riot; an episode happily commemorated in the photograph *20 dollar bill*. Brian Kerstetter, who plays this profligate character, says: 'When I go to the movies, sometimes I think, "A monkey could have made that." But you'd be surprised.

It's difficult to make a movie, even a really bad one. It takes preparation – organising flights, booking hotels, finding food, and speaking foreign languages – just to tell your story that some Neanderthal thinks was made by a monkey. Then there are the scenes that never make it to screen, due to the frailty of a human toe or the dignity of an entire country...'

In the photograph *collage family*, the curious eye will discover obscene carrots, a woman with three buttocks, a child sliding down a cheese grater, and much worse. It is as if the collaged elements were scavenged from *The National Enquirer* as lampooned by *Mad Magazine*, and almost no potential to offend is missed.

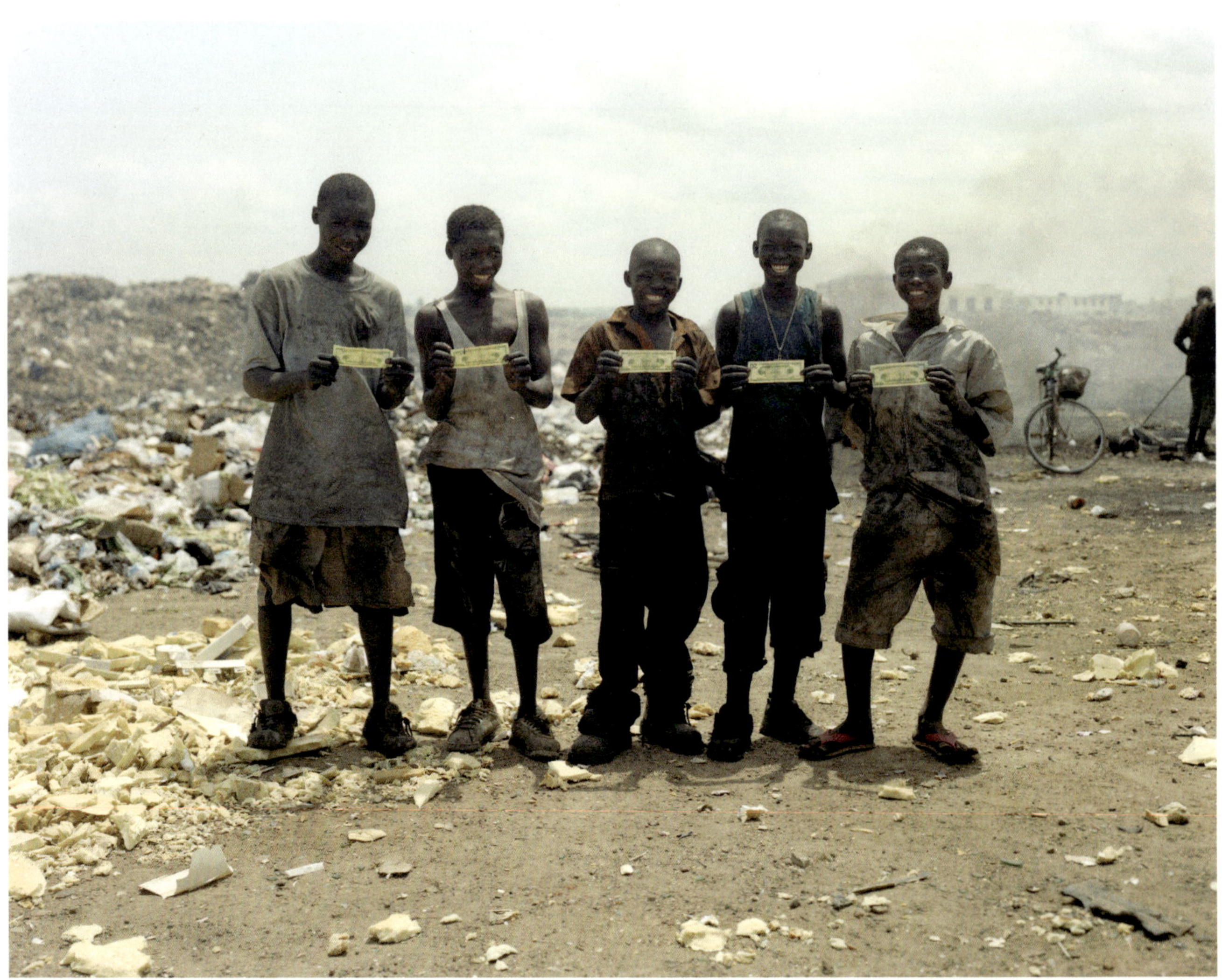

9 Olaf Breuning, *20 dollar bill*, 2007

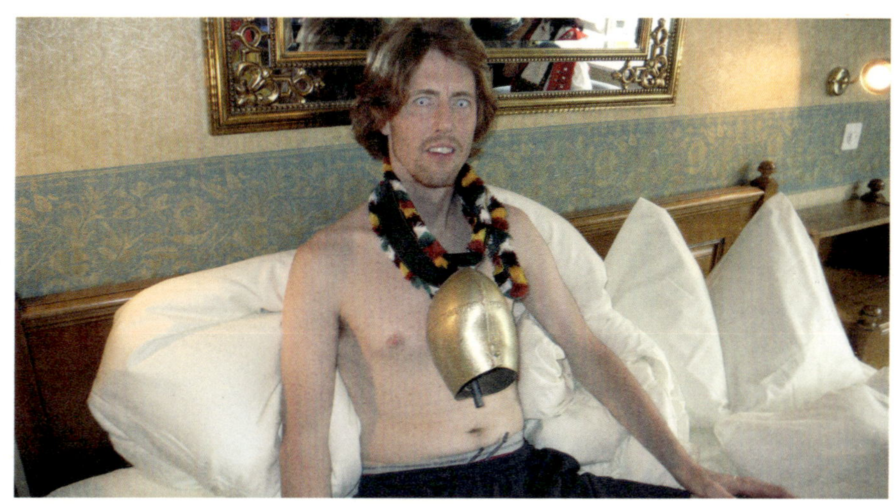

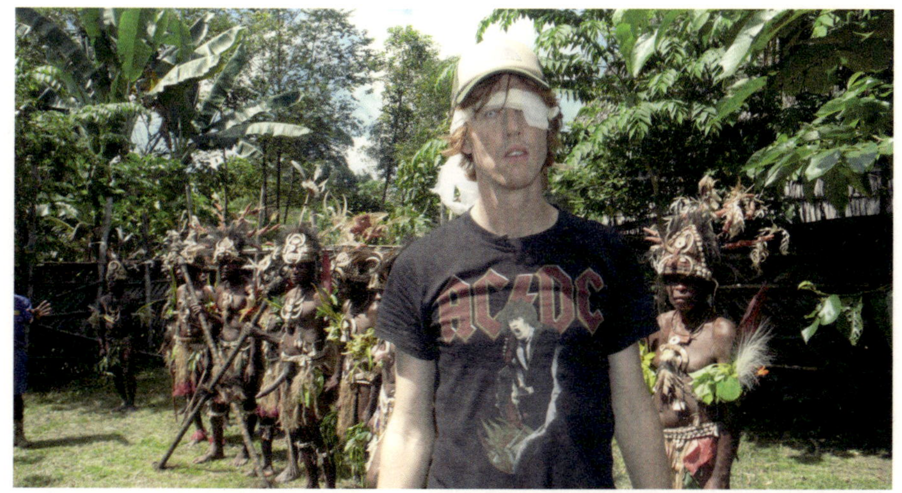

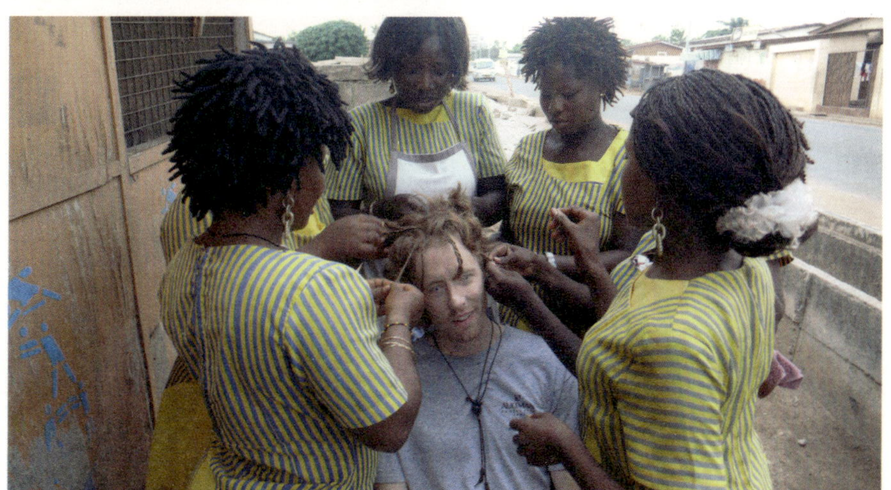

ABOVE / 11 Olaf Breuning, *Home2*, 2007, stills

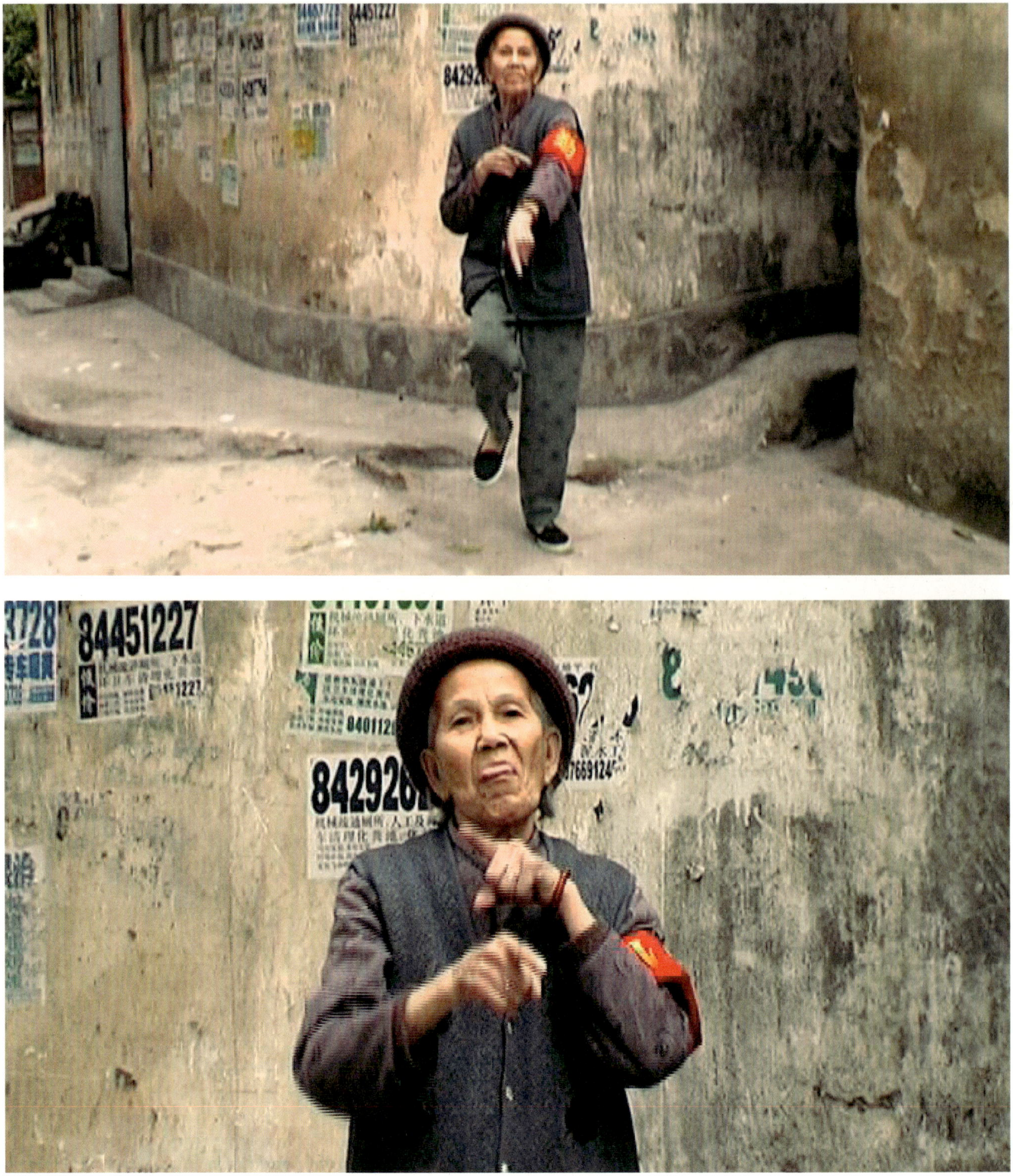

13 Cao Fei, *Hip Hop: Guangzhou*, 2003, stills

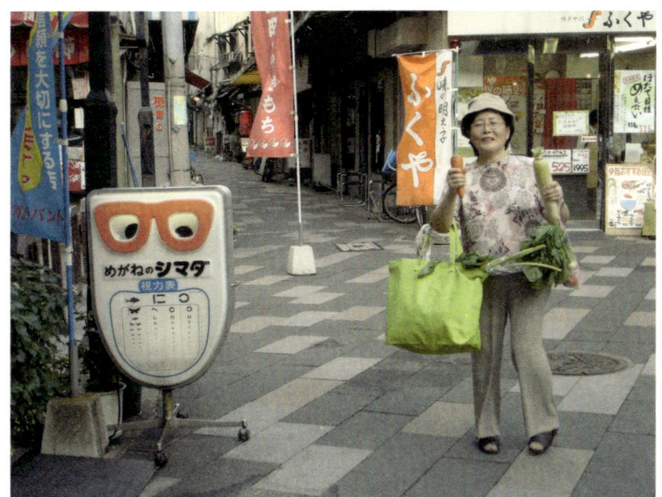

Cao Fei, *Hip Hop: Fukuoka*, 2005, still

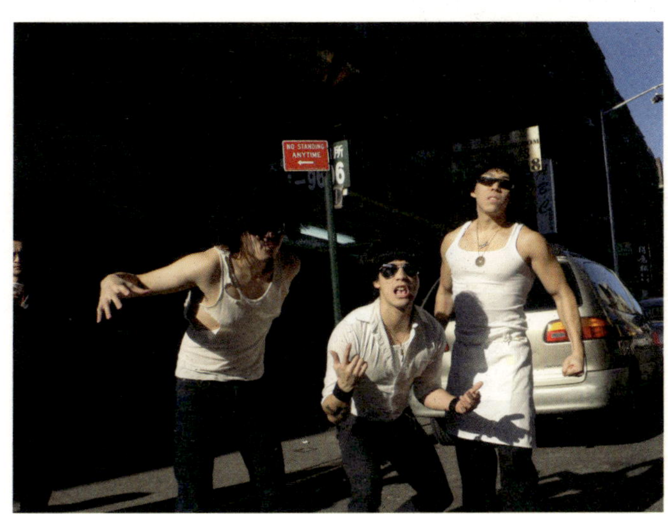

Cao Fei, *Hip Hop: New York*, 2006, still

CAO FEI

Born in 1978, Guangzhou, Guangdong Province, China
Lives and works in Beijing, China

Cao Fei works with performance, photography, writing and sound, and has made both short films and feature-length productions. Much of her work looks at the social consequences of globalisation. Born in the southern Chinese city of Guangzhou, not far from Hong Kong, Cao Fei grew up in a hybrid culture: 'I saw lots of MTV when I was young,' she comments. 'I learned a great deal through TV, especially Hong Kong television that was broadcast in Guangzhou. It was a mix of Hong Kong and Western programming.'

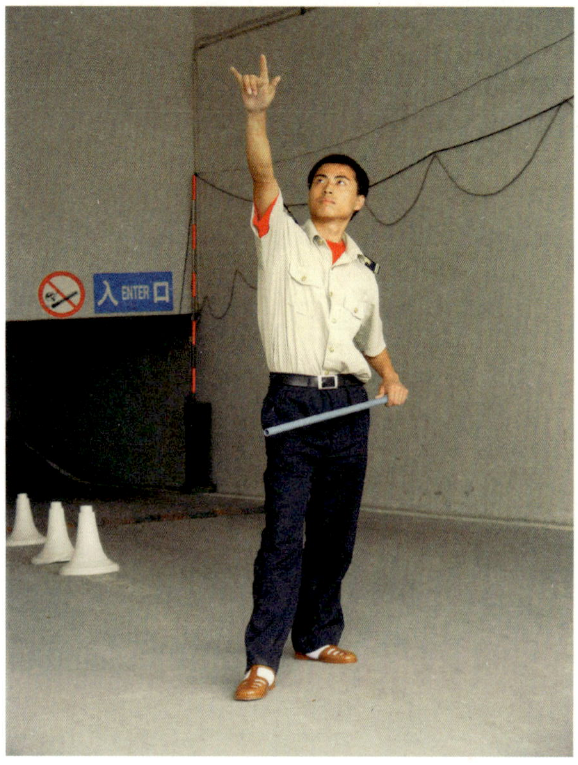

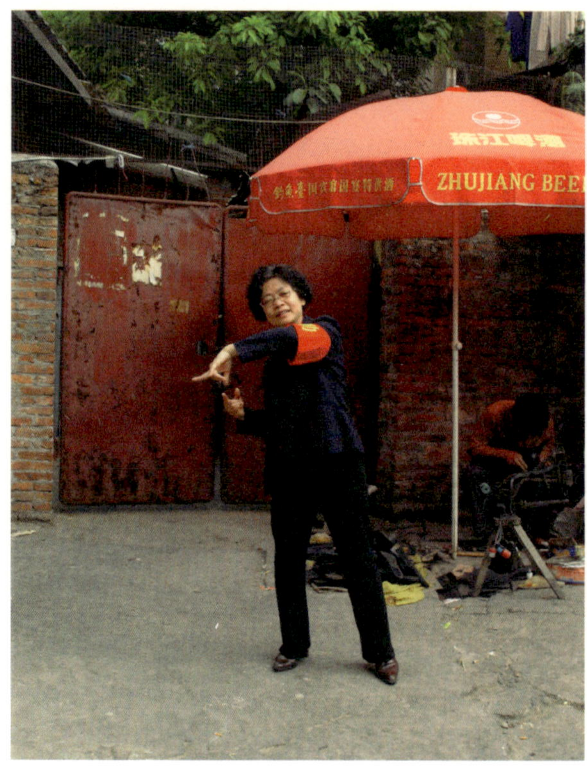

ABOVE AND RIGHT / 13 Cao Fei, *Hip Hop: Guangzhou*, 2003, stills

In *Hip Hop*, Cao Fei combines her own experience of street dancing with her interest in the lives of the ordinary men and women whom posterity never remembers. 'The nation's history always credits the good hero,' she points out. 'I am more interested in common people.' Here, construction workers, students, police and elderly people from Guangzhou are lured from their everyday activities by the siren sound of American-style hip hop music and break into proto-electro dance movements. Cao Fei believes that, despite its African-American origins, there is something universal about hip hop culture, and that beneath its casual surface this dance form expresses the rougher side of suffering. The dancers in *Hip Hop* appear to be controlled both by a higher power and a will to survive. Cao Fei's message is, 'Take it easy. Be simple and happy.

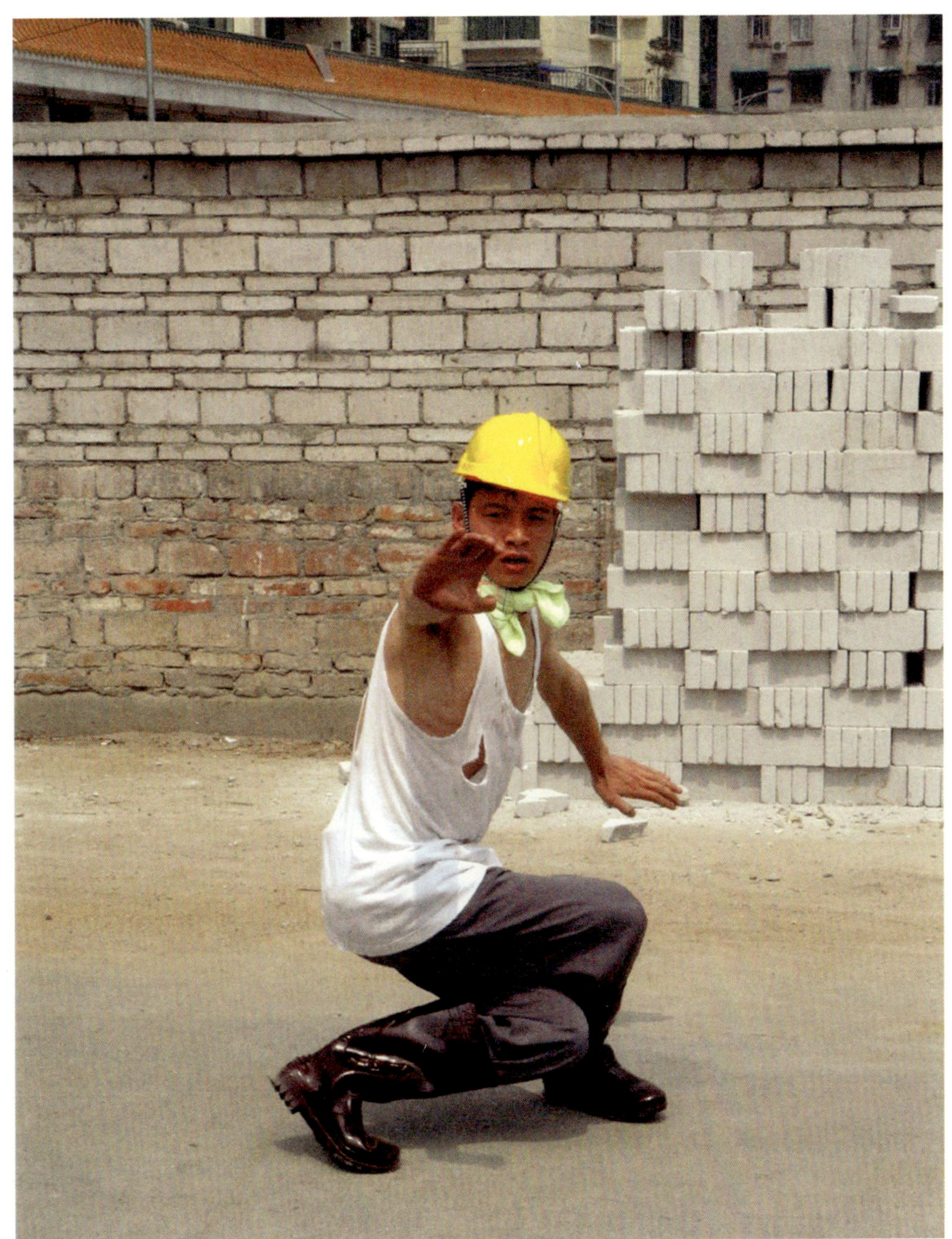

We don't have to carry burdens. Nothing is important anymore. All that people need is to form a [harmonic] whole, to dance without care and catch the eternity of happiness in a flash.' Since making *Hip Hop: Guangzhou*, Cao Fei has taken her hip hop project to New York's Chinatown, to Fukuoka in Japan, and to Berlin.

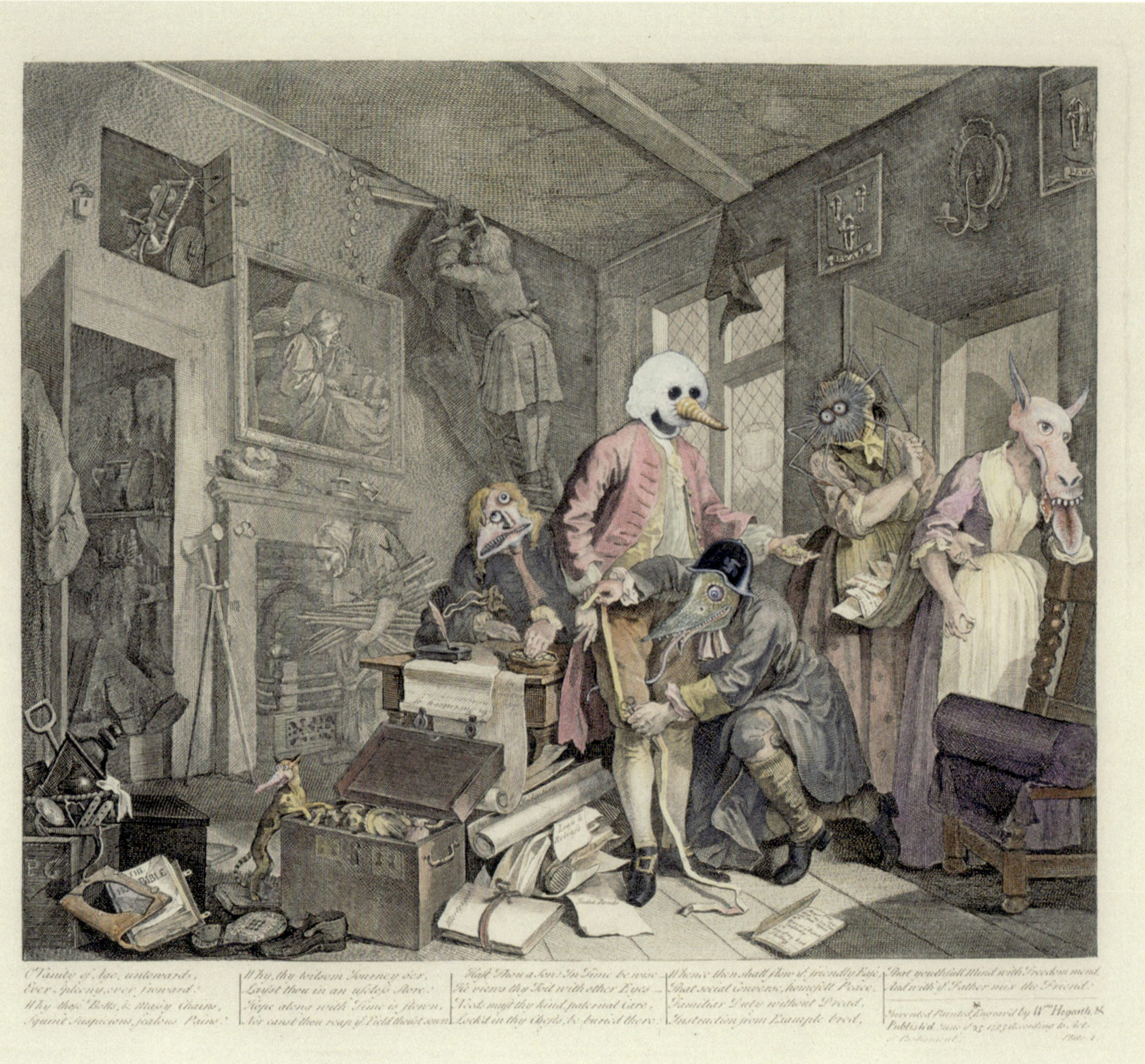

14 Jake and Dinos Chapman, *Dinos and Jake's Progress Plate 1*, 2007

JAKE AND DINOS CHAPMAN

JAKE CHAPMAN
Born in 1966, Cheltenham, UK
Lives and works in London
DINOS CHAPMAN
Born in 1962, London, UK
Lives and works in London

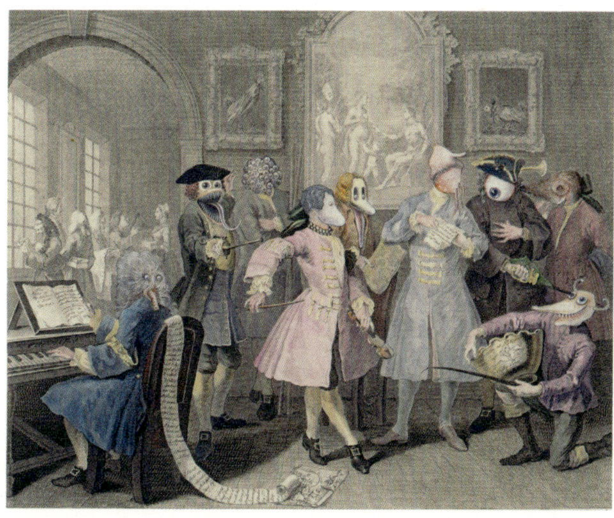

15 Jake and Dinos Chapman, *Dinos and Jake's Progress Plate 2*, 2007, detail

From the very outset of their joint career in the early 1990s, Jake and Dinos Chapman became notorious for their iconoclasm, and quickly gained reputations as the bad boys of contemporary art. In *Insult to Injury*, they 'reworked and improved' a complete set of Goya's harrowing *Disasters of War*, one of the most revered series of prints ever created. 'We always had the intention of "rectifying" it,' said Dinos. 'We've gone very systematically through the entire 80 etchings, and changed all the visible victims' heads to clowns' heads and puppies' heads.' Two years later, they 'reworked and improved' Goya's first major work of social commentary, *Los Caprichos*, and, in 2007, they turned their attention to William Hogarth's *Rake's Progress*, a critique of the corrupting effects of eighteenth-century consumerism and one of his best-known 'Modern Moral Subjects'.

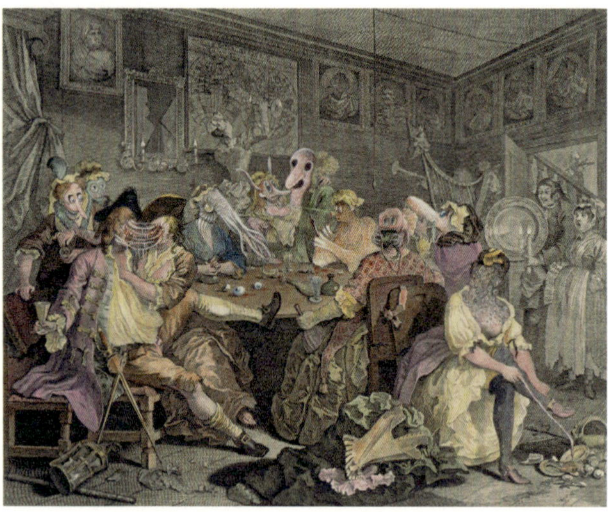

16 Jake and Dinos Chapman, *Dinos and Jake's Progress Plate 3*, 2007, detail

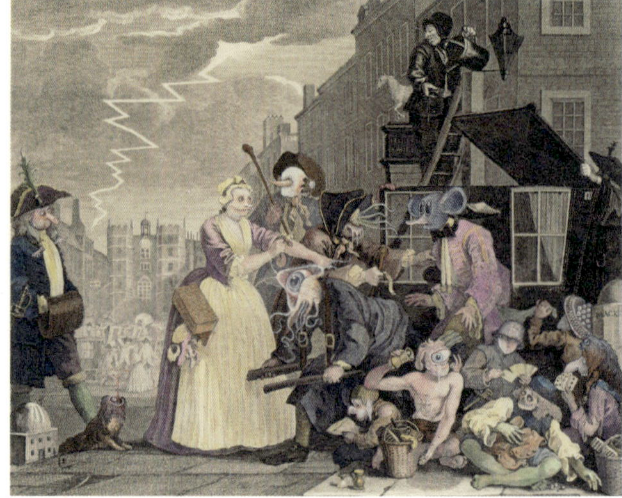

17 Jake and Dinos Chapman, *Dinos and Jake's Progress Plate 4*, 2007, detail

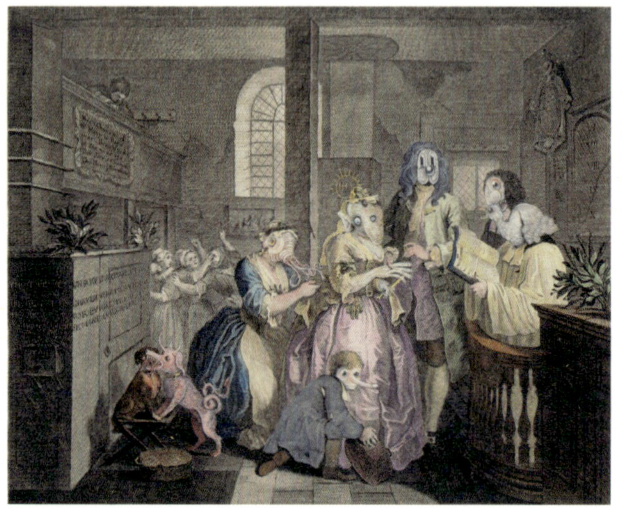

18 Jake and Dinos Chapman, *Dinos and Jake's Progress Plate 5*, 2007, detail

Originally published in 1735, Hogarth's series of eight prints follows the fortunes of a young wastrel who is ruined by his own extravagance and quickly descends from folly to vice. Based on paintings that Hogarth completed in 1733, the prints underwent various changes; Hogarth 'improved' the later states, altering shading, faces and details and adding inscriptions, accessories and even a whole new group of figures. At the end of his life, he made a further revision to the final plate. Nearly two and a half centuries later, the Chapmans have made their own reworkings and improvements, transforming characters into creatures that seem to have been born from a strange meeting between Walt Disney and Hieronymus Bosch.

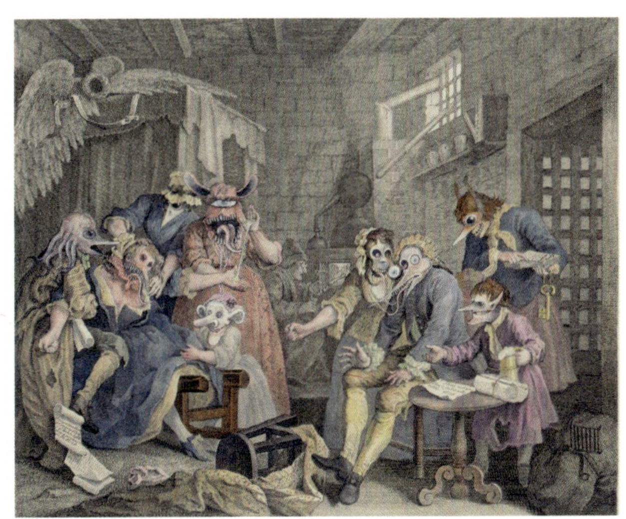

20 Jake and Dinos Chapman, *Dinos and Jake's Progress Plate 7*, 2007, detail

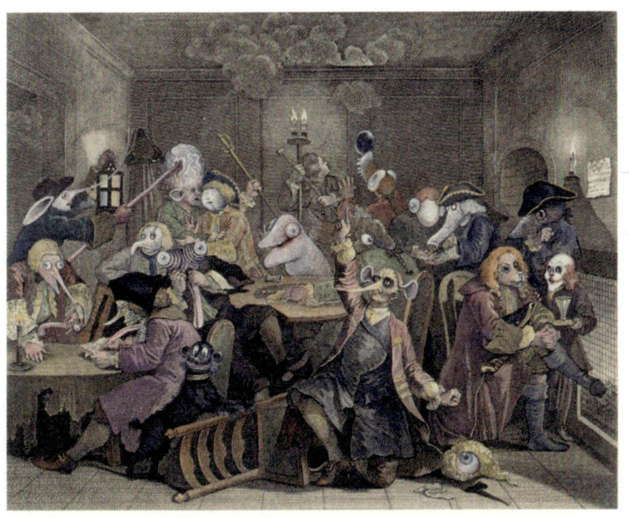

19 Jake and Dinos Chapman, *Dinos and Jake's Progress Plate 6*, 2007, detail

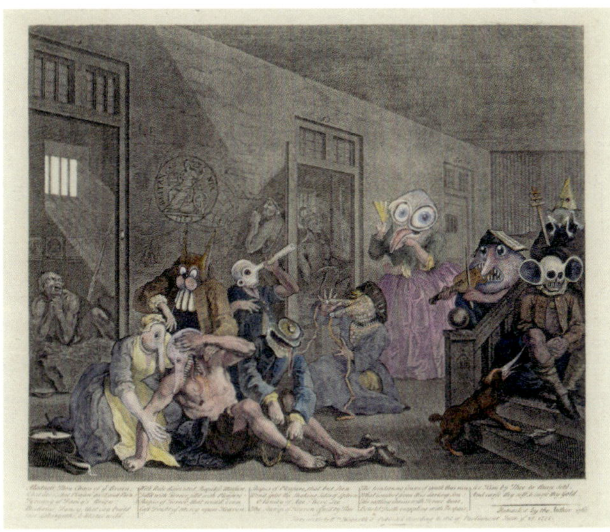

21 Jake and Dinos Chapman, *Dinos and Jake's Progress Plate 8*, 2007

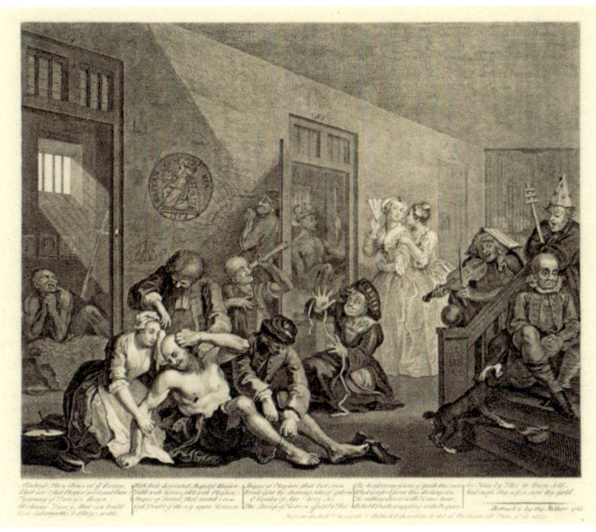

William Hogarth, *A Rake's Progress, plate 8*, 1735, 'improved' in 1763

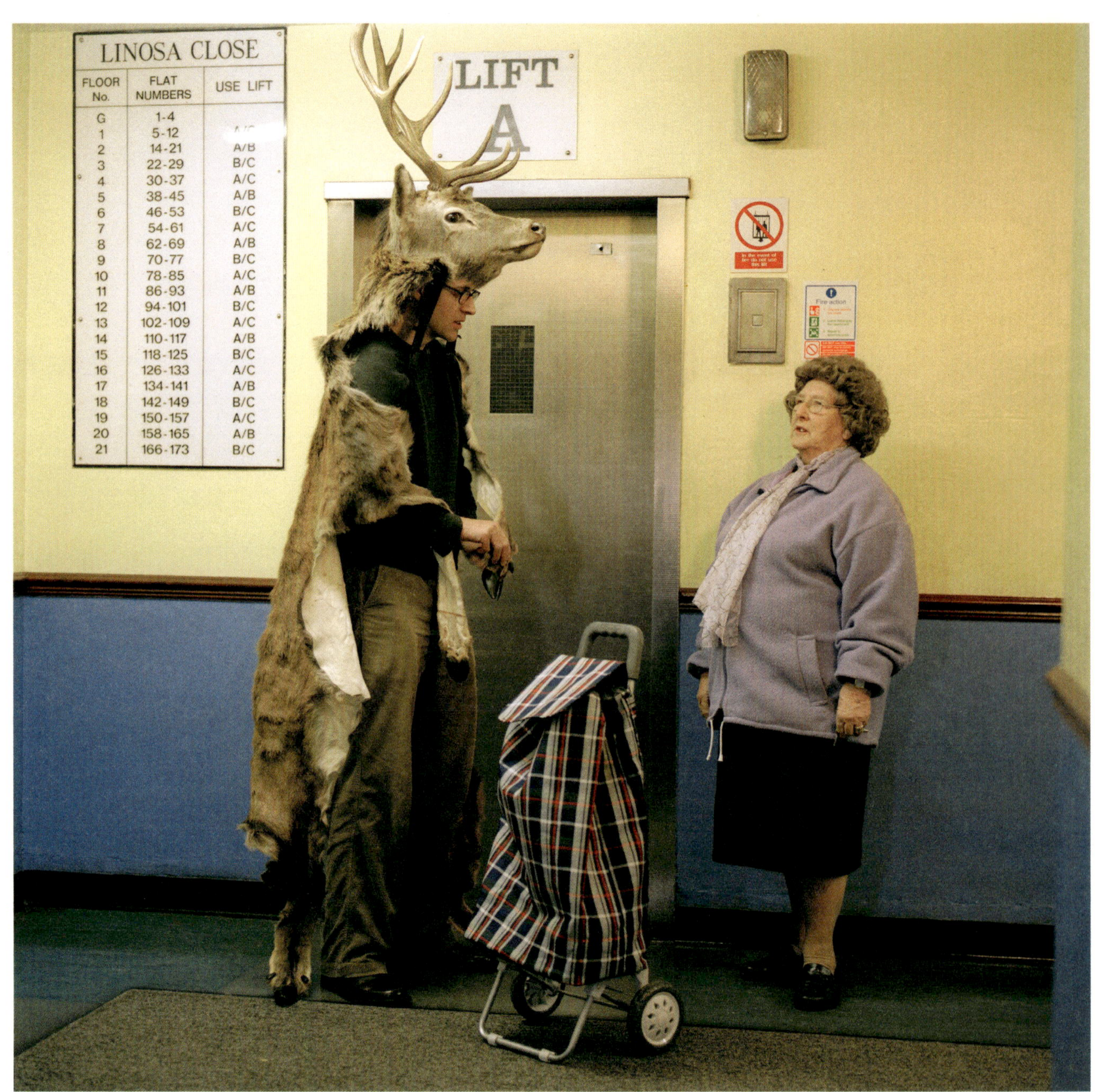

ABOVE AND RIGHT / 22 Marcus Coates, *Journey to the Lower World*, 2004, production stills

MARCUS COATES

Born in 1968, London, UK
Lives and works in London

A keen amateur ornithologist and naturalist, Marcus Coates has always been interested in crossing the boundaries separating the human psyche from animal consciousness. In his videos, photographs, installations, performances and other works he has explored what it is like to be a creature of another species, 'becoming' such different animals as a fox, hawk, seal, stoat and red deer and subjecting himself to ludicrous situations in the process. The comedy lies in the fact that however plausible the transformation may be, as Coates points out, 'you can't escape your humanness'.

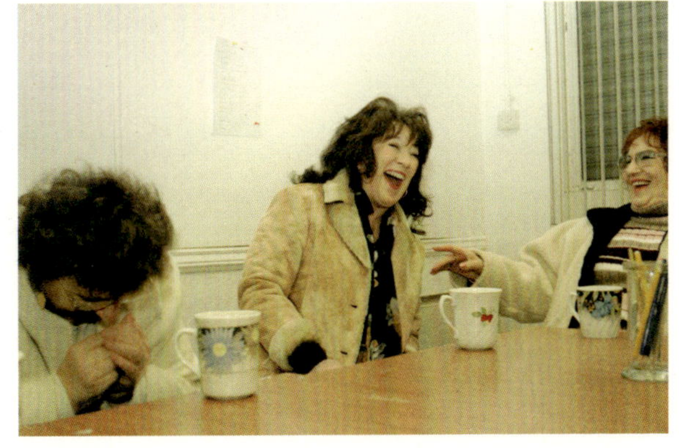

In *Journey to the Lower World*, the first of Coates' shaman works, he performs a traditional Siberian Yakut ritual for a group of residents in a condemned tower block in Liverpool. Historically, the shaman would have been brought in to solve the everyday problems of a community. In this case, the anxiety was about how the residents' lives would change after the demolition of their flats and their relocation. Their question was: 'Do we have a protector for this site, and what is it?' With some trepidation (he was expecting a simpler inquiry about the practicalities of their predicament), Coates makes preparations for his journey

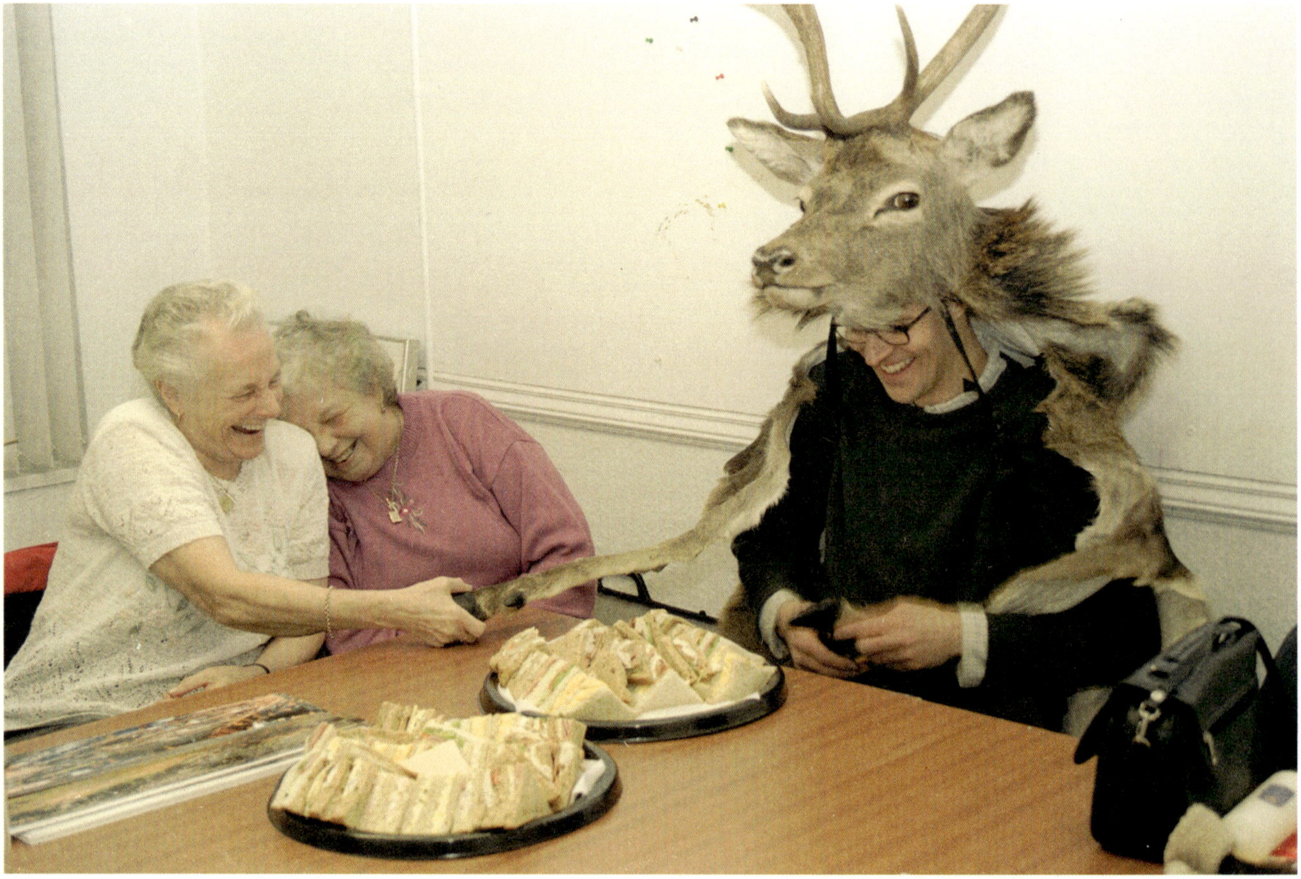

22 Marcus Coates, *Journey to the Lower World*, 2004, **ABOVE** production still, **BELOW** stills

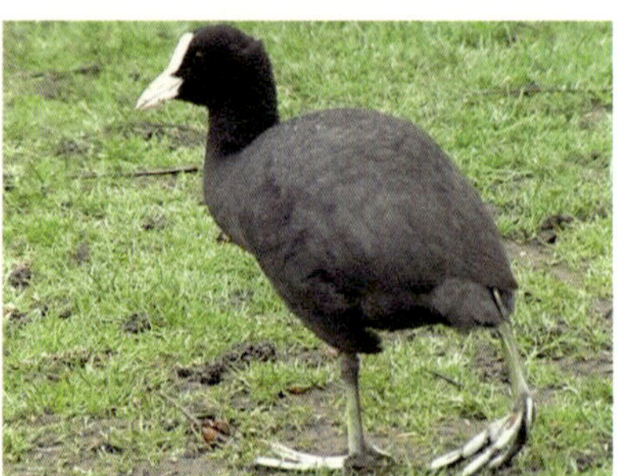

to the lower world to consult animal spirits. During his shamanic journeying, the residents' nervous giggles escalate into ribald laughter as he utters an incantation of strange feral sounds. 'I took the ritual and occasion very seriously,' Coates remarks, 'but I didn't want to take myself seriously, because I wasn't in a position to. It was up to the audience how serious the event was. They laughed all the way through.'

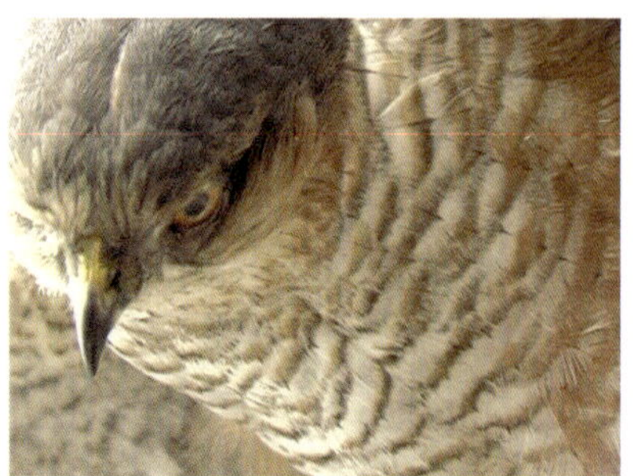

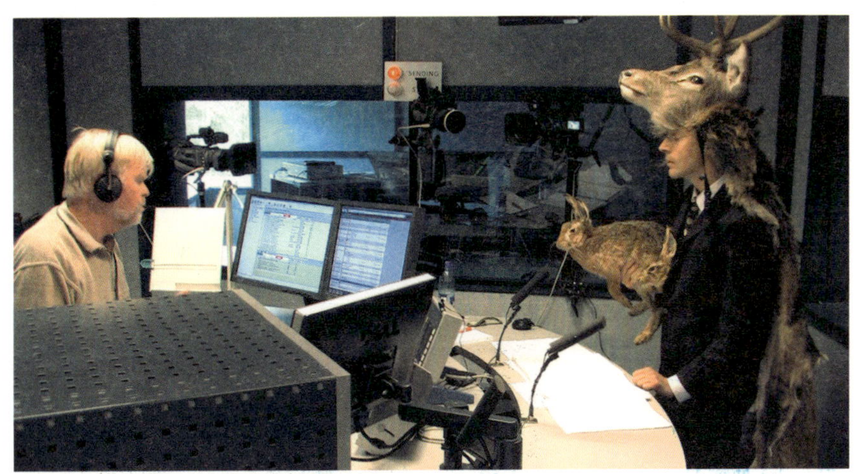

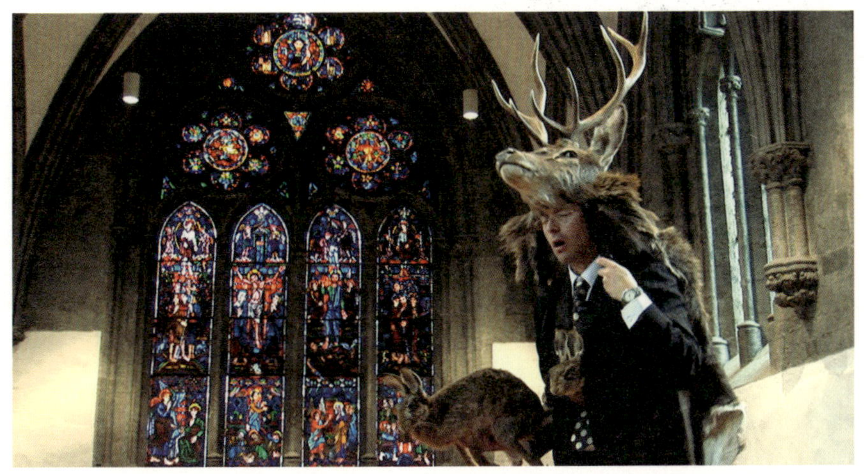

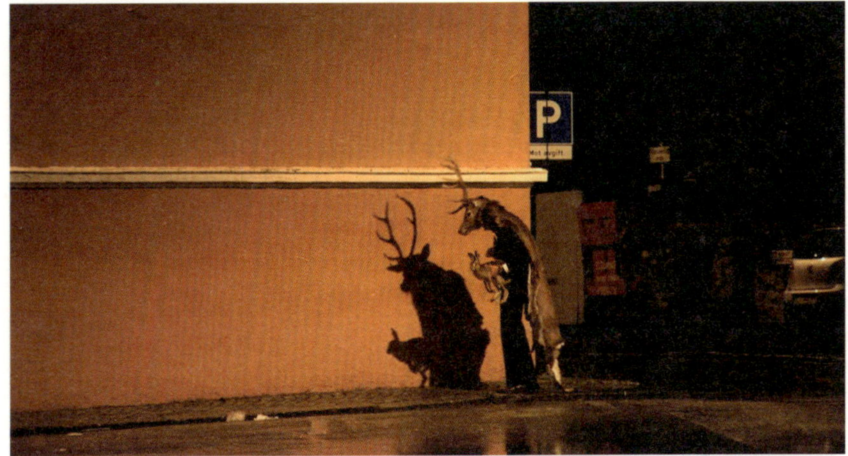

ABOVE Marcus Coates, *Radio Shaman*, 2006, stills

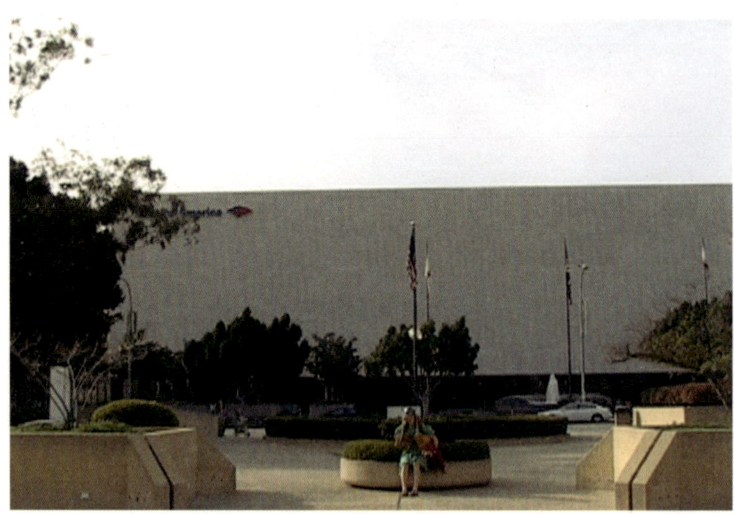

ABOVE AND RIGHT / 23 Harry Dodge and Stanya Kahn, *Can't Swallow it, Can't Spit it Out*, 2006, stills

HARRY DODGE AND STANYA KAHN

HARRY DODGE
Born in 1966, California, USA
Lives and works in Los Angeles, USA
STANYA KAHN
Born in 1968, California, USA
Lives and works in Los Angeles, USA

The performance artists Harriet 'Harry' Dodge and Stanya Kahn make collaborative videos in which Kahn performs in front of the camera while Dodge, who actually does the filming, plays the part of an unseen cameraman. *Can't Swallow it, Can't Spit it Out*, begins with the dawn encounter between a bloody-nosed Valkyrie carrying a giant wedge of cheese and a guy with a video camera trying to 'catch some action'. Their chance meeting outside a hospital begins badly, with the Valkyrie berating and threatening the hapless cameraman. Then, overcoming her reluctance to be filmed, she takes him on a day-long wander around Los Angeles. He fails to find the 'action' he is looking for – police brutality or any other abuse of authority – and instead ends up recording her rambling soliloquies, during which she continues to goad him. Ultimately, it is the Valkyrie's violent memories, fantasies or hallucinations that provide the spectacle.

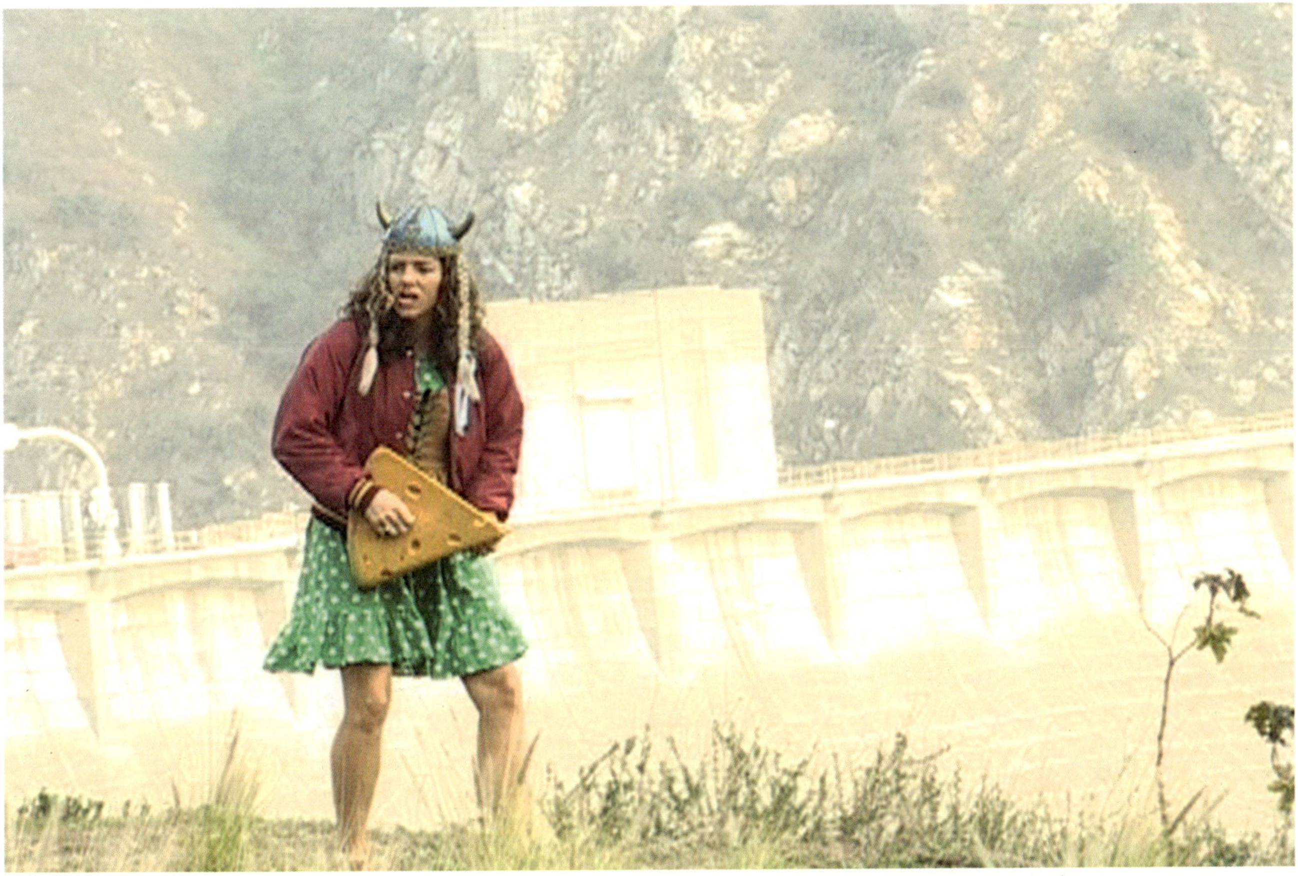

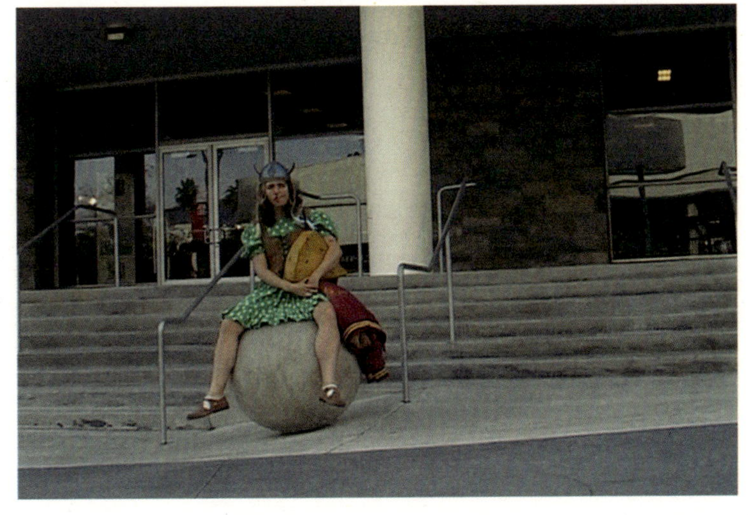

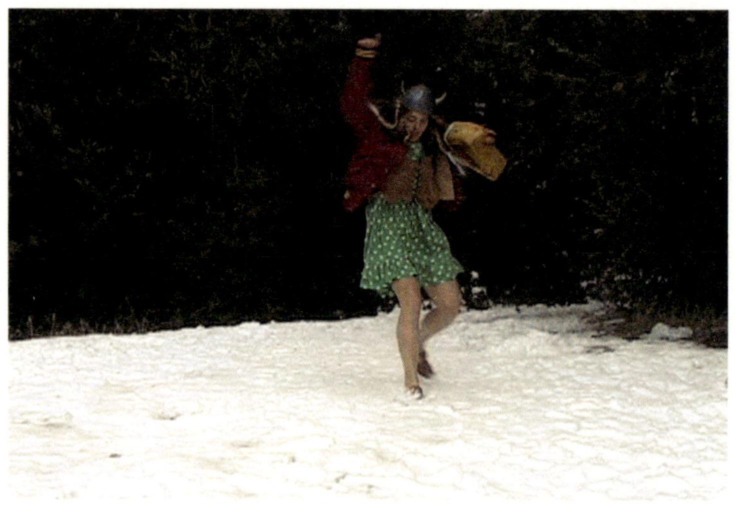

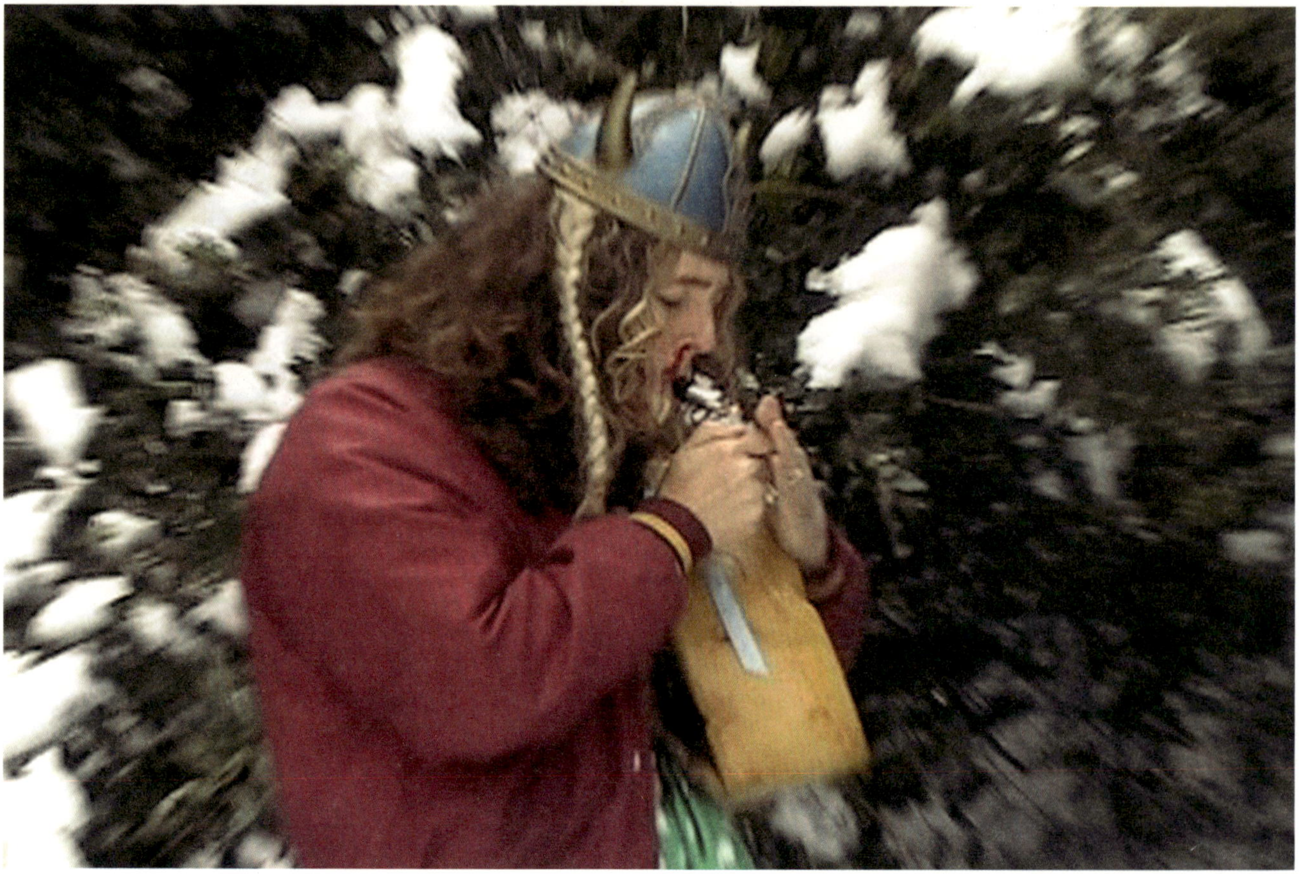

ABOVE AND RIGHT / 23 Harry Dodge and Stanya Kahn, *Can't Swallow it, Can't Spit it Out*, 2006, stills

Made during the third year of the Iraqi war, *Can't Swallow it, Can't Spit it Out* operates on multiple levels. Dodge and Kahn state that 'it is basically a portrait of civilian anxiety in a time of war.' Pointing out that the Valkyrie is a 'kind of double, or even triple entendre,' they ask: 'Is she a person who works at the county fair or a theme park? Can she, as a Viking type, be a symbol of Anglo war imperatives? And is there this hazy possibility that she might be an actual Valkyrie, come to usher spirits of slain heroes to Valhalla?'

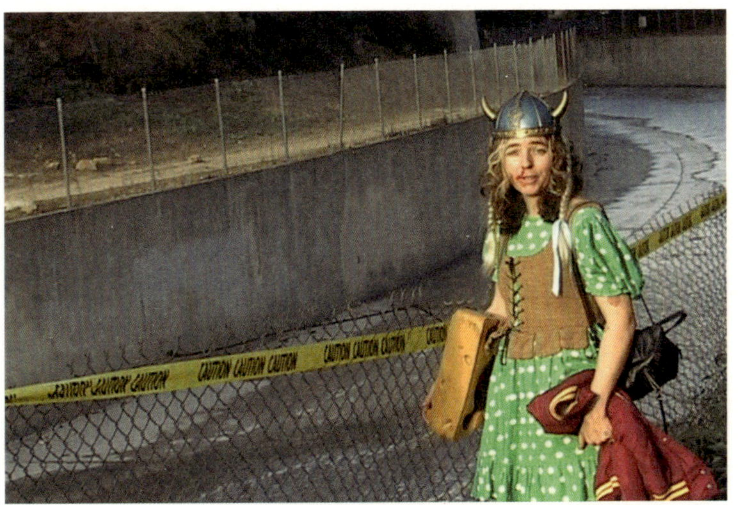

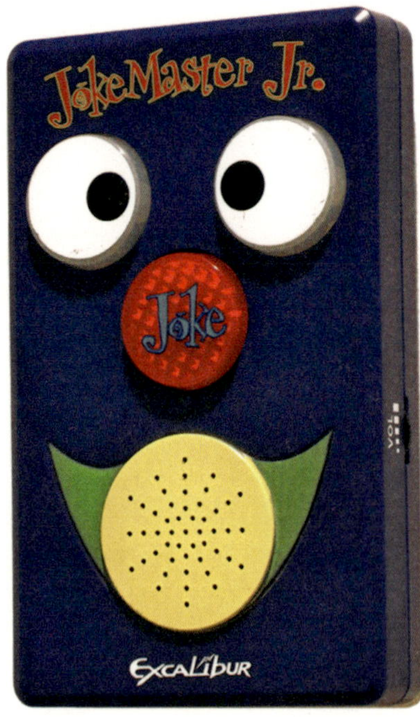

Doug Fishbone, *Joke Master Jr*, 2006 (see cat. 26)

DOUG FISHBONE

Born in 1969, New York, USA
Lives and works in London, UK

Doug Fishbone's videos and installations invite the viewer, as he says, 'to consider some of the more unseemly aspects of modern living in an amusing and disarming way.' Co-opting the strategies of stand-up comedy, he surfs the internet for off-colour jokes, one-liners, visual gags and Freudian slips, which he appropriates and recycles in videos resembling cack-handed slide shows or corporate PowerPoint presentations. His narratives are delivered as nerdy, deadpan voice-overs, adding verbal absurdity to visual incongruity. You laugh, even when you know you shouldn't.

Describing *Towards a Common Understanding* as 'a narrative filled with bizarre anecdotes and filthy jokes, homespun proverbs and strange social analysis,' Fishbone explains that, 'the narrator wallows in the grey area of copyright violation, recontextualizing stolen images to reflect some of the many failures of modern consumer capitalism – greed, perversity, violence, ignorance, obscenity, and above all, indifference – not to mention obesity.' Following a similar format, the images in *Everybody Loves a Winner* range from the personal to the political, featuring hunchbacks, trepanation, an actual 'frog king', Bill Clinton stagemanaging the Yitzhak Rabin-Yasser Arafat handshake, soldiers beating civilians, various polytheistic gods and idols, the mass suicide of the followers of Jim Jones' People's Temple cult, and jokes about the 'agnostic dyslexic insomniac' who stays up all night wondering whether there really is a dog. Fishbone comments that 'all of the images in the video turn the vulgarity of our society's freely available visual language back on itself.'

Joke Master Jr and its successor *Joke Master Jr 2* are Fishbone's new and improved versions of commercially available electronic joke machines. He has replaced the original child-friendly gags with his own collection of two-bit jokes and one-liners, commenting: 'The subtle inflections of a classic Jewish joke, or the extreme poor taste of some of the dirtier remarks, are made very strange by the utter incongruousness of the locale. Humour, after all, is a function of context ... In an environment like The Hayward, with all of its attendant cultural gravitas, the *Joke Master Jr* is very much out of place.'

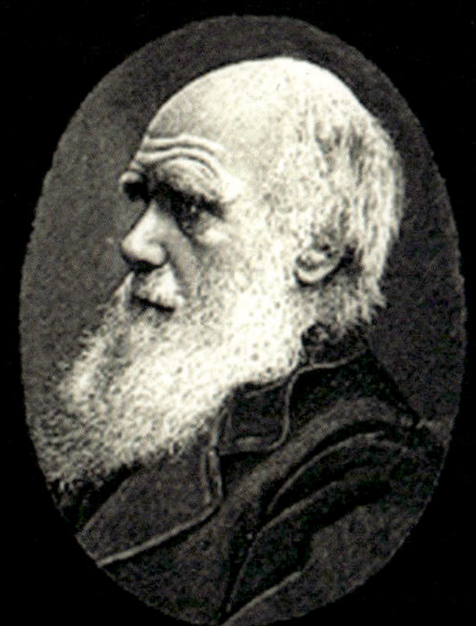

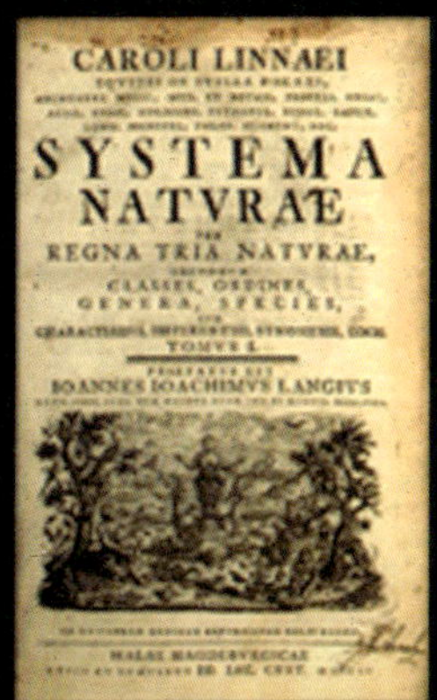

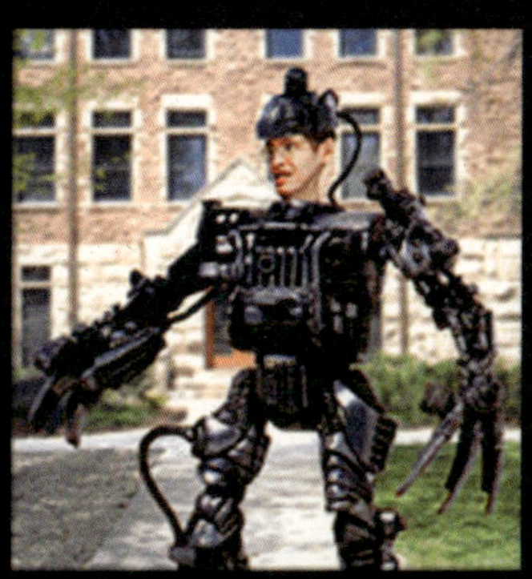

Some folks like to make up fancy systems of classification with big Latin words, and think they've got the world all neatly organized.

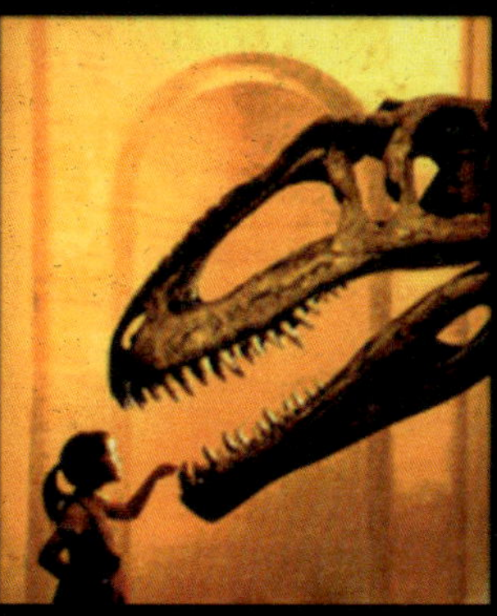

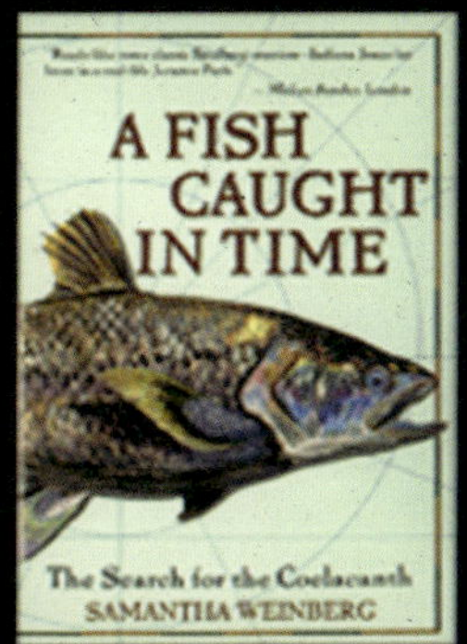

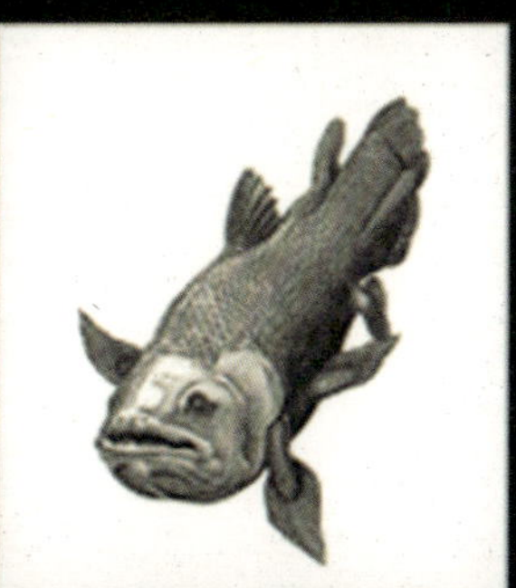

But then they discover evidence of a new dinosaur, or some strange fish that was thought to be extinct,

25 Doug Fishbone, *Towards a Common Understanding*, 2005, excerpt

OVERLEAF / 24 Doug Fishbone, *Everybody Loves a Winner*, 2004, excerpt

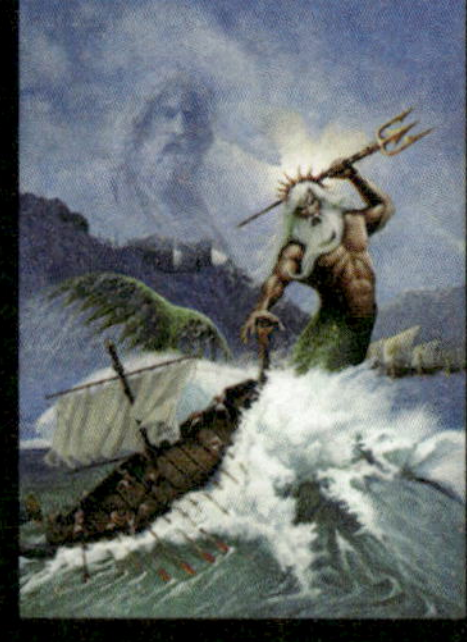

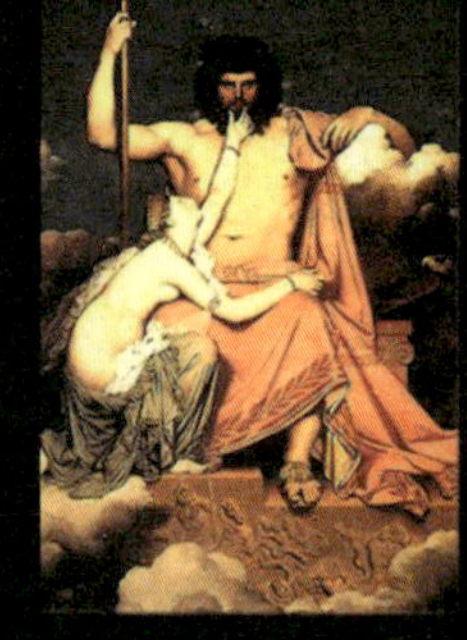

The Greeks used to worship Poseidon and Zeus, and tried to predict the future by reading the entrails of birds.

You had your Norse gods.

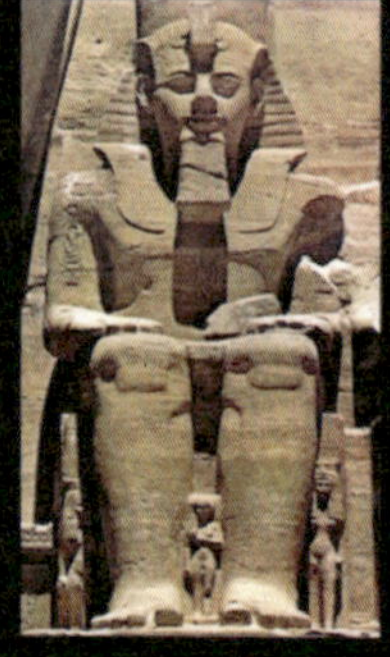

...and Egyptian gods...

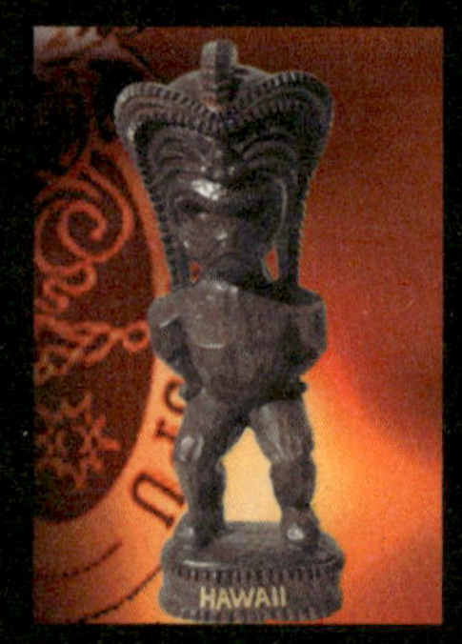

...ancient Hawaiian spirits like Kanoa...

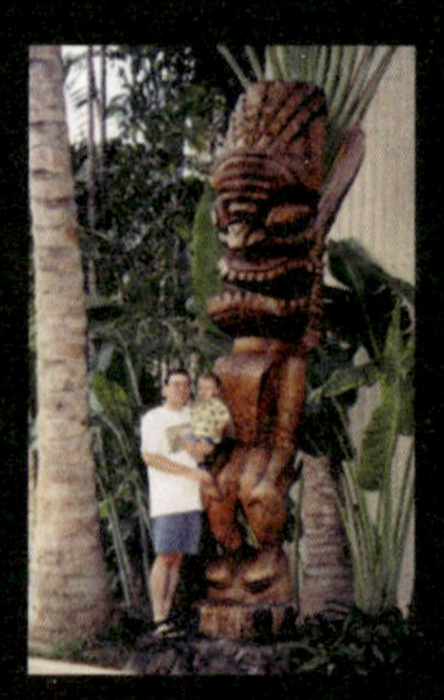

...and Hina-puku-a'i.

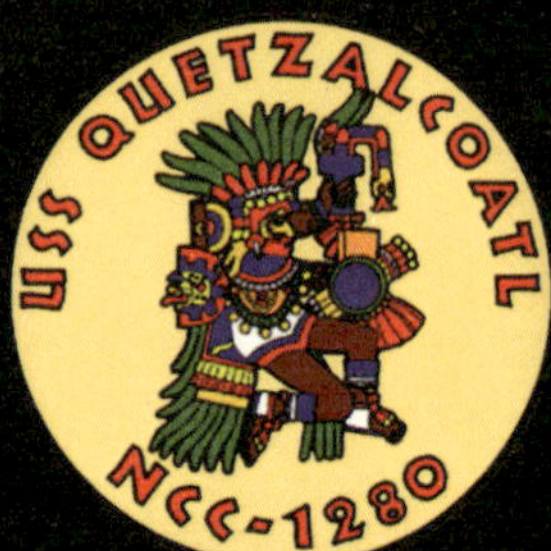

The Aztecs worshipped a giant snake called Quetzalcoatl, and engaged in human sacrifice.

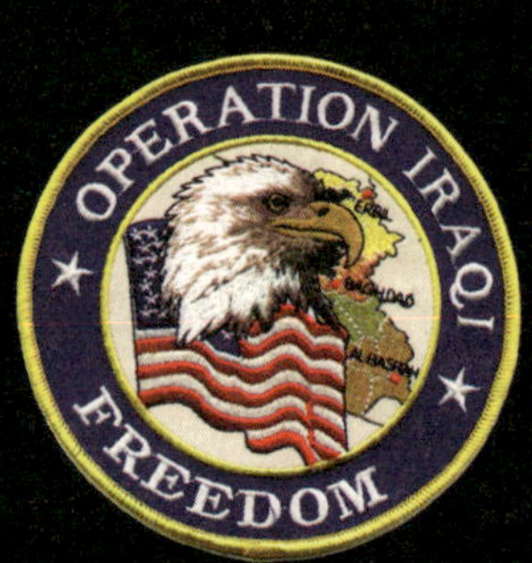

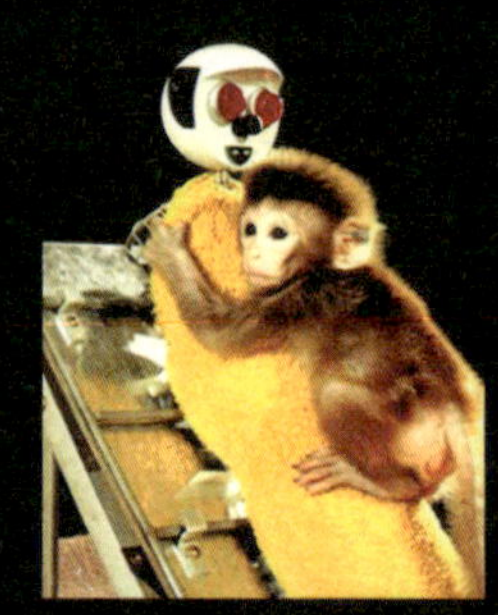

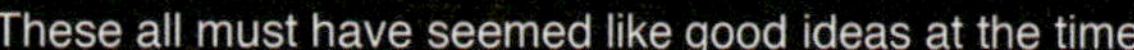

These all must have seemed like good ideas at the time, but now we just think they're a crock.

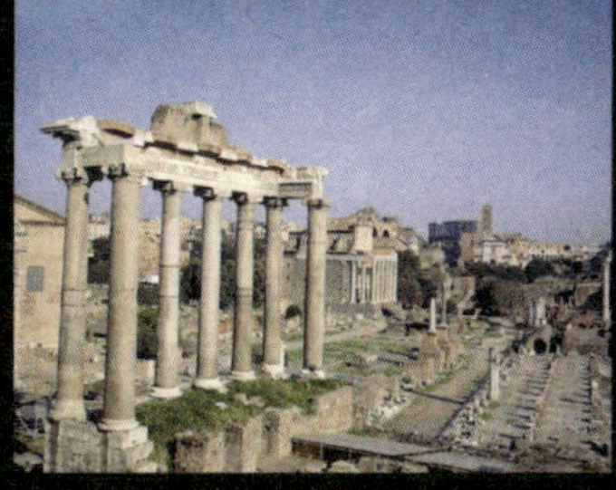

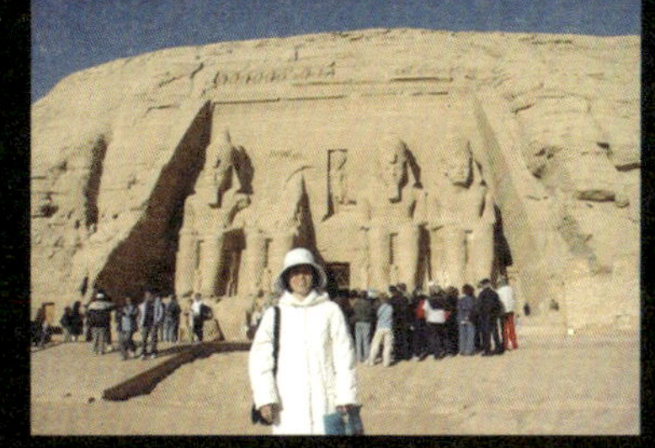

But what if everything we think today turns out to be just as wrong-headed?

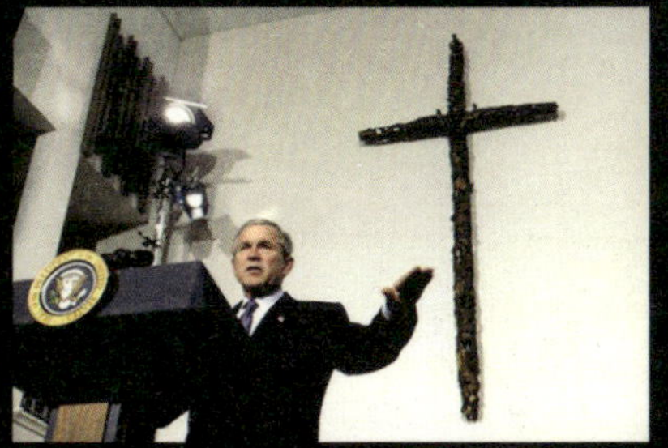

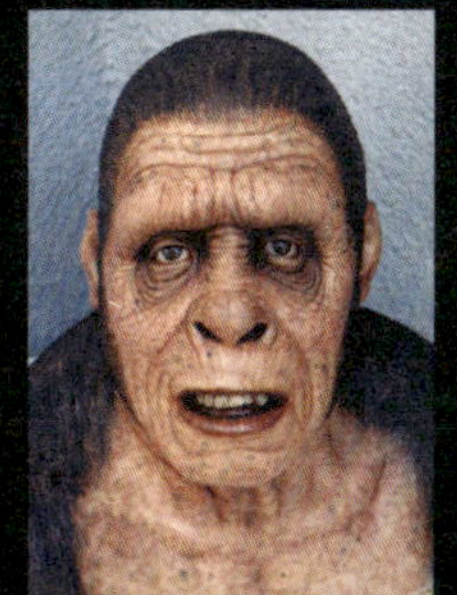

Maybe worshipping Jesus is as ridiculous as anything the cave men did?

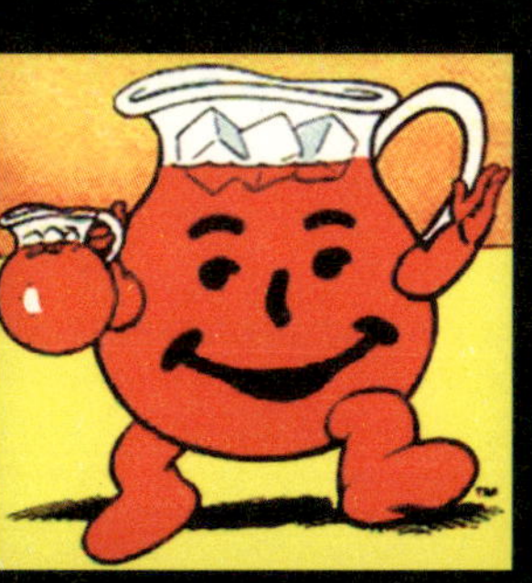

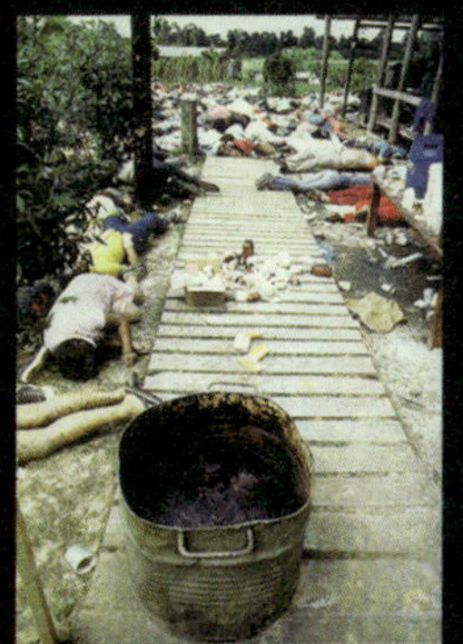

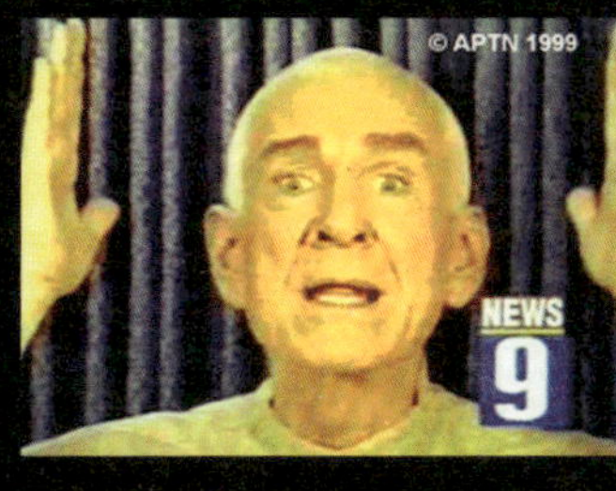

Or those wackos with the Kool Aid back in Guyana in the Seventies?

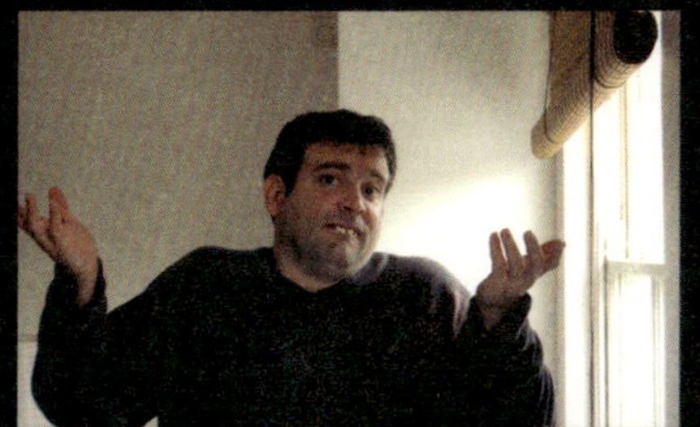

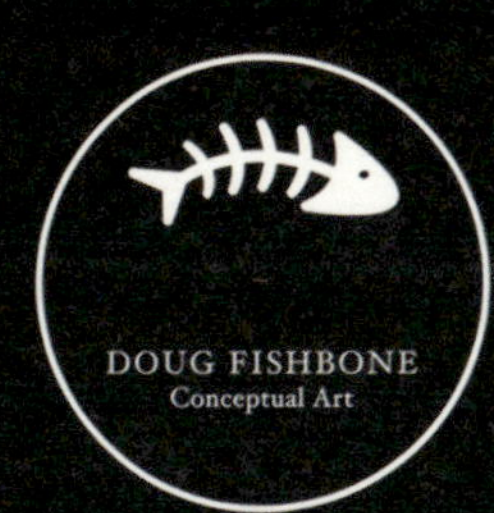

Maybe it's impossible to know anything with any certainty at all?

GHAZEL

Born in 1966, Tehran, Iran
Lives and works in Paris, France

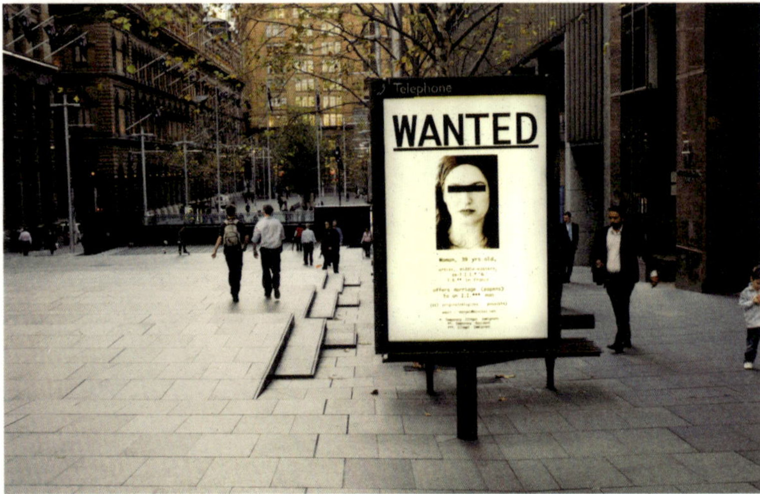

Ghazel, *Wanted*, 2006, installation view: Sydney, Australia, 2006 (see cat. 31)

The starting point for Ghazel's art is identity; her work is triggered, she says, by 'my multiple imperfect identities, though it has evolved into being more and more universal.' An Iranian who had studied and lived in France since 1986, her ongoing series *Wanted* began in 1997 when, denied a residence permit by the French immigration authorities, she was given 15 days to leave the country. In response, she decided to make posters advertising for a husband. A version of this work, made in 1998 and handed out in the streets, reads: 'WANTED Woman (31 yrs. old) (middle-eastern) seeks a non-racist and understanding HUSBAND (passport) (EU citizenship, preferably French).'

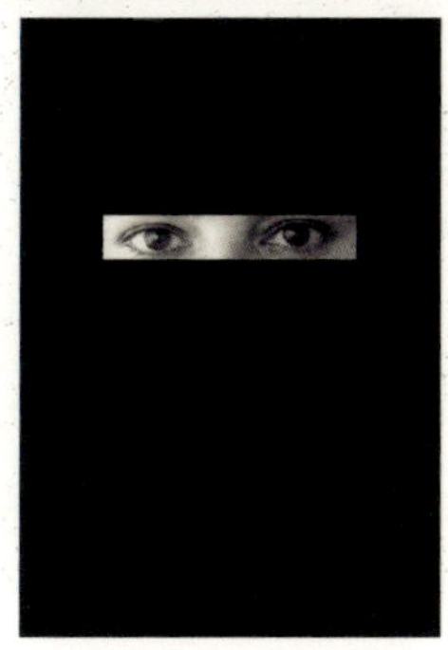

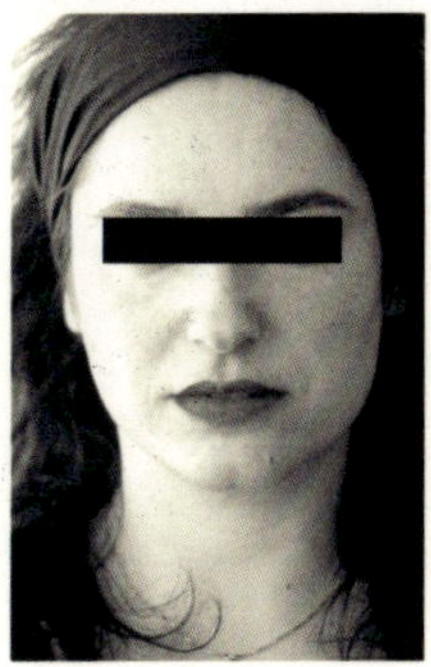

31 Ghazel, *Wanted*, 2007

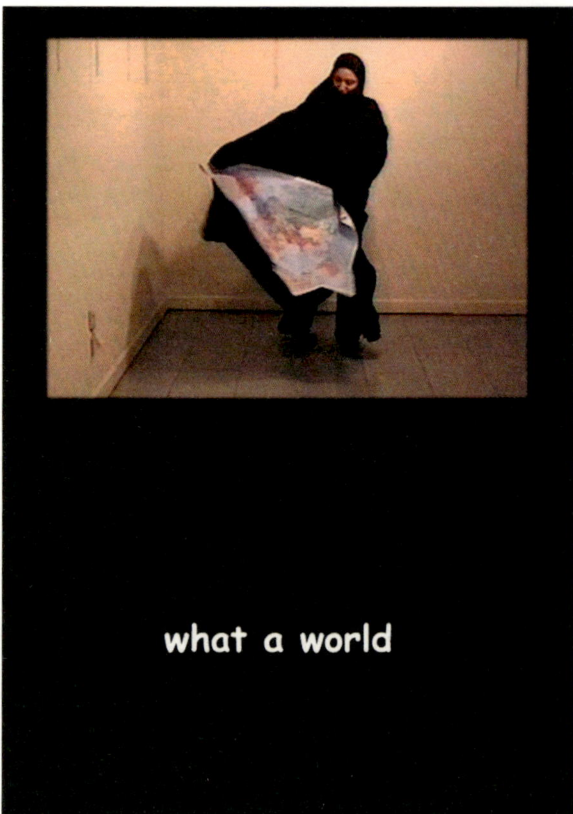

30 Ghazel, *Olé*, 2004, *Me* series

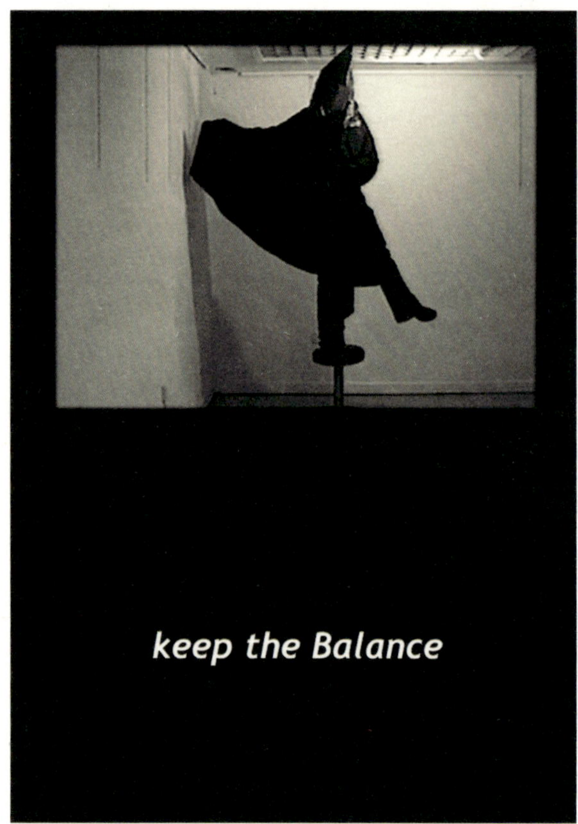

29 Ghazel, *Keep the Balance*, 2004, *Me* series

Ghazel eventually received a ten-year permit for residency in France in 2002. Since then she has continued her poster campaign but now, instead of advertising for a husband who will enable her to have a *carte de séjour*, she offers herself in marriage to illegal immigrants so that they can become eligible for residency in France. She has exhibited this work internationally, adapting it to each country in which it is shown.

In 1997, Ghazel also started another ongoing series, *Me*, which began as an autobiography, illustrating her life 'in between', spent half in Tehran and half in Montpellier. In these self-portraits she appears dressed in a black chador which she refers to as a 'timeless Iranian icon', explaining that it provides not only a link between the images but also gives 'a local colour - much like the black humour that I use in my work.' She adds that, 'through the pretext of autobiography, I try to portray a human (regardless of gender, and ethnic or racial background) in our world today.'

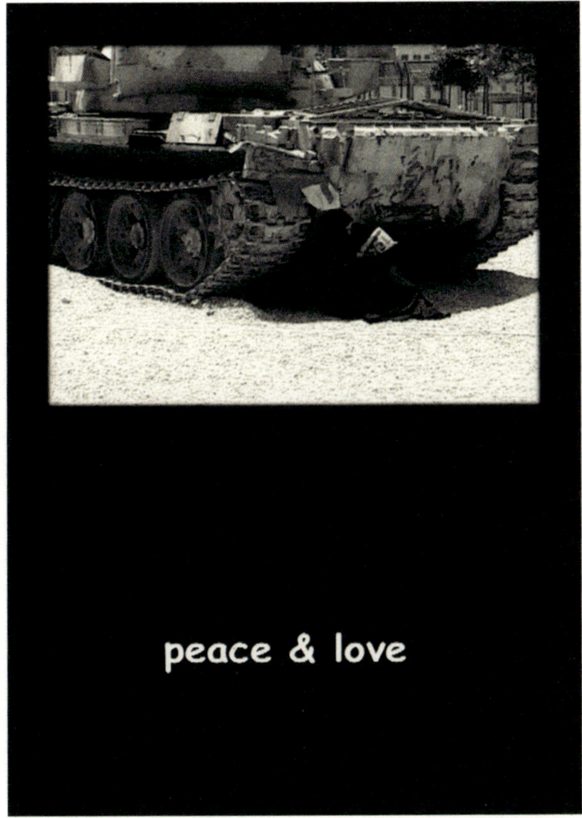

27 Ghazel, *Peace & Love*, 2001, *Me* series

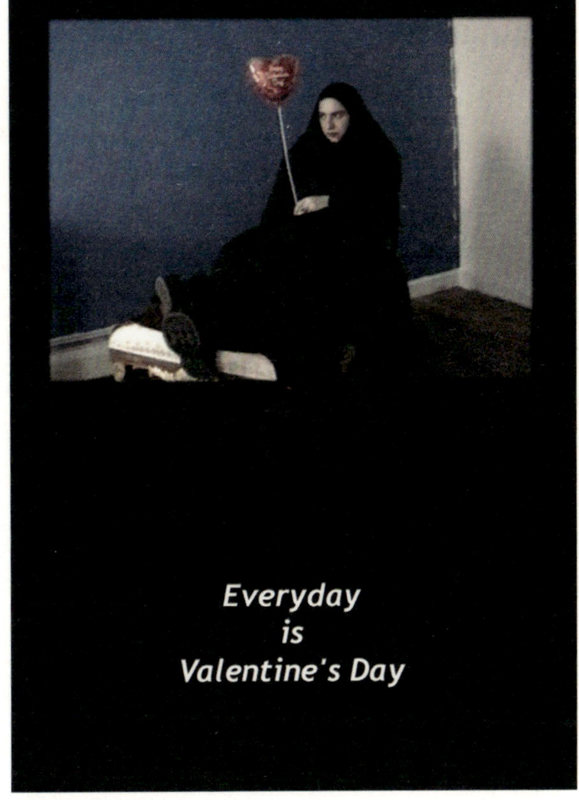

28 Ghazel, *Valentine's Day*, 2001, *Me* series

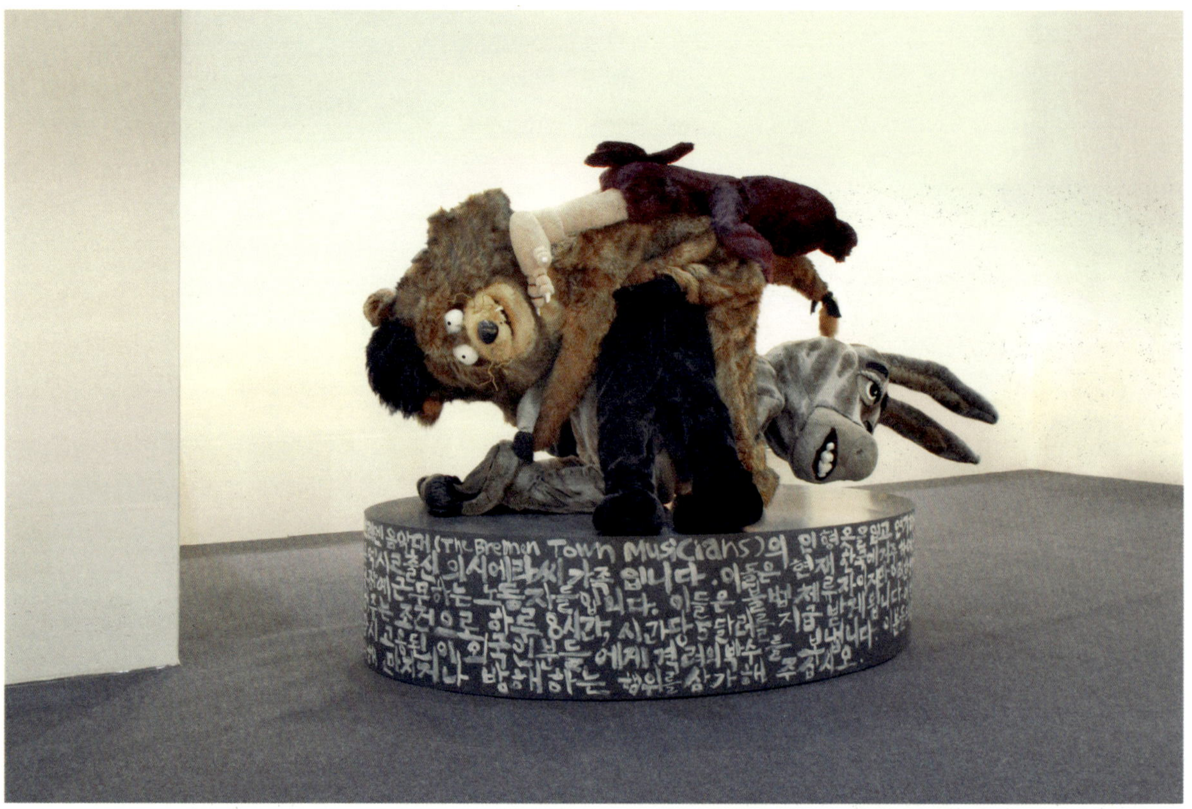

32 Gimhongsok, *The Bremen Town Musicians*, 2006–07, installation view

GIMHONGSOK

Born in 1964, Seoul, South Korea
Lives and works in Seoul

Working in a variety of media, including film, video, sculpture and installation, Gimhongsok often uses everyday materials to engage his audience in dialogues about nationalism, the economy and cultural divisions. Language and the problems of translation are some of his central concerns. In *The Bremen Town Musicians*, he takes a tale from the Brothers Grimm about a donkey, a dog, a cat and a rooster – all of which have been mistreated by their masters – and persuades us that it is being acted out by a group of illegal immigrants. Wearing appropriate animal costumes, they are collapsed in a heap, like one of those little push-button wooden toys or marionettes whose strings have been cut. The text around the base tells us that the performers are the Sierra family from Mexico, who work in a shoe factory and are being hired to work in the exhibition at the rate of 5 dollars per eight-hour day.

Gimhongsok extends the joke, by suggesting that these exhausted and exploited actors are, in fact, contemporary artists. In a version of this work exhibited at the 2006 Gwangju Biennale in South Korea, the parts of the donkey, dog and cat were ascribed to the Spanish artist Santiago Sierra, who lives in Mexico City and whose work reflects on the uselessness of capitalism; the Italian sculptor Maurizio Cattelan, who has made several sculptures on the theme of the Bremen town musicians, featuring real animals, either stuffed or reduced to skeletons; and the British neo-conceptualist artist Liam Gillick, whose on-going project concerns a fictitious group of ex-factory workers. The part of the rooster remained undecided.

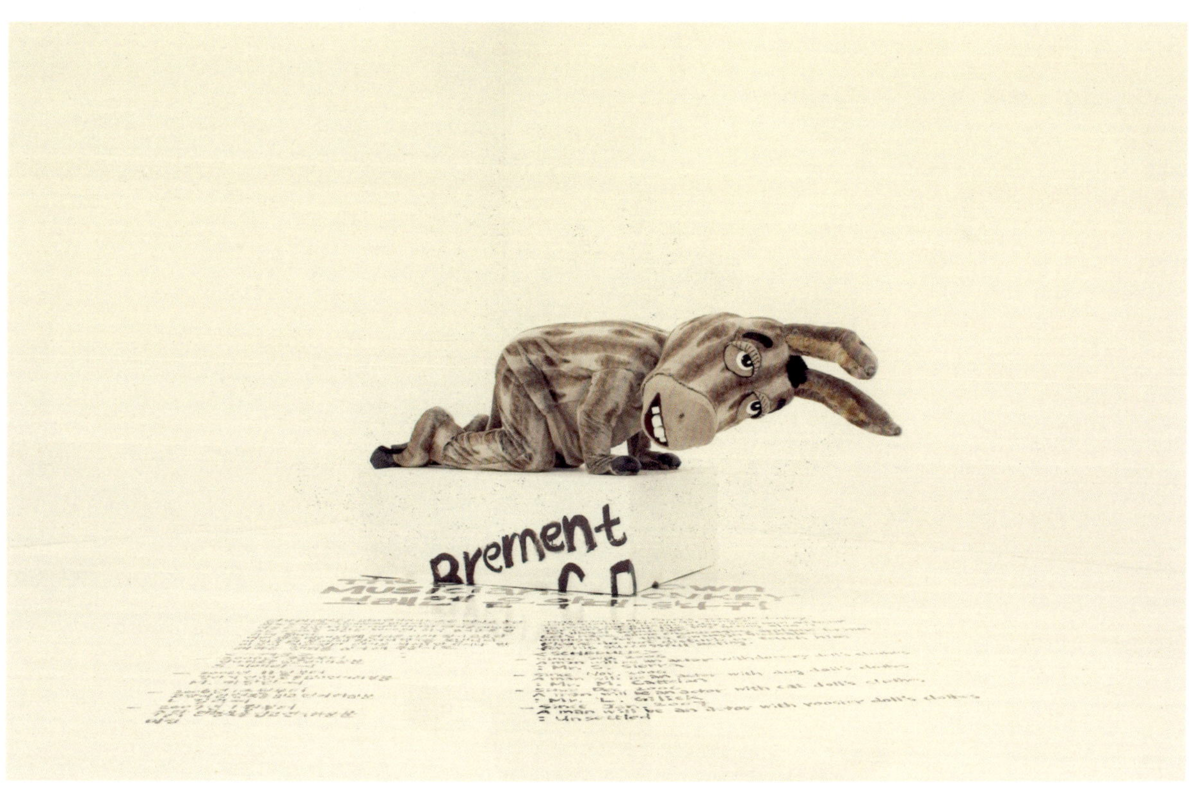

Gimhongsok, *The Bremen Town Musicians – Donkey*, 2006, installation view: 6th Gwangju Biennale, 2006

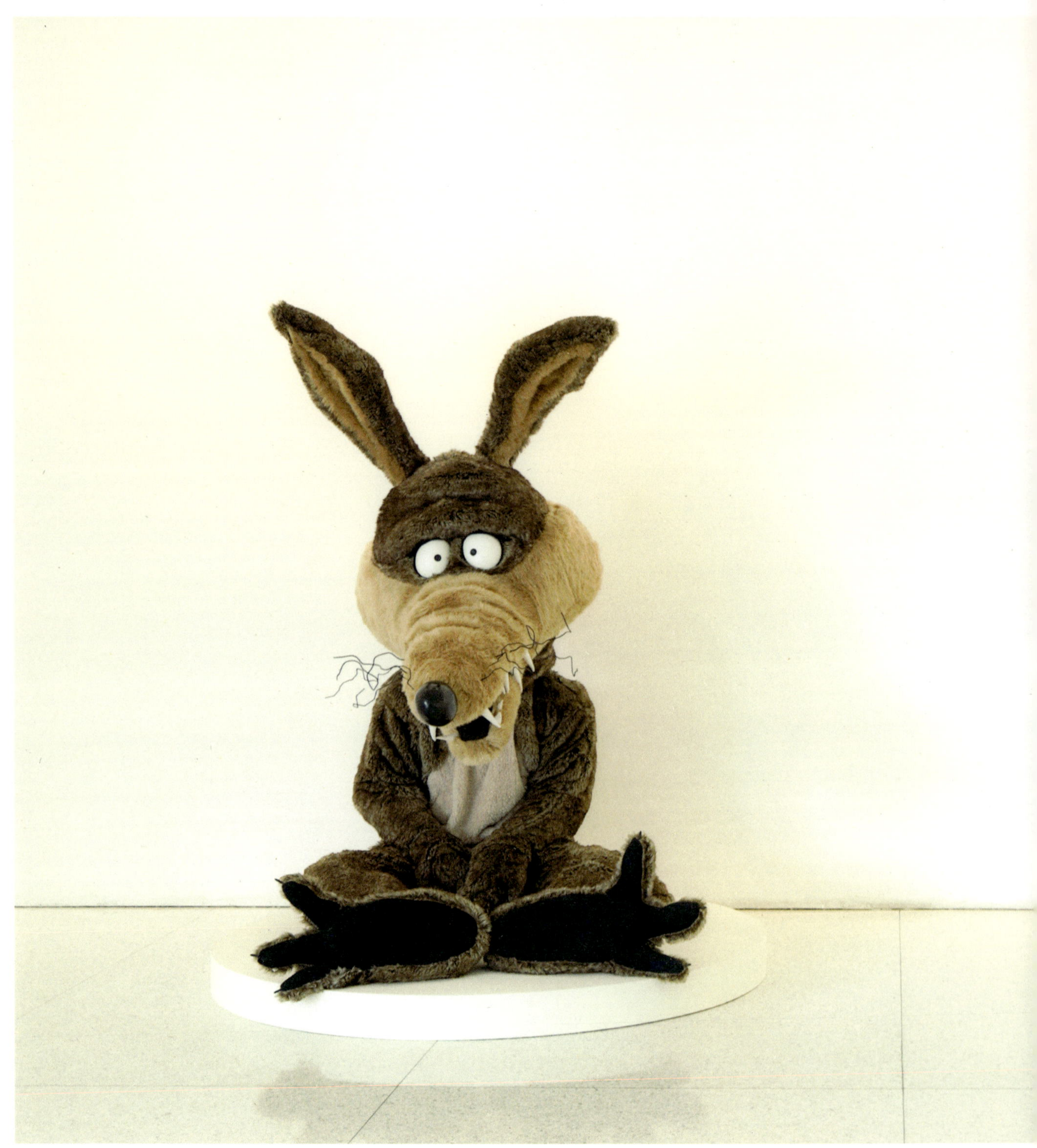

Gimhongsok, *This is Coyote*, 2006, installation view

The wall text exhibited alongside *This is Coyote* reads:

This is Kim Jun-il, who performs in a coyote costume. He is a defector from North Korea, now settled in Japan. Mr Kim is not subject to any legal protection from any country and is seeking recognition by Japanese government as a political refugee.

This foreign national is temporarily employed for this exhibition, and will be paid 5 dollars per hour for the eight-hour long performance per day.

I would like to applaud Mr Kim for encouragement. Please refrain from touching or any act that can be of impediment to the performer's successful performance.

(Note: Kim Jong-il is the leader of North Korea, and is the only person who is allowed to make jokes in that country. According to officials, he is 'a priceless master of witty remarks'.)

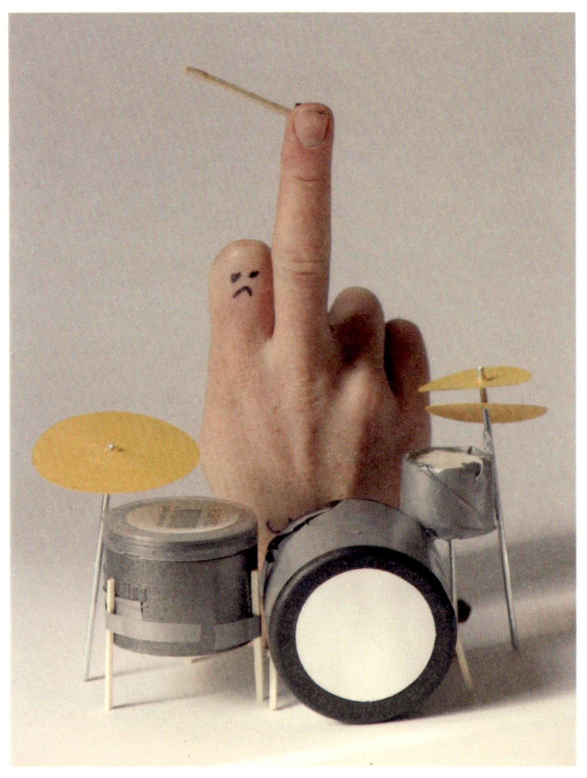

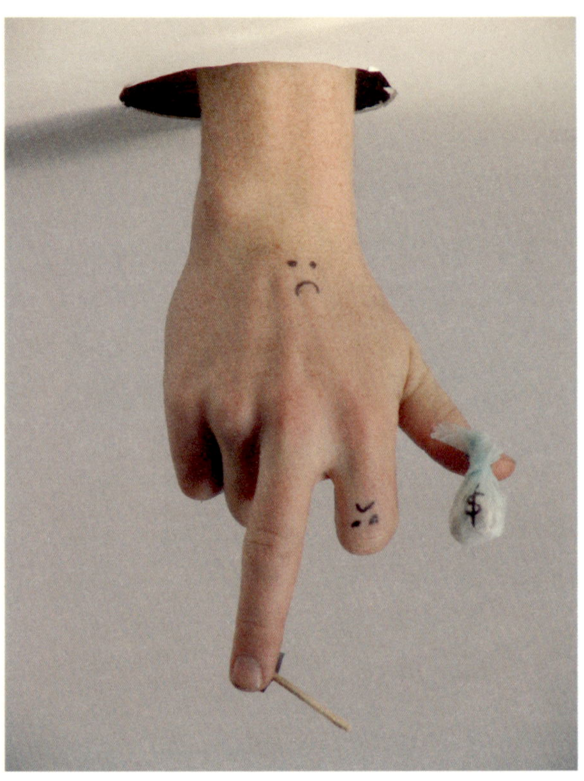

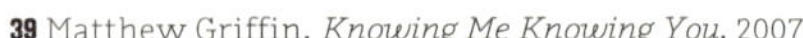

39 Matthew Griffin, *Knowing Me Knowing You*, 2007

Using a wide range of media, including painting, photography, video, installation, zines and wall-drawing, Matthew Griffin's work is an extended exploration of subculture, idolisation, myth-making and deviance. 'I like to explore how an underground culture becomes mainstream and what is lost in that,' he explains. 'It's about profundity and stupidity existing together.' He goes on to say, 'Living in Australia you are always aware of your distance both physically and culturally from "what's happening". I make work about things I like (hip-hop, drugs, Black Metal, tattoos, etc.) using people that I know. I guess that it's a way for me to personalise subjects that I don't have any firsthand experience with. Most of my work comes from daydreams or jokes.'

MATTHEW GRIFFIN

Born in 1976, Bendigo, Australia
Lives and works in Melbourne, Australia

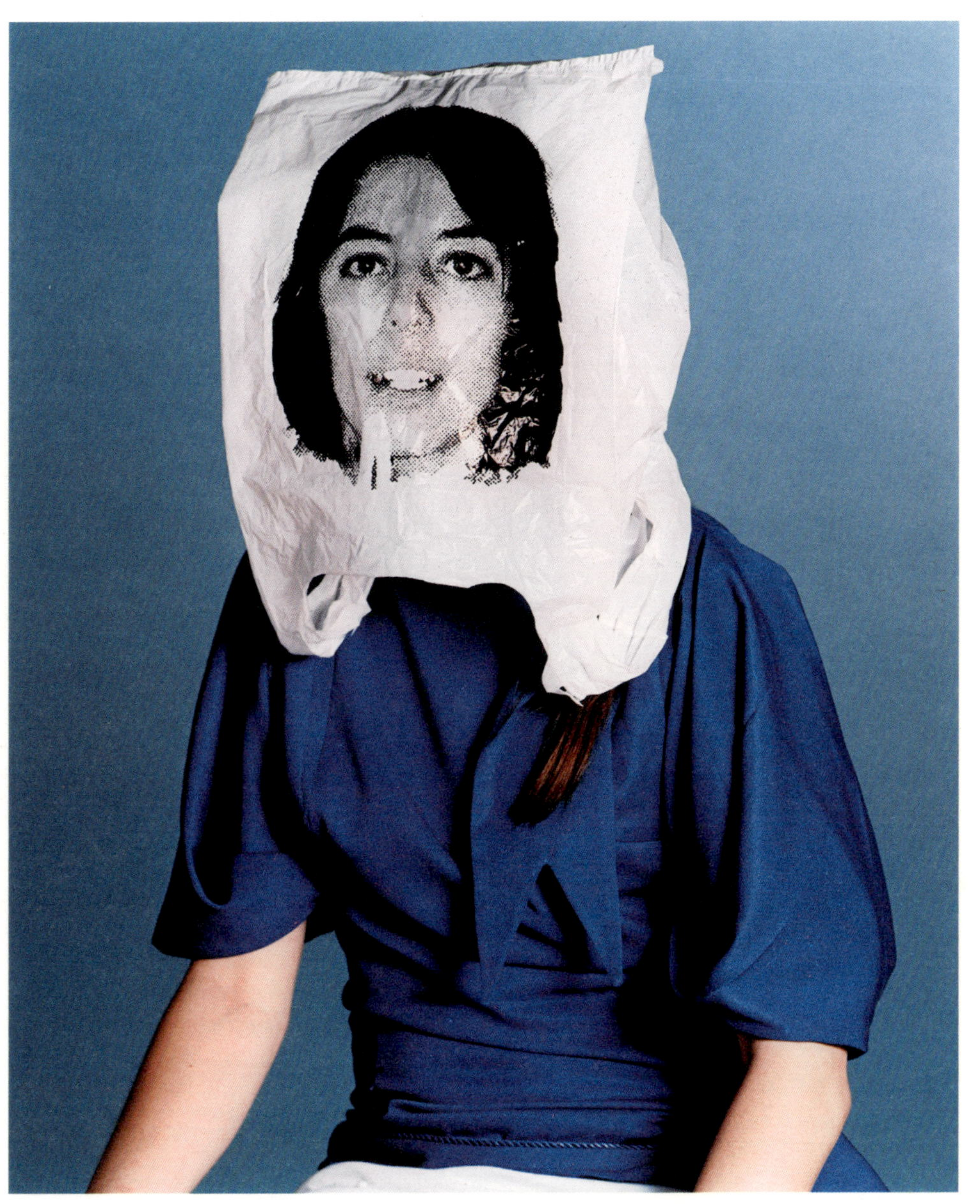

33 Matthew Griffin, *Spare Girlfriend*, 2004

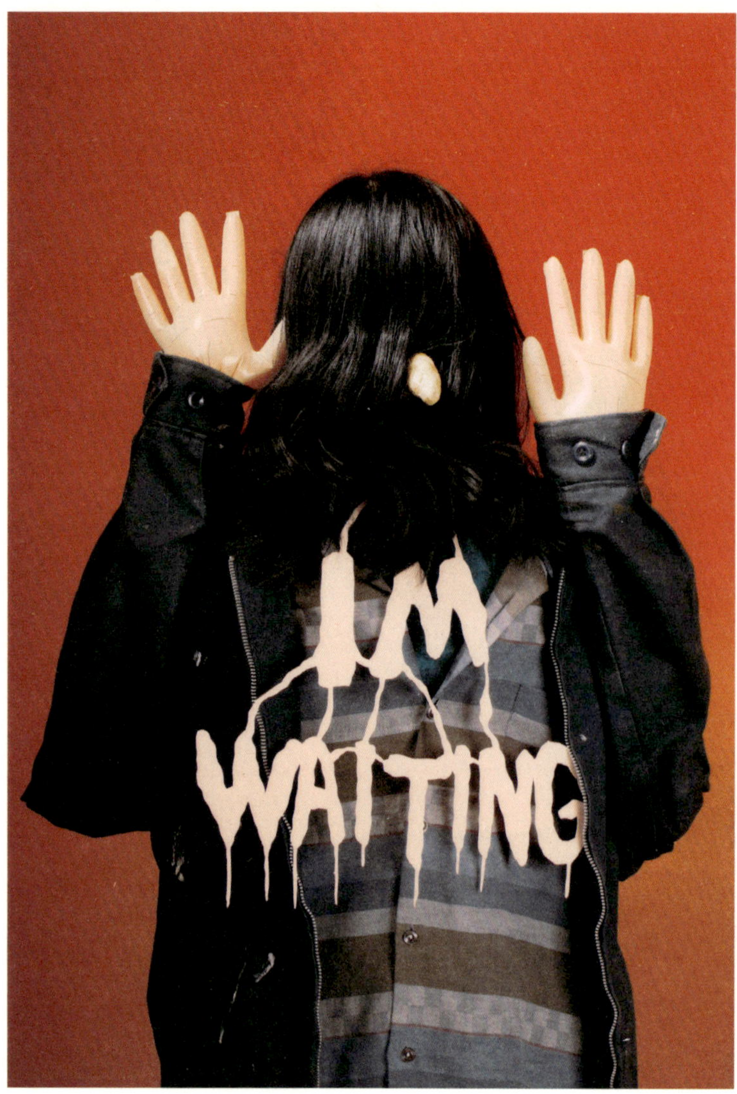

38 Matthew Griffin, *I'm Waiting*, 2007

Griffin's work has featured such counter-culture heroes as hip hop legend Tupac Shakur and Burzum, the Norwegian Black Metal act created by Varg Vikernes, who was later convicted of the murder of Mayhem guitarist Euronymous and for the arson of several churches. Often combining image and text, with words appearing like ectoplasm or graffiti, dribbling from mouths or dripping from back-to-front or upside-down faces, Griffin's visual jokes include fingers impersonating people and giant Mickey Mouse hands bearing subversive messages. For the *Laughing in a Foreign Language* exhibition at The Hayward, he has combined photographs with a new large-scale wall drawing.

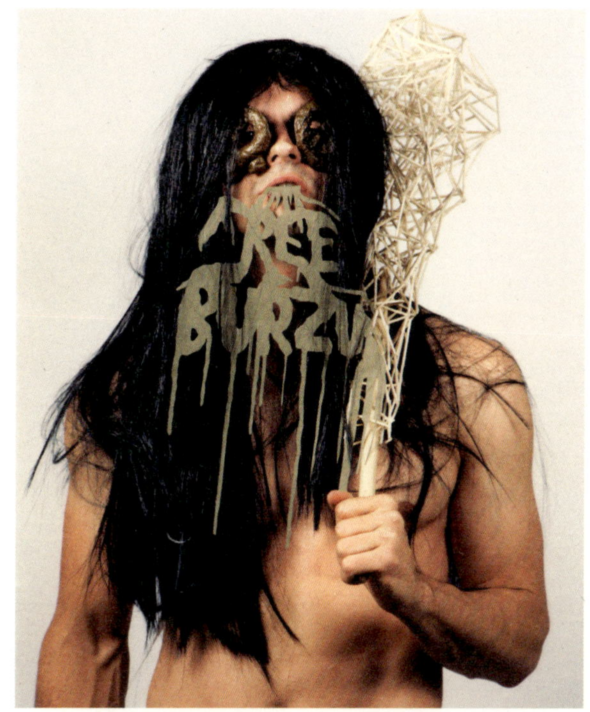

34 Matthew Griffin, *Free Burzum*, 2005

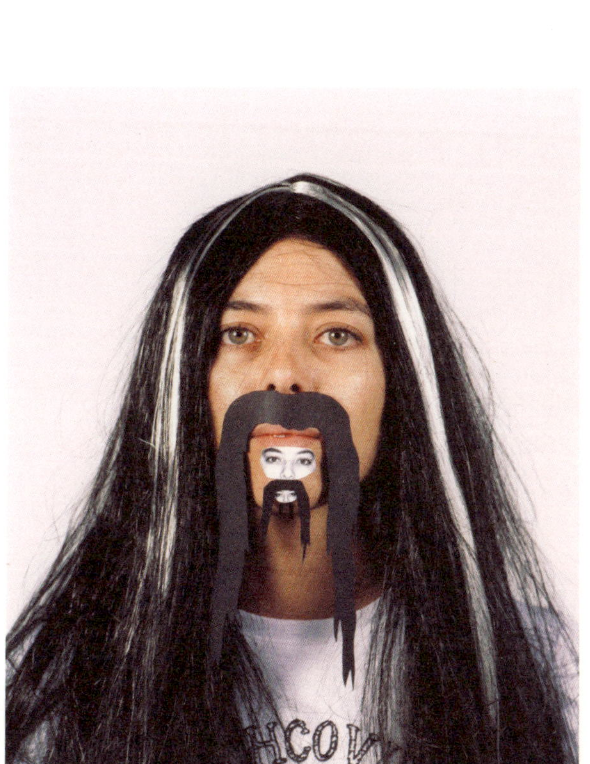

35 Matthew Griffin, *Infinity Hombre*, 2005

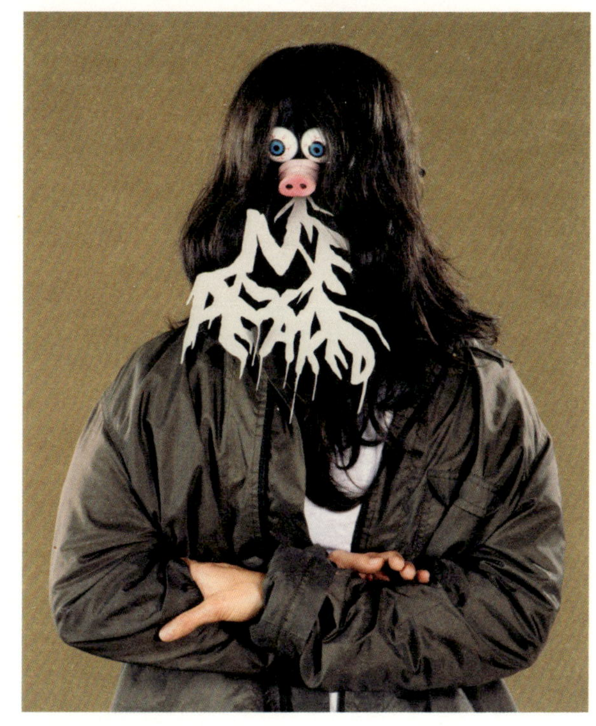

37 Matthew Griffin, *I've Peaked*, 2005

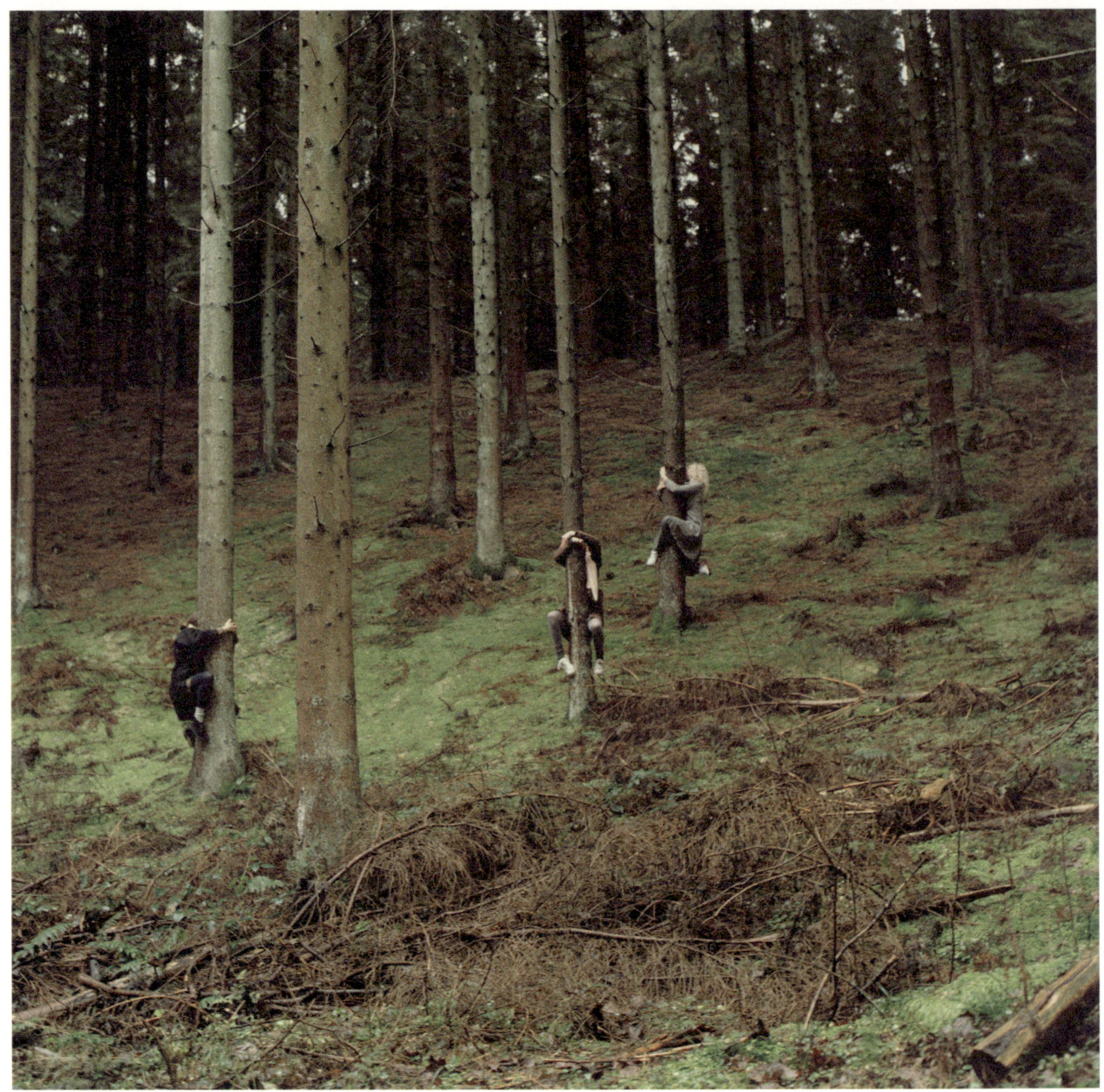

Nina Jan Beier and Marie Jan Lund, *The Play me series (Hang on for as long as you all can)*, 2006

NINA JAN BEIER AND MARIE JAN LUND

NINA JAN BEIER
Born in 1975, Denmark
Lives and works in Copenhagen, Denmark, and London, UK
MARIE JAN LUND
Born in 1976, Denmark
Lives and works in Copenhagen and London

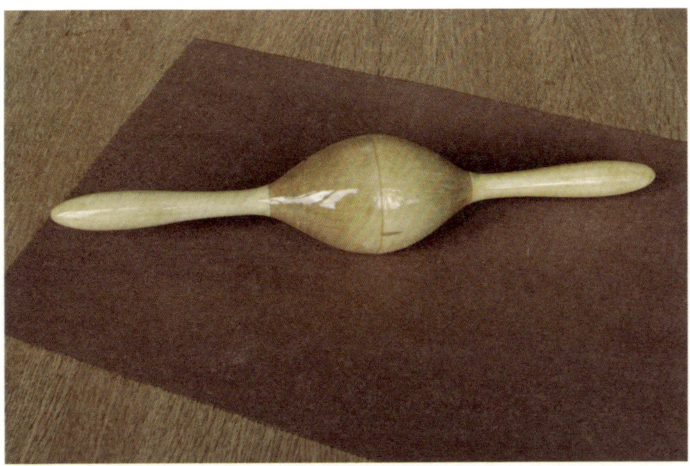

49 Nina Jan Beier and Marie Jan Lund, *One on One (The Maraca)*, 2007

Fascinated by group dynamics and the ways in which individuals relate to each other, Nina Jan Beier and Marie Jan Lund work collaboratively, creating particular social situations that are carefully choreographed and then documented on film and in photographs. In the ongoing *Play me* series, they instigate a range of abstract games for different groups to act out. Reminiscent of playground challenges, instructions such as 'Hang on to the trees for as long as you all can', or 'Look in the window until someone looks back at you', provoke individual competitiveness at the same time as encouraging collective effort.

The concept behind *Les Sabots* was to ask a group of Danish people to pause what they were doing and make a face at the camera for as long as the film lasted. As Beier and Lund remark, this act of rebellion is a kind of multiple portrait of themselves and symbolises 'our attempts at revolutionary activities in our art. We are interested in the validity of privileged revolt ... Can you be in genuine opposition when you have all you need?' The title refers to acts of subversion during the Industrial Revolution, when workers would disrupt production by throwing their wooden shoes or clogs (known in French as *sabots*, hence the term sabotage) into the machinery.

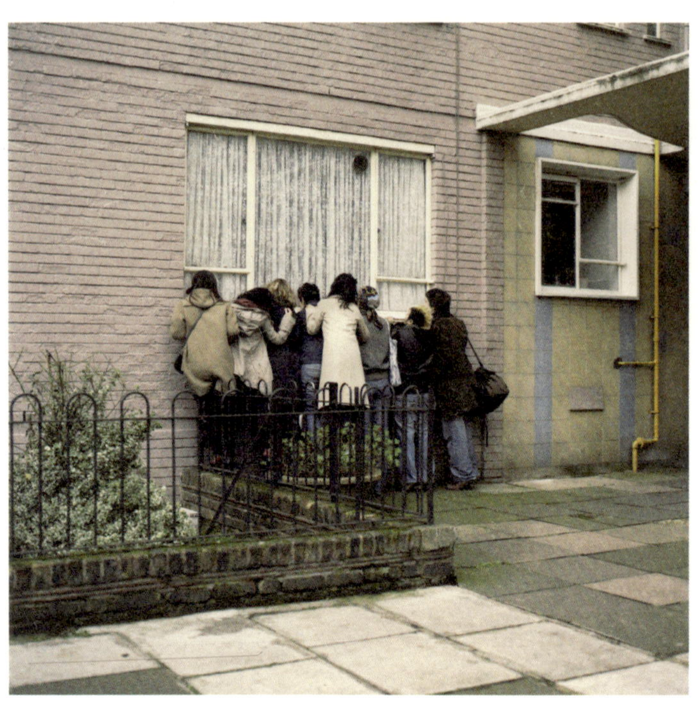

Nina Jan Beier and Marie Jan Lund, *The Play me series (Look in the window until someone looks back at you)*, 2006

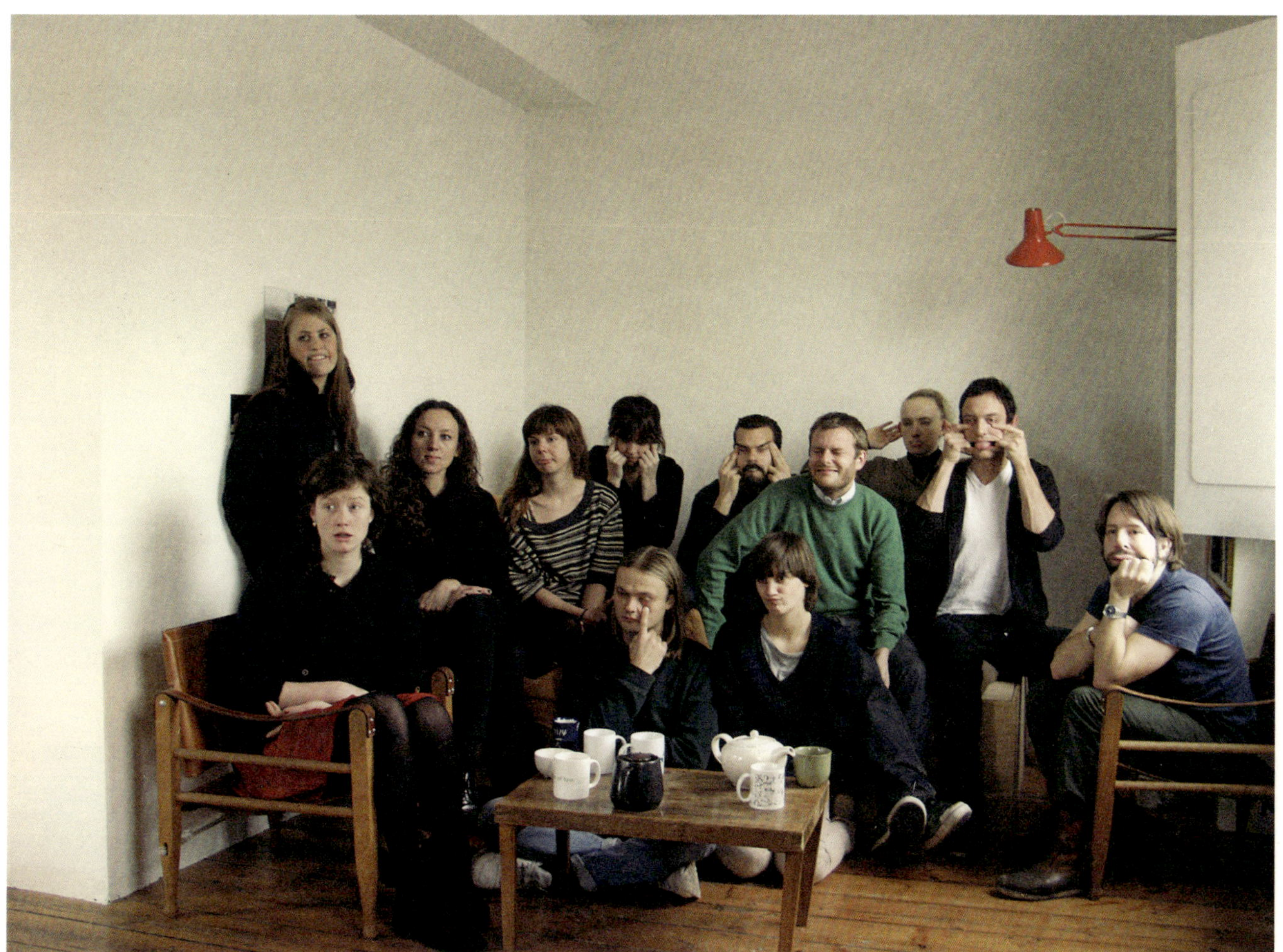

47 Nina Jan Beier and Marie Jan Lund, *Les Sabots*, 2007, still

Beier and Lund adopt a different strategy in their series of double objects, *One on One*. Each of these second-hand items, which would have been perfectly usable on its own, either malfunctions or ceases to work when it is conjoined with its twin. When the two-handled maraca is used by a couple of people the sound becomes irregular and the action becomes a convulsive handshake. With *The Dedication (For Elizabeth Bishop – For Robert Lowell)* two separate books, each containing a poem by one author dedicated to the other, are glued together so that the pages interleave and 'speak' to each other but the poems cannot be read.

Confessing that for him, 'humour is still a deep mystery,' Taiyo Kimura observes: 'No animals laugh except humans. I wonder why only human beings laugh?' He finds the impetus for his art in the oddities of everyday life and uses the ordinary stuff that surrounds us as materials for his interactive installations.

Typical Japanese-English involves two performances – the viewer's and the artist's. To see the work, you have get down on your hands and knees and sort through a pile of clothes. Peering into a shirt, you discover a secret world of absurdities captured on a tiny monitor – Kimura holding chopsticks with his eyelids and trying to pick up little objects; brushing the teeth of a fish held in his mouth; tossing a steak into a washing machine set to 'wash cycle'; spewing out coins like a slot machine. These and other equally inscrutable actions are interspersed with televised footage from a game of Go.

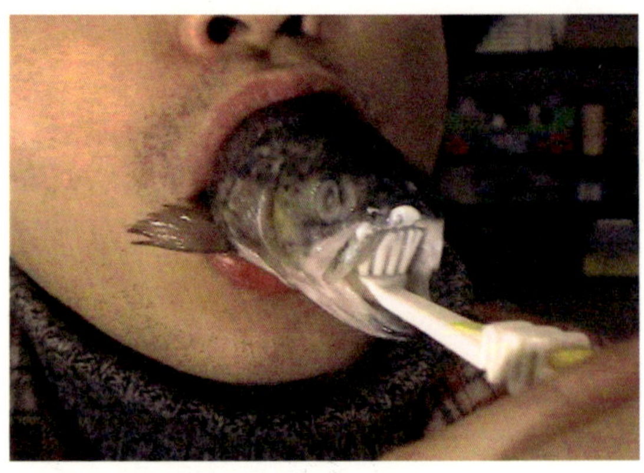

TAIYO KIMURA

Born in 1970, Kamakura, Japan
Lives and works in Kamakura

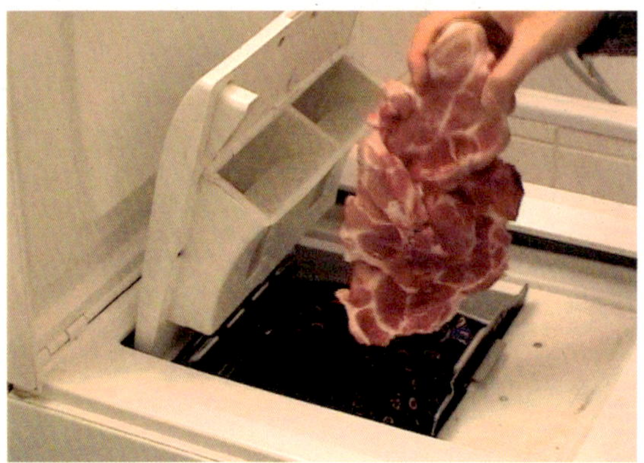

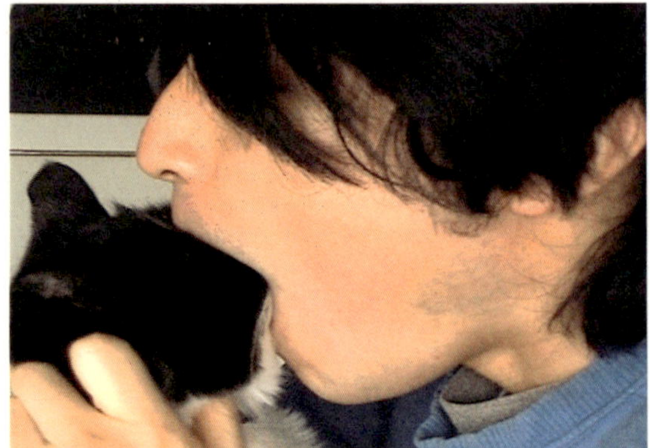

ABOVE AND RIGHT / 53 Taiyo Kimura, *Typical Japanese-English*, 2005, stills

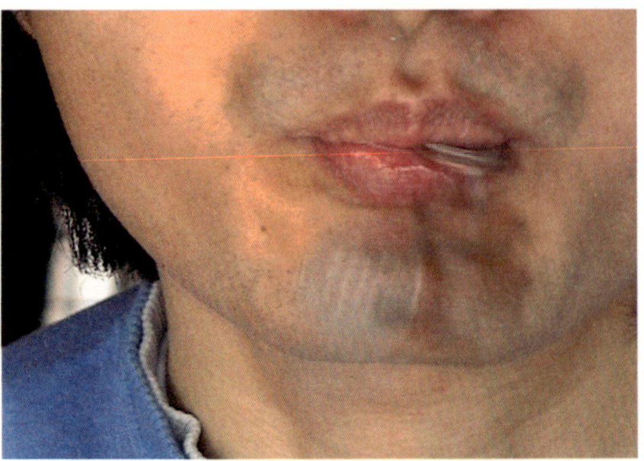

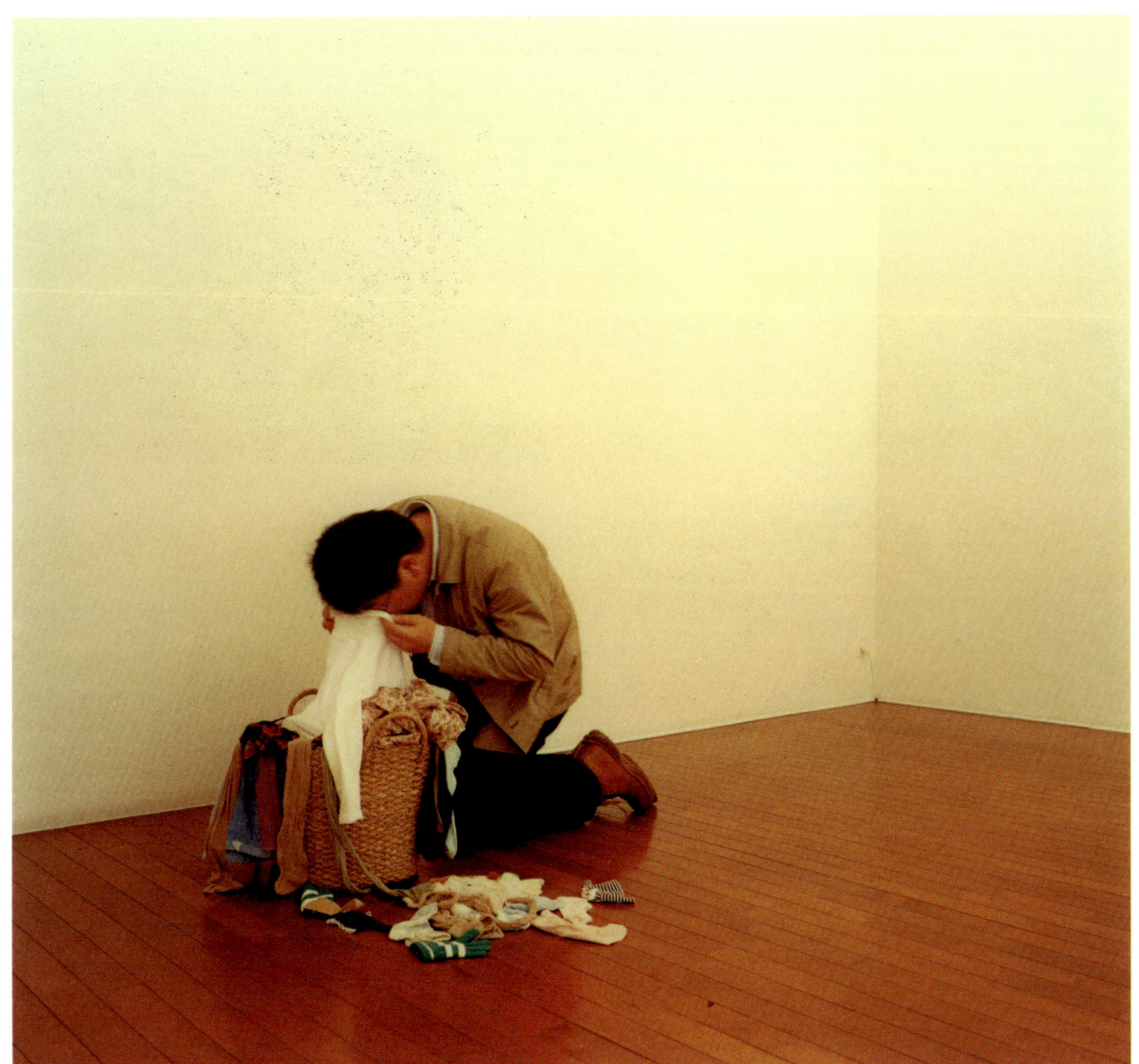

53 Taiyo Kimura, *Typical Japanese-English*, 2005, installation view

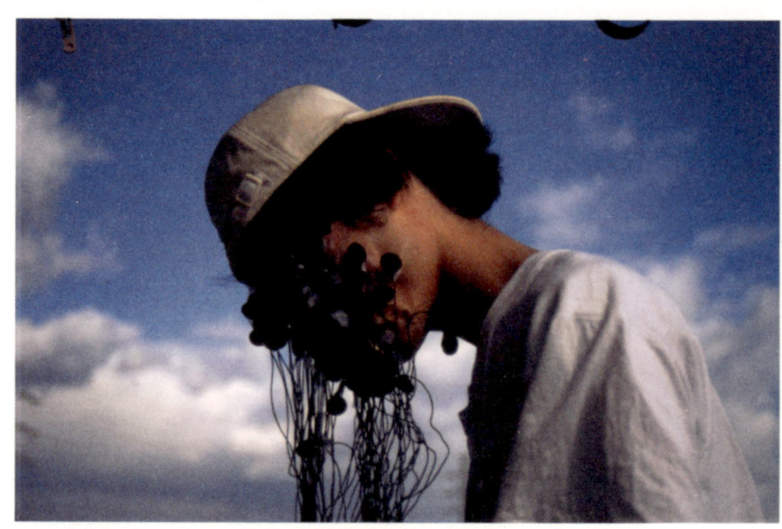

52 Taiyo Kimura, *Untitled (performance photo 1996)*, 1996–2007

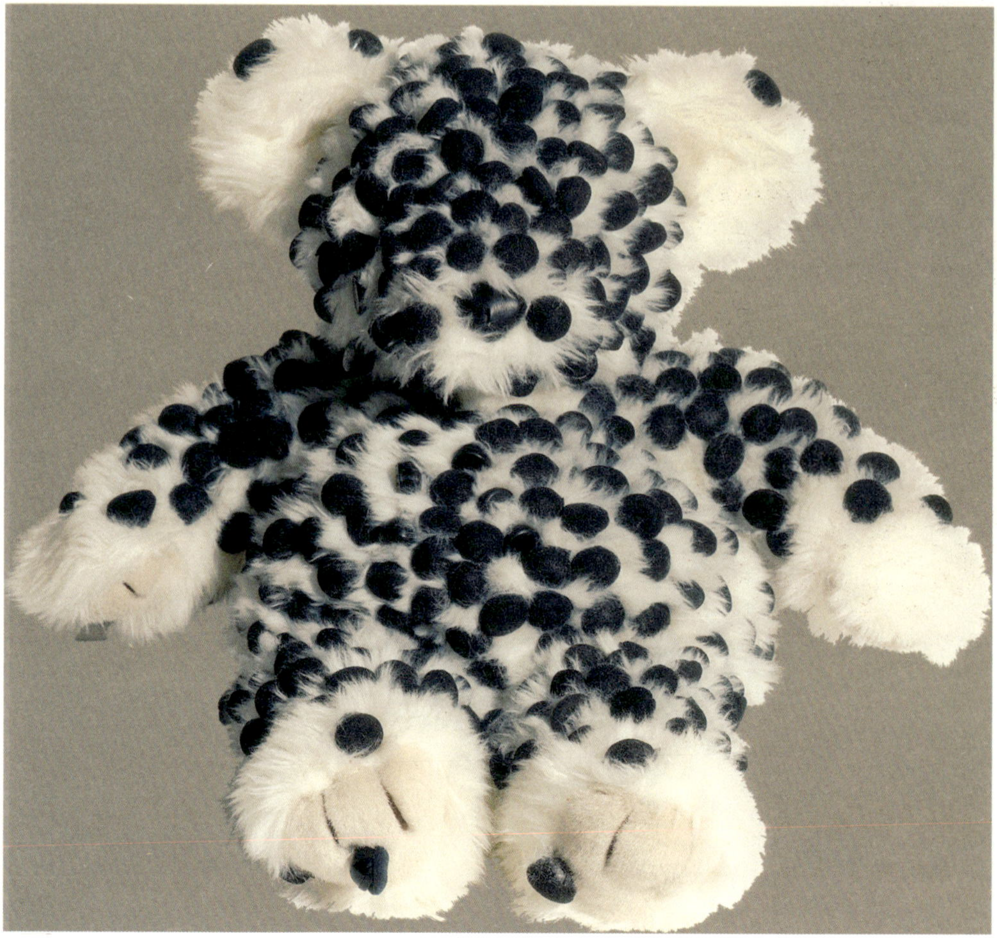

51 Taiyo Kimura, *Black Hole*, 1995–2005

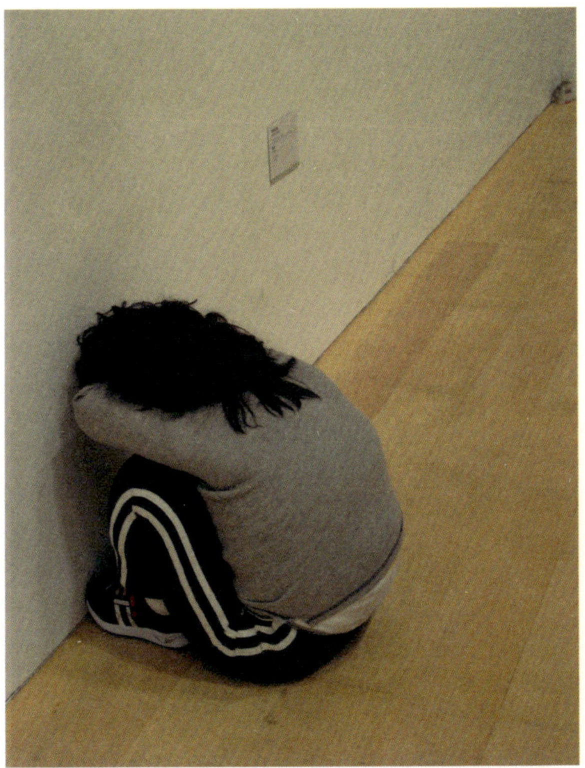

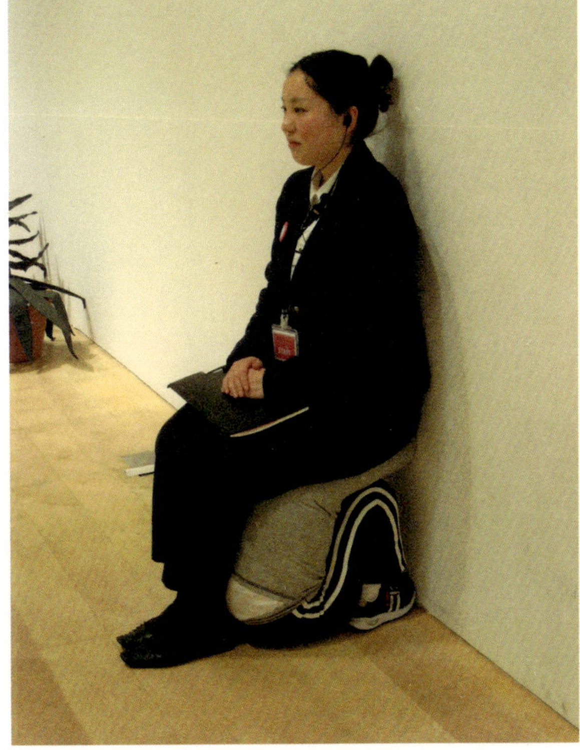

54 Taiyo Kimura, *Untitle me (stool for guard)*, 2007, installation view

Kimura comments: 'Through making my art I have come to think of my "life" as an extremely strange thing. What possible sort of meaning is there in living the way we do?' He often uses sound and earphones in his installations and admits to being typical of the 'Walkman generation': 'I actually can't make my art without listening to music ... I always listen to music by earphones when I concentrate internally and see and interpret reality through the inner side. Since the earphones can be so close to the brain, I believe there must be a certain effect.' Kimura has responded to the cosmopolitan Babel of foreign-language radio stations in the earphone-studded *Black Hole*, and in a related performance work in which he stuck earphones all over his face.

In *Untitle me (stool for guard)*, a disconsolate figure sits huddled, face to the wall, reciting the names of all the stations on Tokyo's busy Yamanote line – and at the same time provides a comfortable seat for a security guard in the gallery.

PETER LAND

Born in 1966, Aarhus, Denmark
Lives and works in Copenhagen, Denmark

Peter Land plays the clown, without the make-up or the funny clothes. His video performances, which feature slapstick and repetition, are both comic and tragic, echoing Samuel Beckett's injunction never to give up: 'Ever tried. Ever failed. No matter. Try Again. Fail again. Fail better.' Speaking of his own particular brand of humour, Land says: 'I've always found it hard to listen to people who insist on being taken seriously by putting on a grave face and using big words. It always makes me want to do something disruptive like fart or make funny noises. We have a saying in Denmark which freely translated into English would be: "He who recognizes fun as only fun and seriousness as only seriousness has actually misunderstood both" (in Danish it rhymes).'

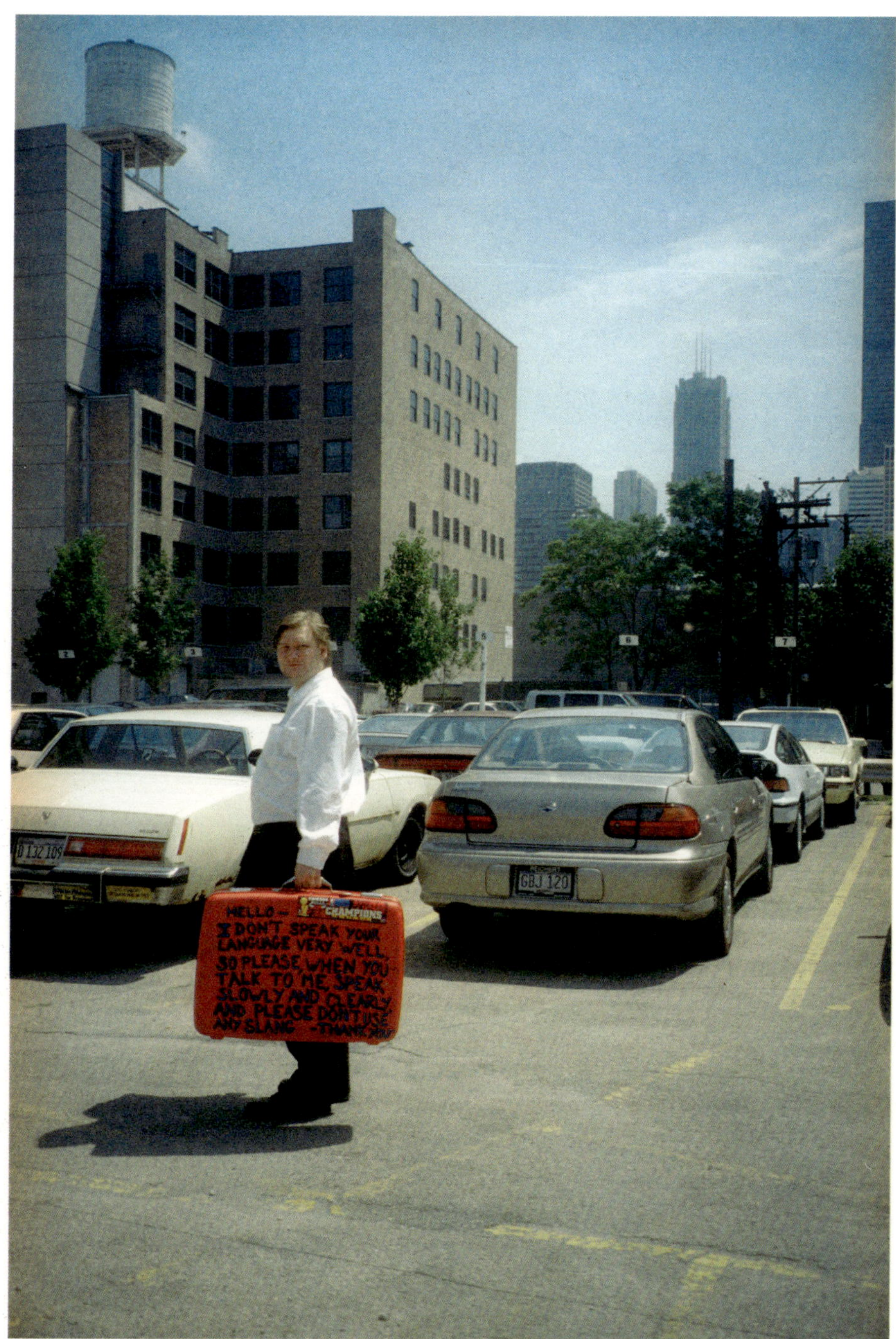

56 Peter Land, *Hello – I don't speak your language very well, so please when you talk to me speak slowly and clearly and please don't use any slang, Thank You. (Chicago)*, 1998

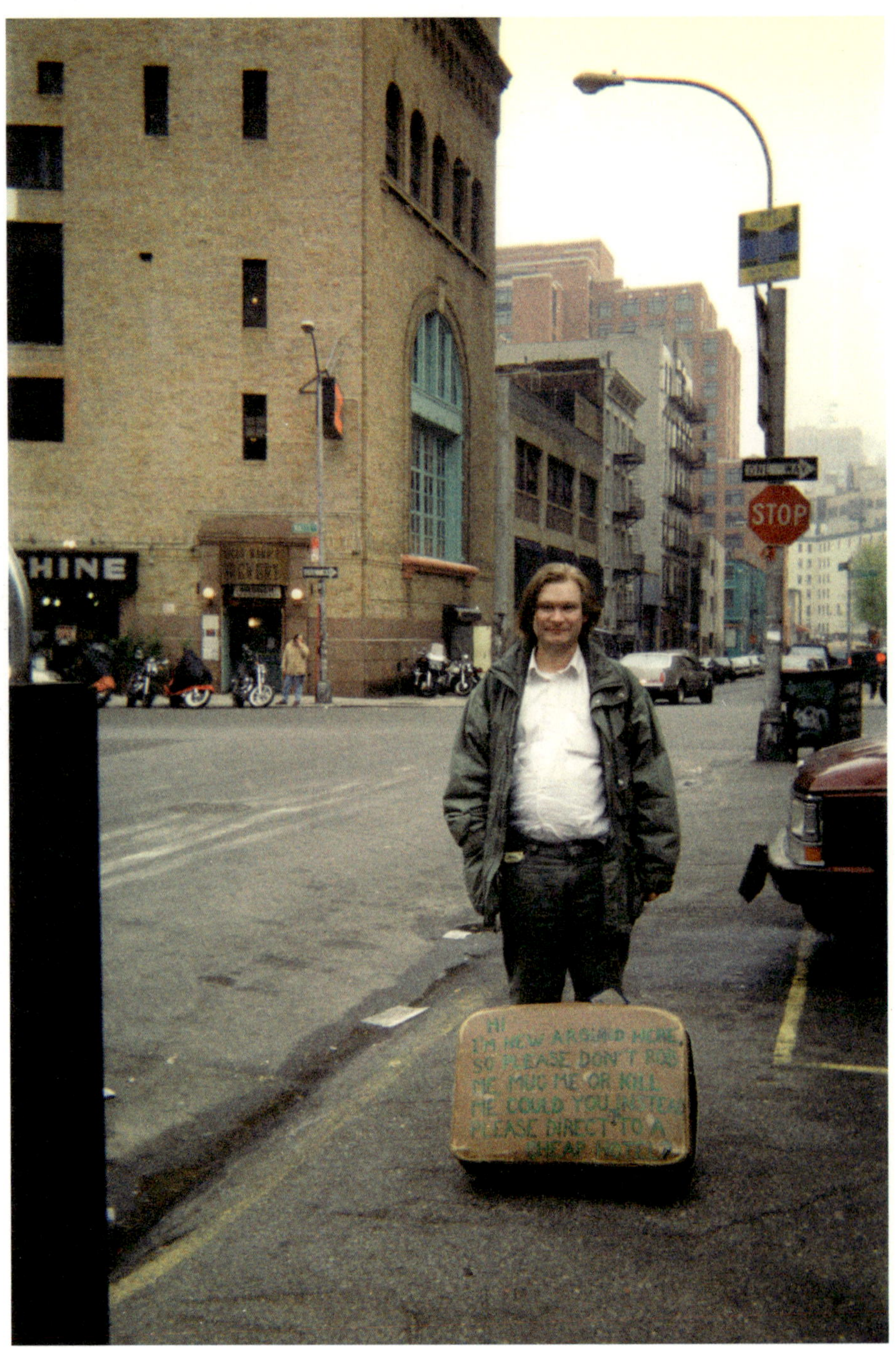

55 Peter Land, *Hi I'm new around here, so please don't rob me, mug me or kill me. Could you please direct me to a cheap hotel? (New York)*, 1996

The idea behind the performance works *Hi I'm new around here...* and *Hello – I don't speak your language very well...* is, he says, 'very much about being a tourist in the USA. I guess it's especially interesting when you go from Europe to the United States because as a European you've often heard, read and seen enormous amounts about the United States through television, movies, etc ... Also, the news we get from the USA is rather selective. In Denmark there was a period where a lot of media time was spent reporting about America's crime rate which gave the Danes the impression that going to the States was the same as asking to be mugged or killed. I guess by parading these suitcases I'm trying to confront some of these preconceptions.'

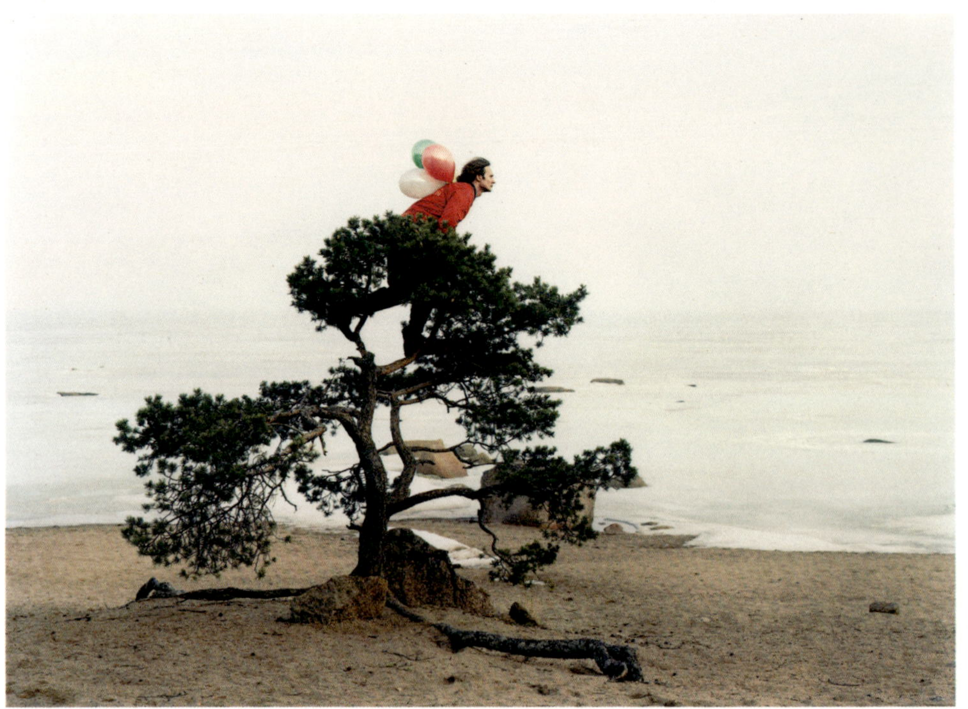

Like Icarus and countless others before and since, the Finnish photographer Janne Lehtinen has dreamed of flying like a bird. His series of photographs, *Sacred Bird*, document his myriad attempts to become airborne, in what he calls 'fictitious scenes from a true story'. Although he never achieves lift-off, Lehtinen, the son of a well-known glider pilot, follows in the tradition of such heroes of aviation history as Ibn Firnas, who in 875, at the age of 65, built his own hang glider and launched himself from the Mount of the Bride, near Córdoba; Eilmer of Malmesbury, 'The Flying Monk' who two centuries later leapt from a monastery tower and flew for 240 yards before falling to earth and breaking both legs; the fifteenth-century mathematician Giovanni Battista Danti of Perugia who, wearing a pair of wood and feather wings, flew over the town square before crashing on a roof; and the French surgeon Charles Bernouin, who in January 1672, equipped with wings and a rocket, leapt from a tower and flew till he fell and broke his neck.

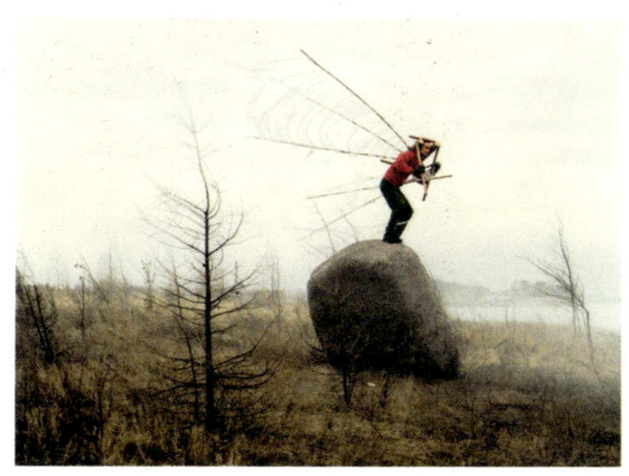

JANNE LEHTINEN

Born in 1970, Karhula, Finland
Lives and works in Loviisa, Finland

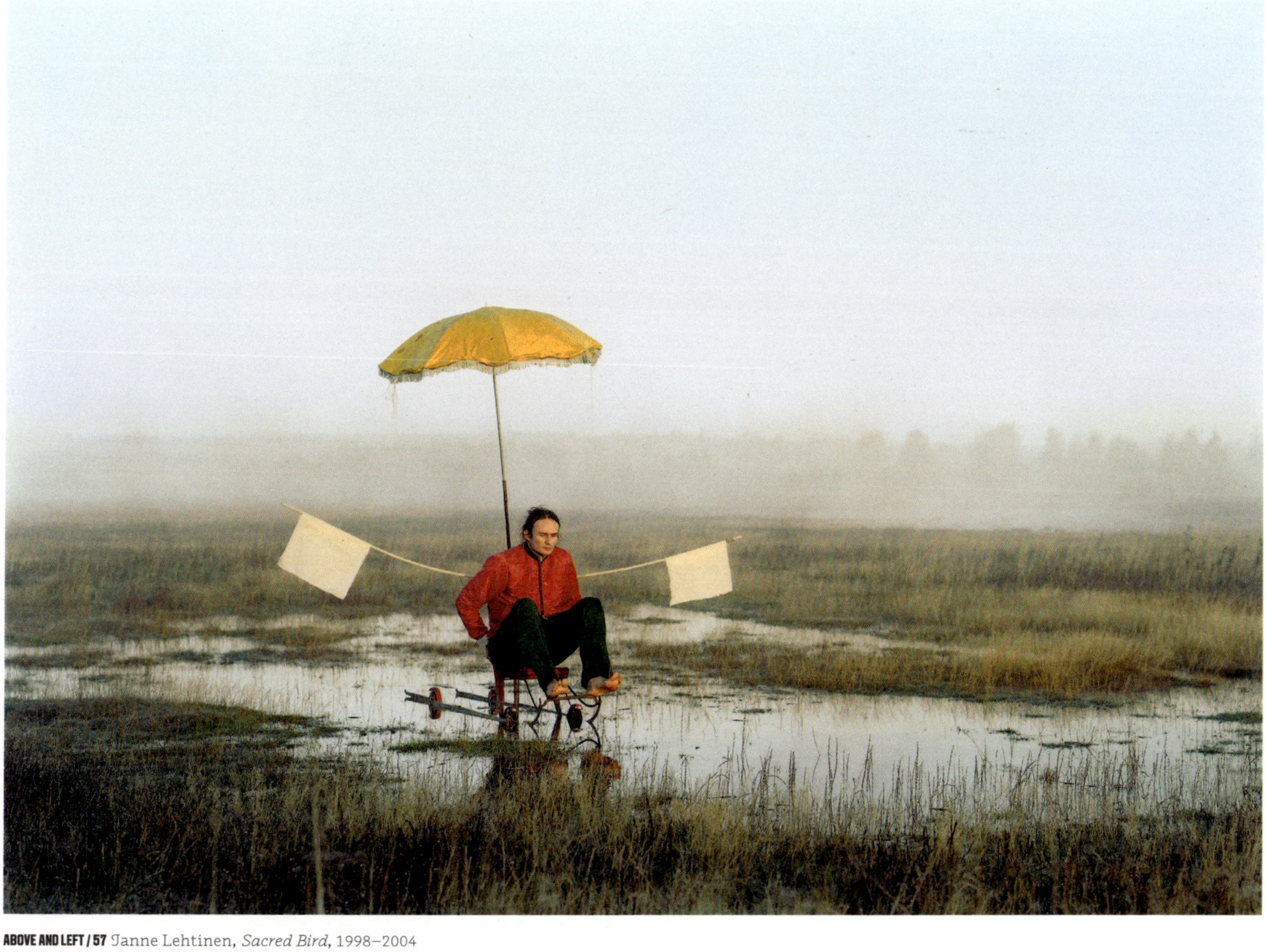

ABOVE AND LEFT / 57 Janne Lehtinen, *Sacred Bird*, 1998–2004

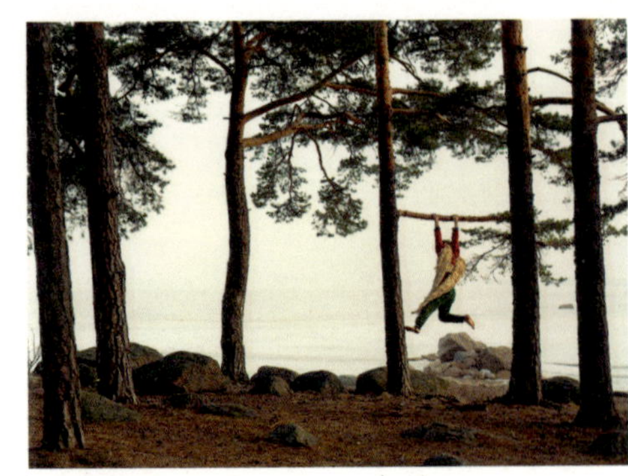

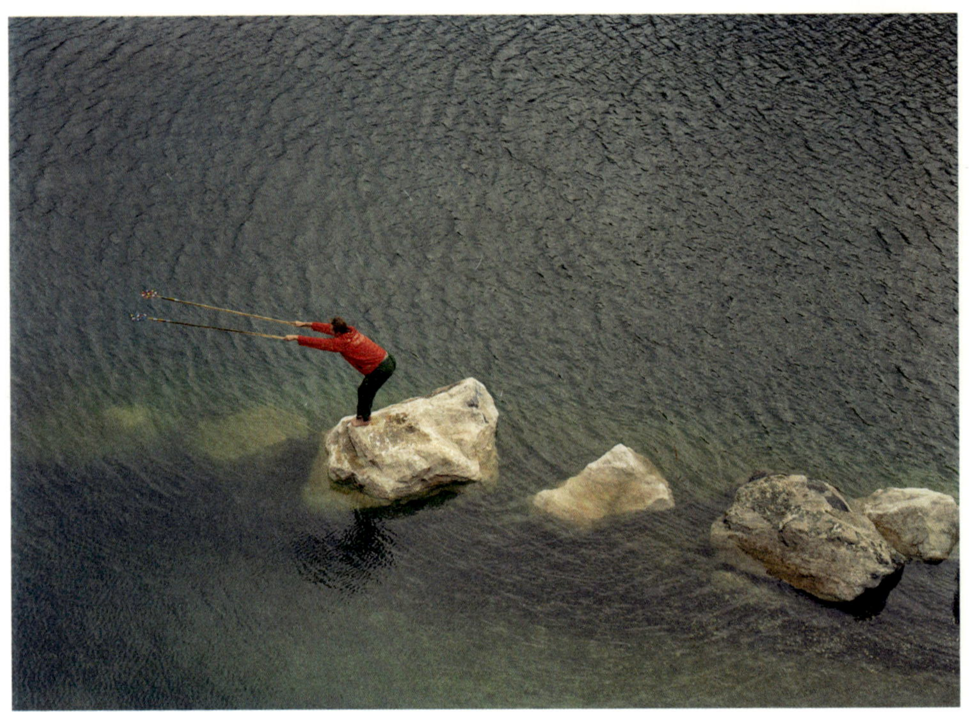

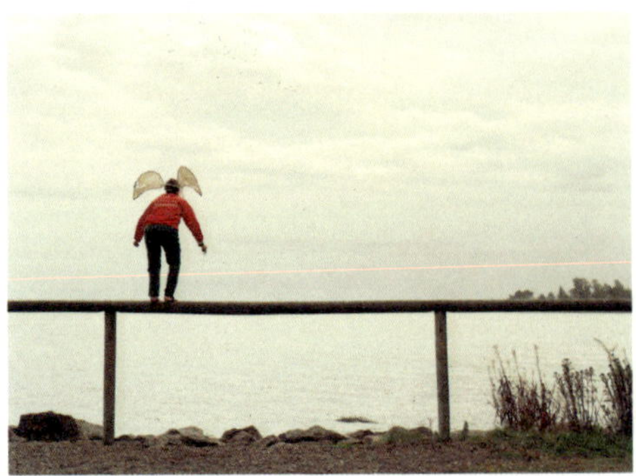

ABOVE AND RIGHT / 57 Janne Lehtinen, *Sacred Bird*, 1998–2004

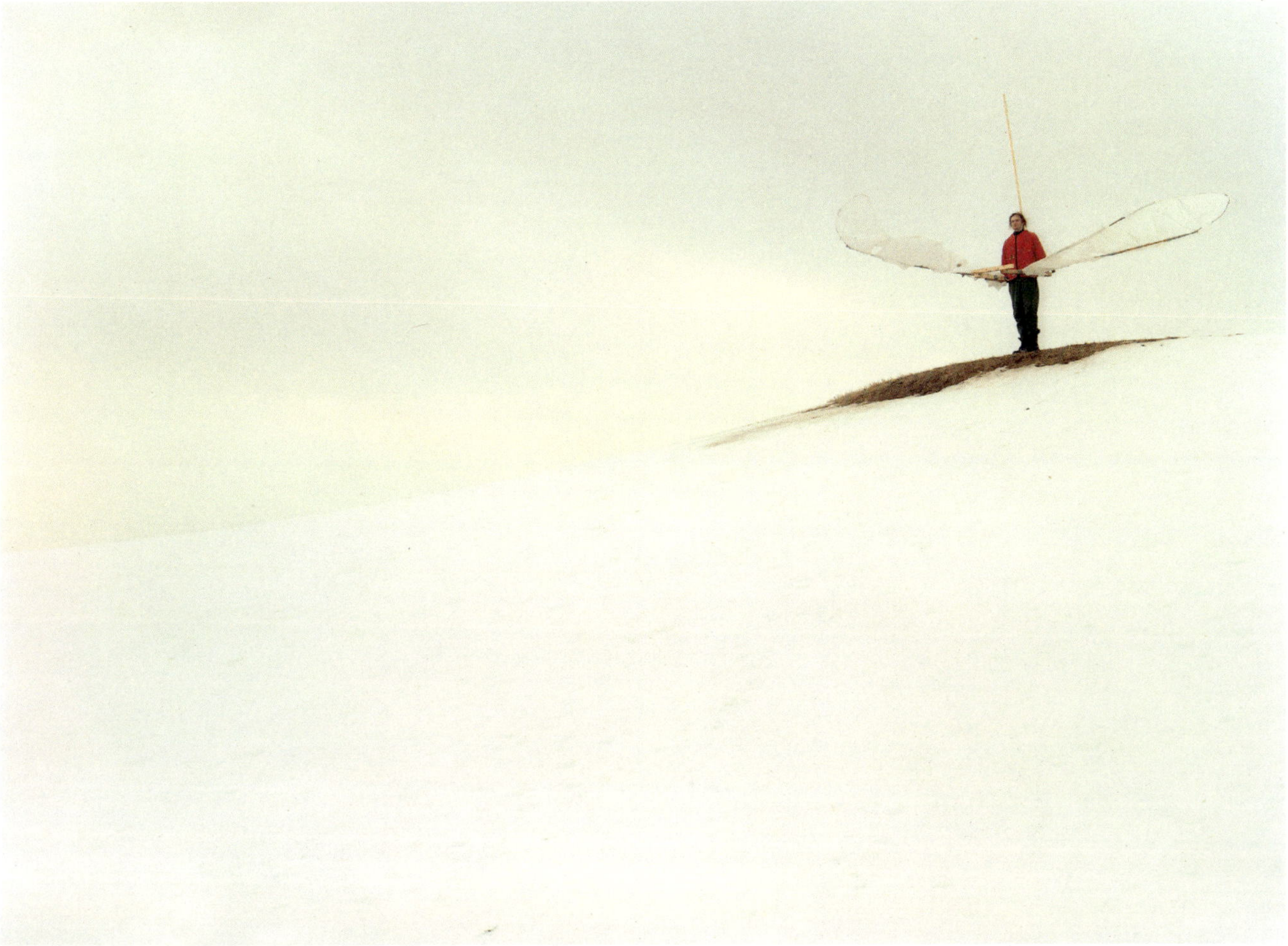

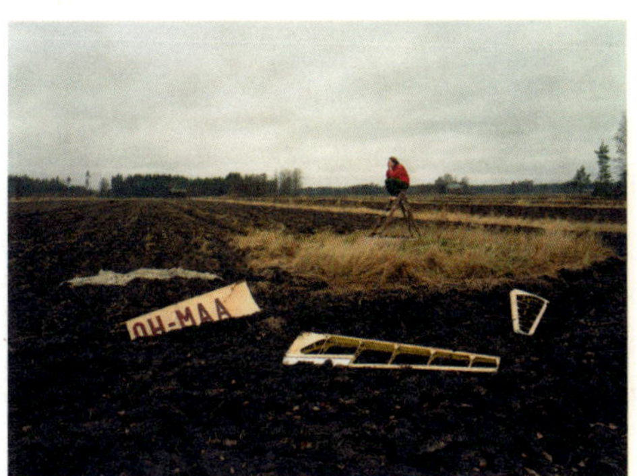

Lehtinen's efforts are, in their own way, no less remarkable. Evoking images as various as angels, insects, Leonardo da Vinci's human-powered ornithopter, and late nineteenth-century flying machines such as Otto Lilienthal's fantastic gliders, his absurd contraptions are poised for calamity; precipitating slapstick and pratfalls which we will not see but can gleefully imagine. The fact that these anti-heroic self-portraits are set in romantically sublime landscapes only reinforces the comic futility of the enterprise.

KALUP LINZY

Born in 1977, Florida, USA
Lives and works in New York, USA

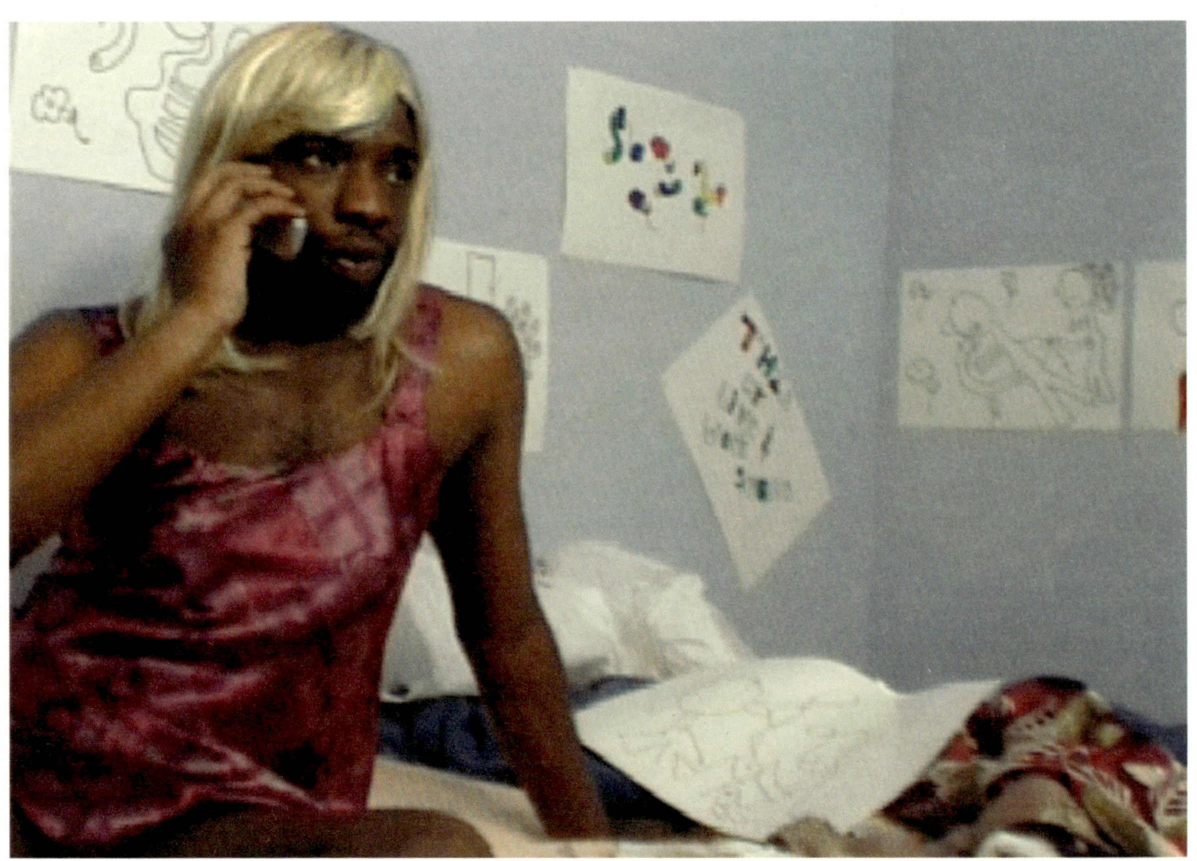

59 Kalup Linzy, *Conversations wit de Churen IV: Play wit de Churen*, 2005, still

Kalup Linzy uses humour to deal with such highly-charged topics as gender, sexuality, race, class, human relationships and art world politics. A performance artist and filmmaker, he began the on-going video series, *Conversations wit de Churen*, in 2002. Taking the television soap opera format and lampooning it, Linzy's approach mixes melodrama, farce and satire, parodying the stereotypical roles of African-Americans in popular culture. The series features Nucuavia, a 'ghetto hoochie mama', and her family, including Jada, the tough, educated, career woman and Taiwan, the gay male stereotype who, Linzy says, is 'most of time used for comedic purposes and sometimes, I guess, openly sad ones'. Besides directing the videos, Linzy also writes the scripts, does the overdubbing, writes the scores and – aided and abetted by a supporting cast of artist-actors – plays many of the characters himself, often in drag.

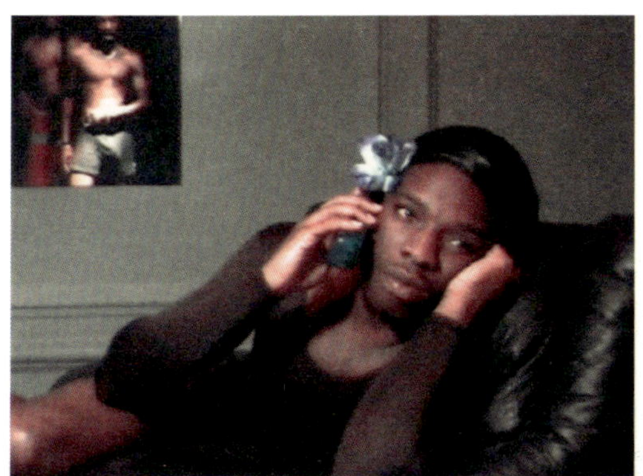

58 Kalup Linzy, *Conversations wit de Churen III: Da Young and Da Mess*, 2005, still

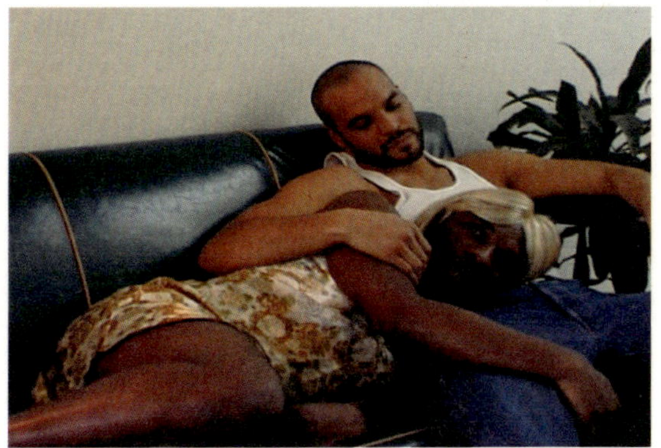

60 Kalup Linzy, *Conversations wit de Churen V: As da Art World Might Turn*, 2006, still

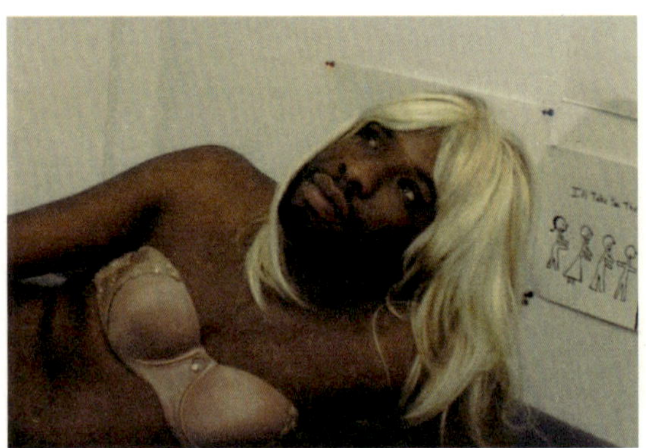

60 Kalup Linzy, *Conversations wit de Churen V: As da Art World Might Turn*, 2006, still

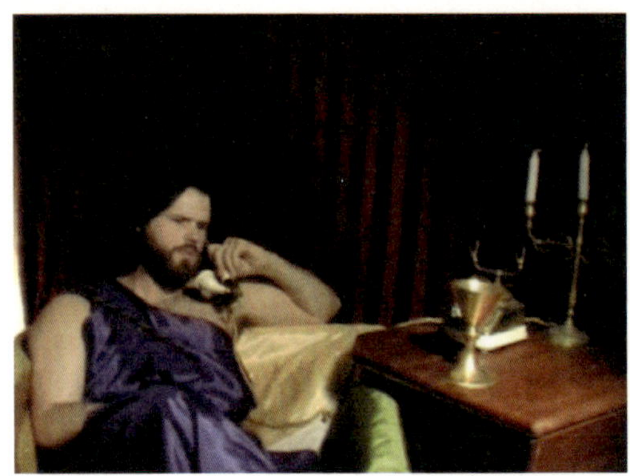

59 Kalup Linzy, *Conversations wit de Churen IV: Play wit de Churen*, 2005, still

Most of the dialogue takes the form of mobile phone conversations. Linzy says: 'Through the contemporary device known as the telephone, characters communicate in a dialect that is primarily Black Ebonics seasoned with a southern accent. The use of the telephone places emphasis on the language that is the center of my work. The soundtracks are pre-recorded, manipulated and performed through lip-syncing by the cast.'

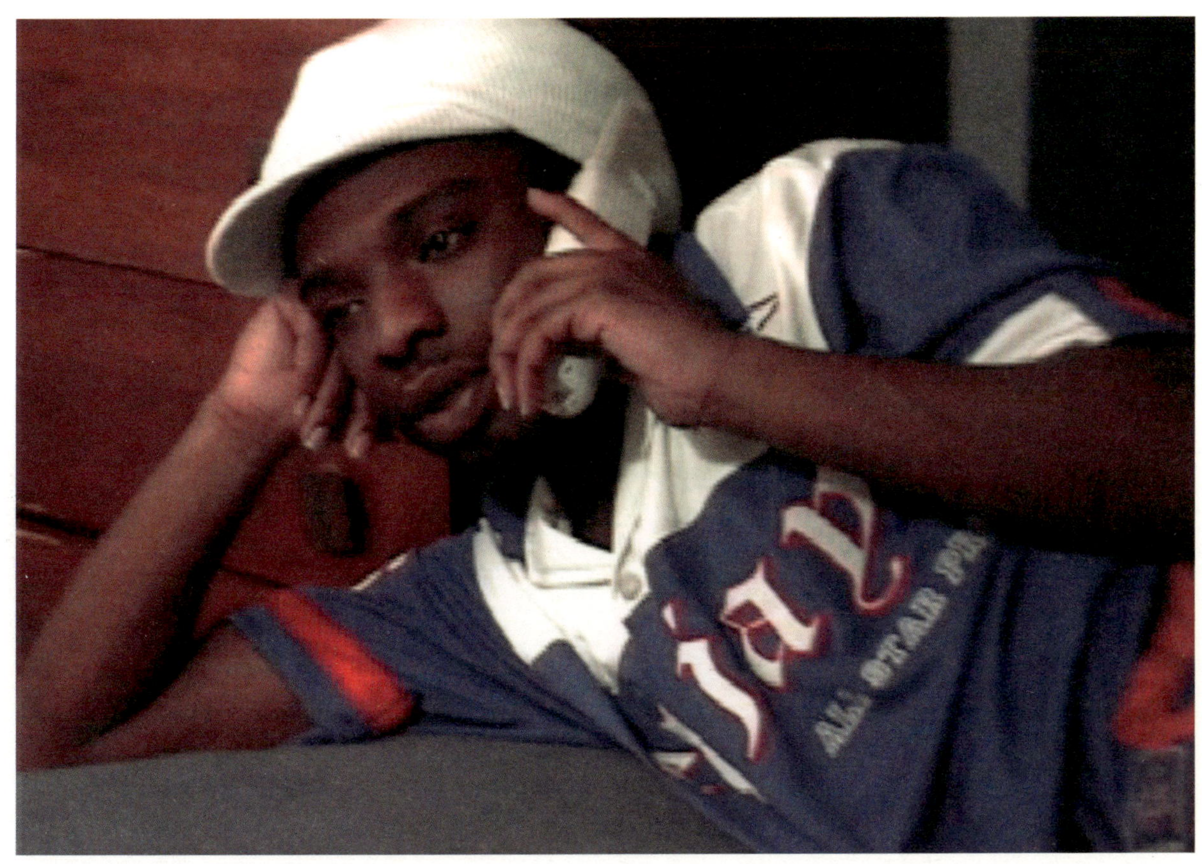

58 Kalup Linzy, *Conversations wit de Churen III: Da Young and Da Mess*, 2005, still

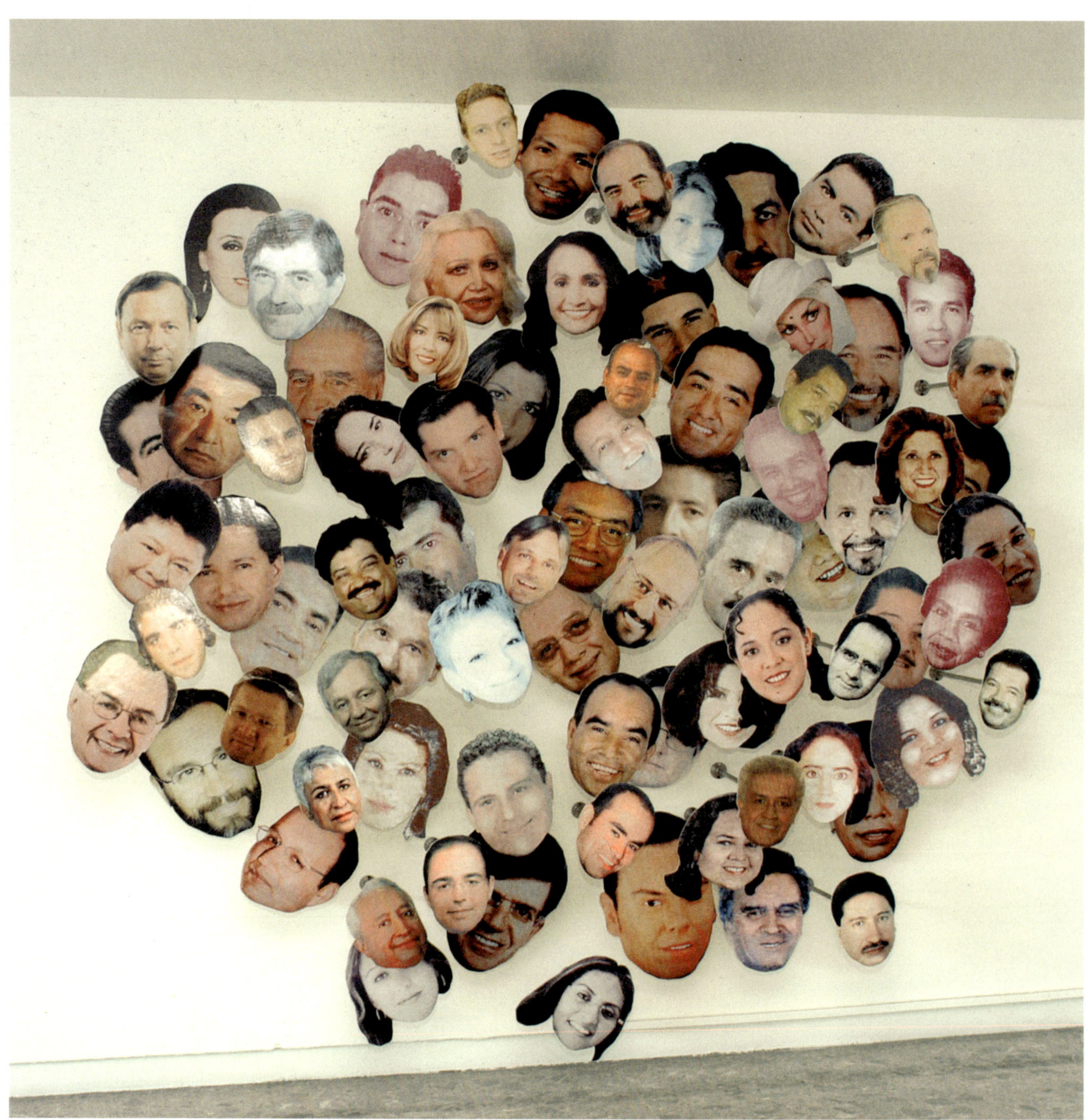

61 Yoshua Okon, *Staphylococcus*, 2004, installation view

YOSHUA OKON

Born in 1970, Mexico City, Mexico
Lives and works in Mexico City, Mexico, and Los Angeles, USA

Alongside improvised and orchestrated video performances, in which he often invites strangers to participate, Yoshua Okon produces installations and photographic works. *Staphylococcus*, a photographic installation that takes the shape of staphylococci bacteria, which can cause a wide variety of diseases through toxin production or invasion, comments on the parasitical nature of politicians. The 80 cut-out portrait heads – taken from political campaigning and propaganda posters around Mexico – are mounted at different distances from the wall, without any references to political affiliations or election promises. Like the staphylococcus bacterium itself, they might be harmless, but they could be deadly.

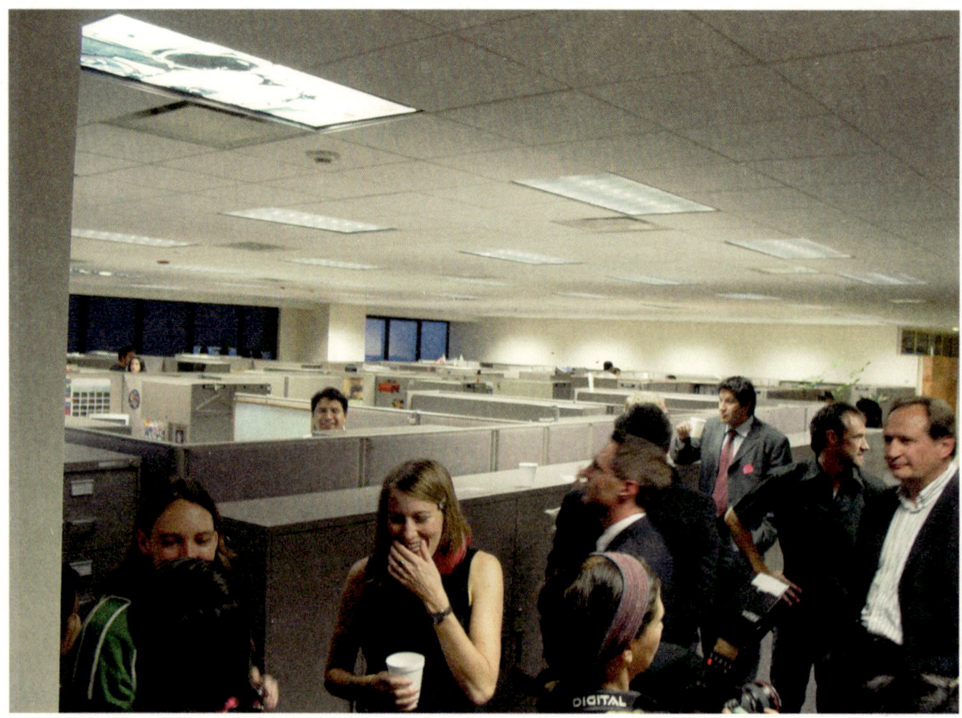

Yoshua Okon, *Office Ceiling Tile*, 2002, installation view: Daimler Chrysler, Mexico City, 2002

Speaking of his staged situations and participatory performances, Okon says, 'these interventions act like detonators that dislocate social codes, bringing about uncontrolled and unexpected effects.' His *Ceiling Tile* project took place at the Daimler Chrysler building in Mexico City in 2002. Playing with the relationship between private transgression and public humiliation, and with personal privacy and corporate surveillance, the resulting installation purported to give an intimate view of office life. Ceiling tiles in one office-space were replaced with photographs, supposedly of the occupants of the workstations above. The candid camera reveals a worm's eye view of bored workers caught misbehaving and flouting business protocol; drinking, having sex, using drugs and painting their toenails.

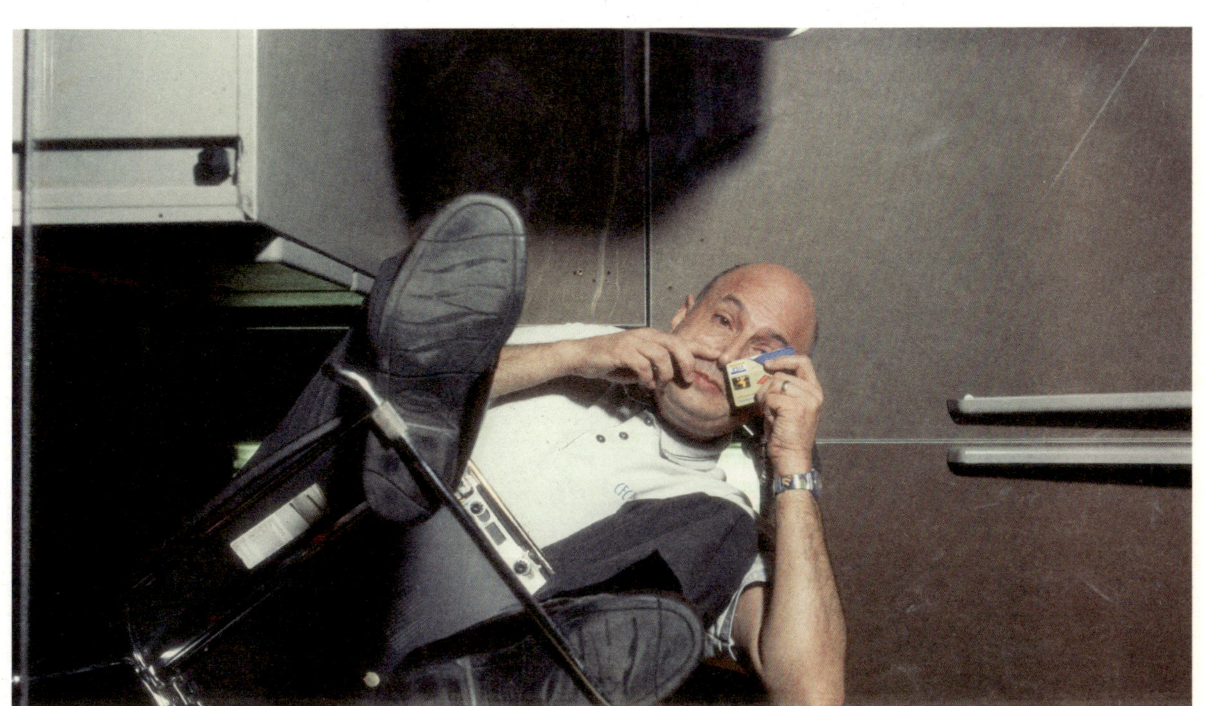

Yoshua Okon, *Office Ceiling Tile*, 2002, detail

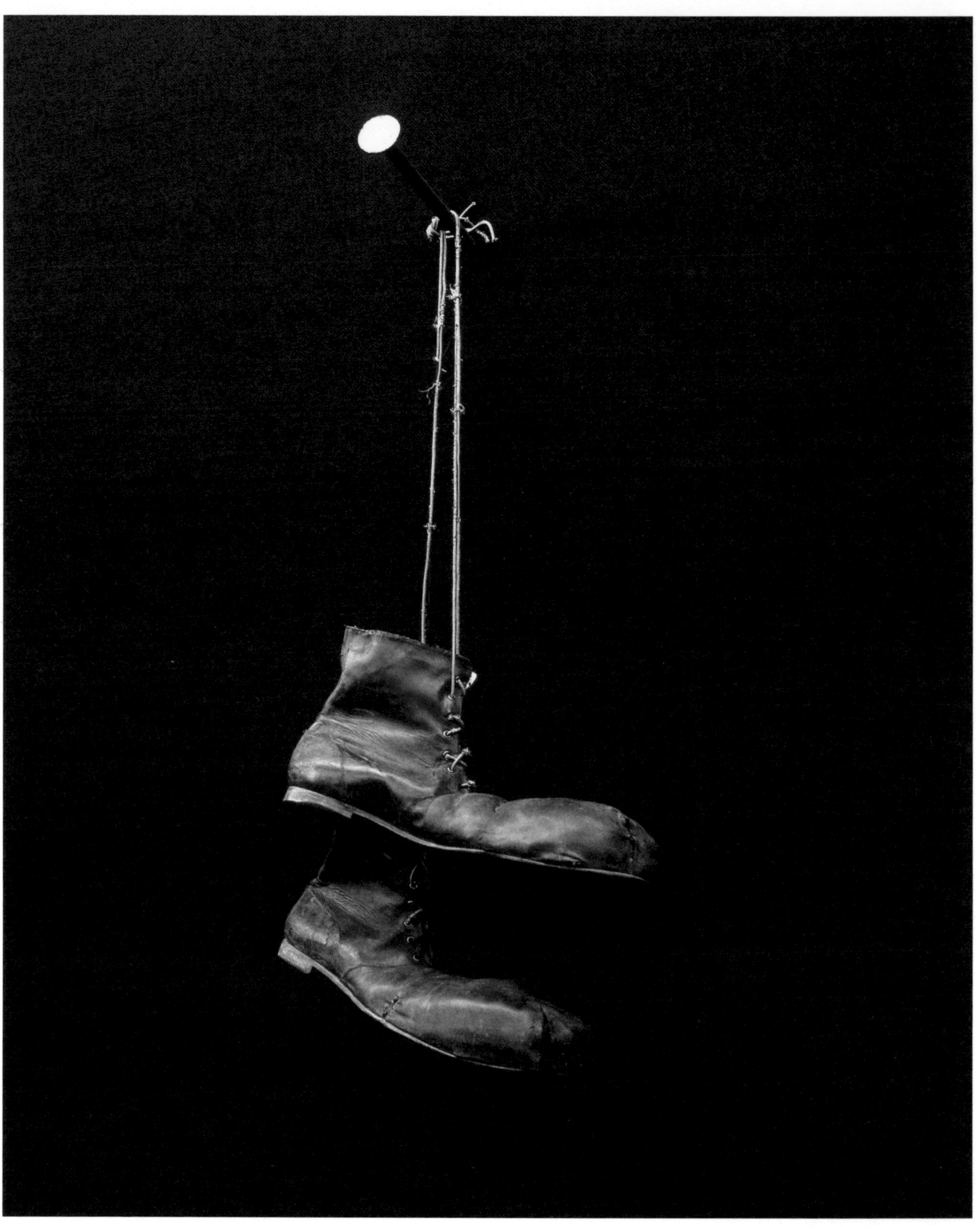

62 Ugo Rondinone, *ZERO*, 2006

UGO RONDINONE

Born in 1964, Brunnen, Switzerland
Lives and works in New York, USA

Clowns are society's truth-tellers and mischief-makers, and exist to pull the rug of propriety from under our feet. But Ugo Rondinone's clowns are different, refusing to behave as we expect them to. Always inactive, sitting around, lazing or sleeping, they made their first public appearance in his work in the mid-1990s, becoming the subject of performances, installations, photographs, videos and sculptures. For the installation *if there were anywhere but desert*, Rondinone made seven fibreglass clowns and titled each of them after a day of the week. All of them, from Monday through Sunday, are in completely passive positions.

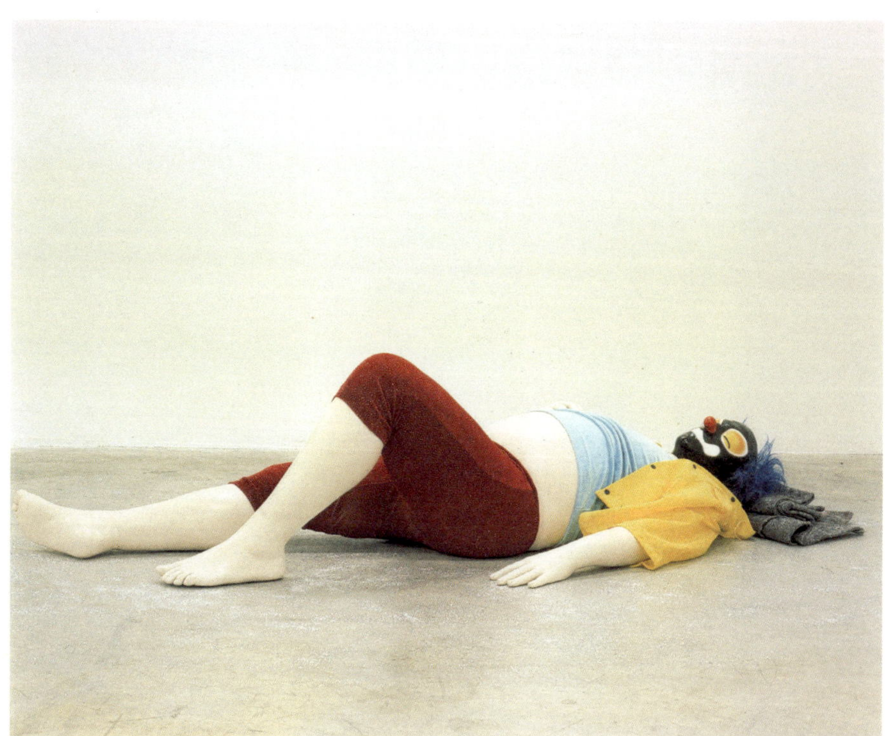

Ugo Rondinone, *if there were anywhere but desert. 0*, 2001, installation view: Galerie Almine Rech, Paris, 2001

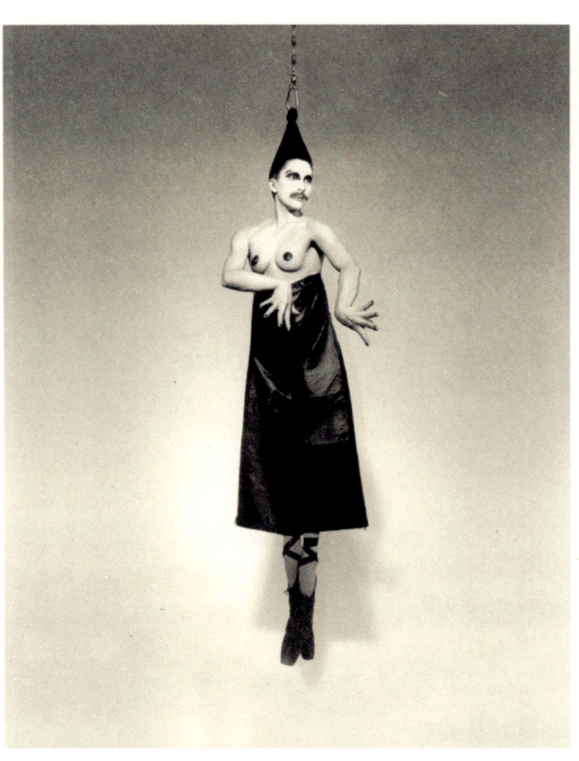

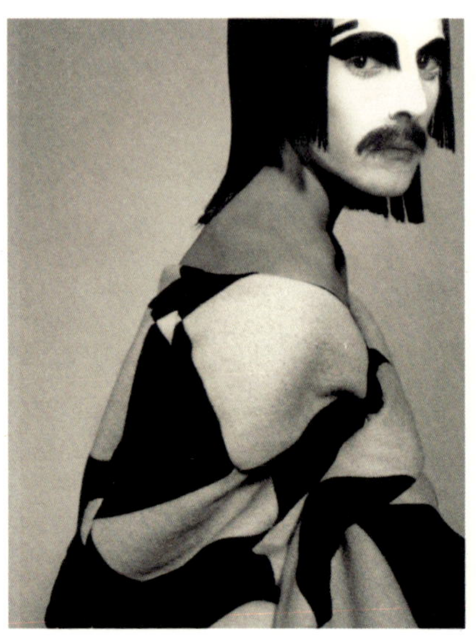

'I like that they aren't doing what they're supposed to as entertainers,' he remarks, 'because the work is about nothingness and doing nothing – how you organise your days doing nothing.' With *ZERO*, Rondinone is signalling that this is the end of nothingness; that the clown has hung up his boots and won't be coming back.

In the series of gender-bending images, *I don't live here anymore*, which dates from the mid- to late-1990s, Rondinone acts the clown by digitally-manipulating fashion photographs and superimposing his own head (and sometimes his arms) onto the model's body. The title alludes to one of Charles Baudelaire's prose poems, in which the poet reflects: 'It always seems to me that I should feel well in the place where I am not.'

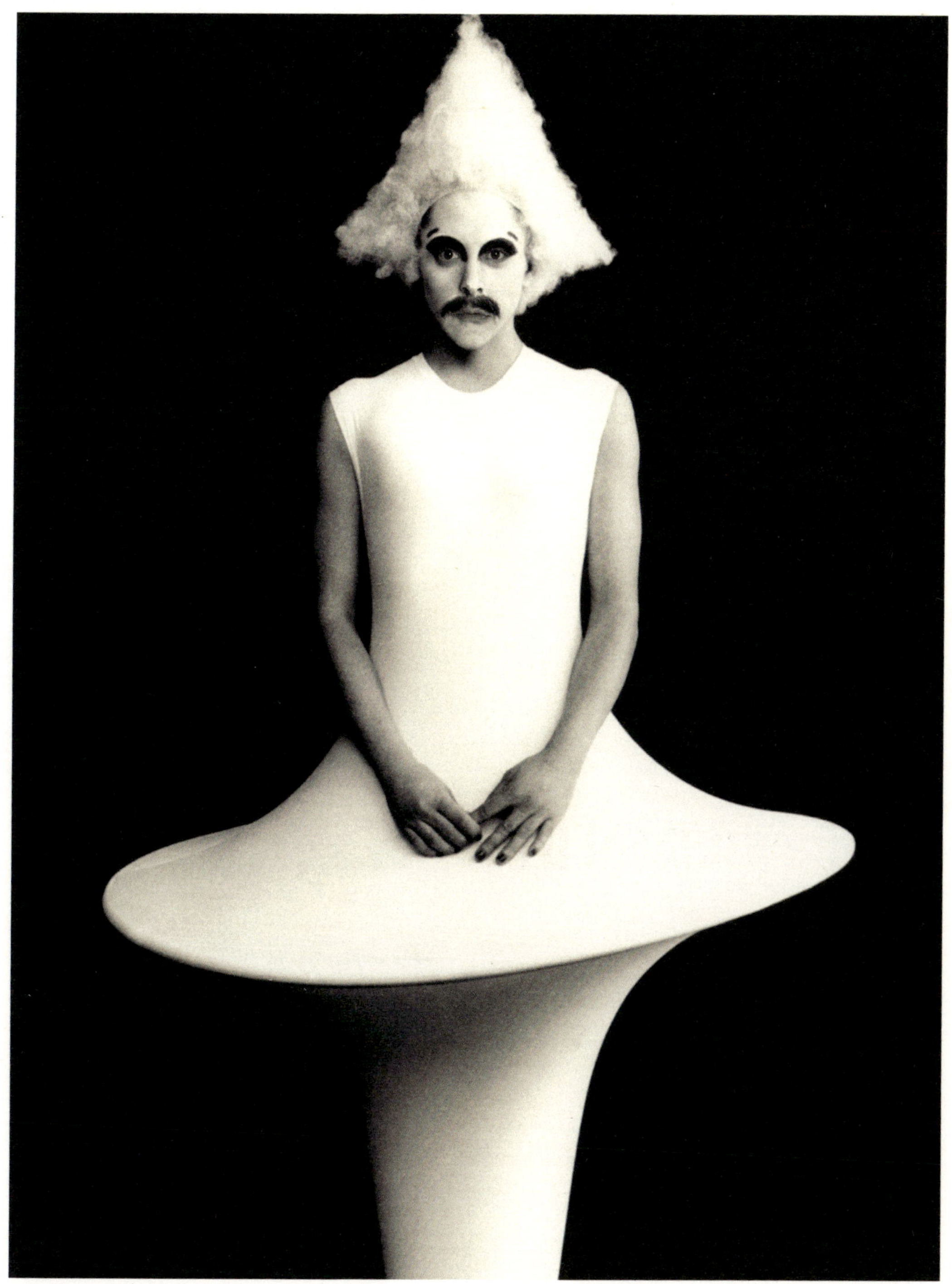

ABOVE AND LEFT Ugo Rondinone, *I don't live here anymore*, 1997

JULIAN ROSEFELDT

Born in 1965, Munich, Germany
Lives and works in Berlin, Germany

Julian Rosefeldt's multiple-screen video installations give a contemporary twist to the Greek myth of Sisyphus, who is condemned for eternity to roll a huge stone uphill; when he reaches the top the stone always rolls down again. In Rosefeldt's *Trilogy of Failure*, the three episodes present surreal fantasies in the purposeless existence of Everyman, mirroring the absurdity of life and the vanity of human endeavour. In each, the protagonist's futile actions are endlessly repeated, stuck in a continuous loop without hope of either fulfilment or reprieve.

In *Clown*, which Rosefeldt considers as the *Trilogy of Failure*'s epilogue, the focus is no longer on the ordinary man-in-the-street and instead we are given brief glimpses of a tragi-comic character dwarfed by nature. The three-screen video projection transports us into the depths of a tropical rainforest. Nothing seems to happen. A leaf falls. There are muted sounds of invisible jungle creatures. Then, in the far distance, a figure emerges. He slowly stumbles into view, crosses from one video screen to another, and disappears. Again, nothing seems to happen. A leaf falls...

Rosefeldt's *Clown* photographs provide an intimate portrait that we are denied in the film. In close-up, momentarily relieved of his incessantly circular traipsing and able to admire the scenery, he is revealed as a traditional circus joey, who might be related to the Big Mac's 'chief happiness officer', Ronald McDonald. But, on screen, his Sisyphean ramblings allow no lingering, no pause, no variation in the routine, no end.

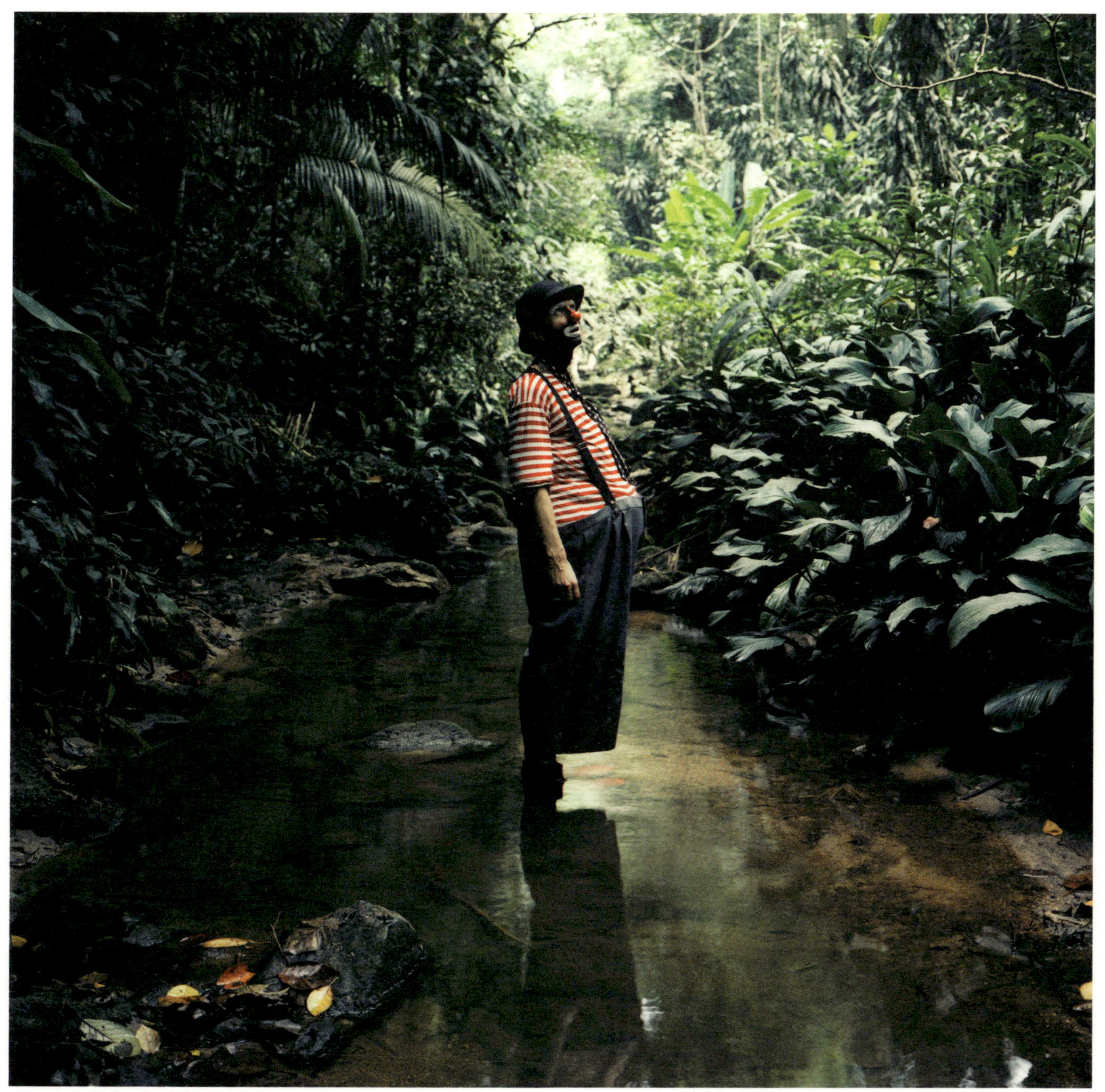

63 Julian Rosefeldt, *Clown*, 2005, production still

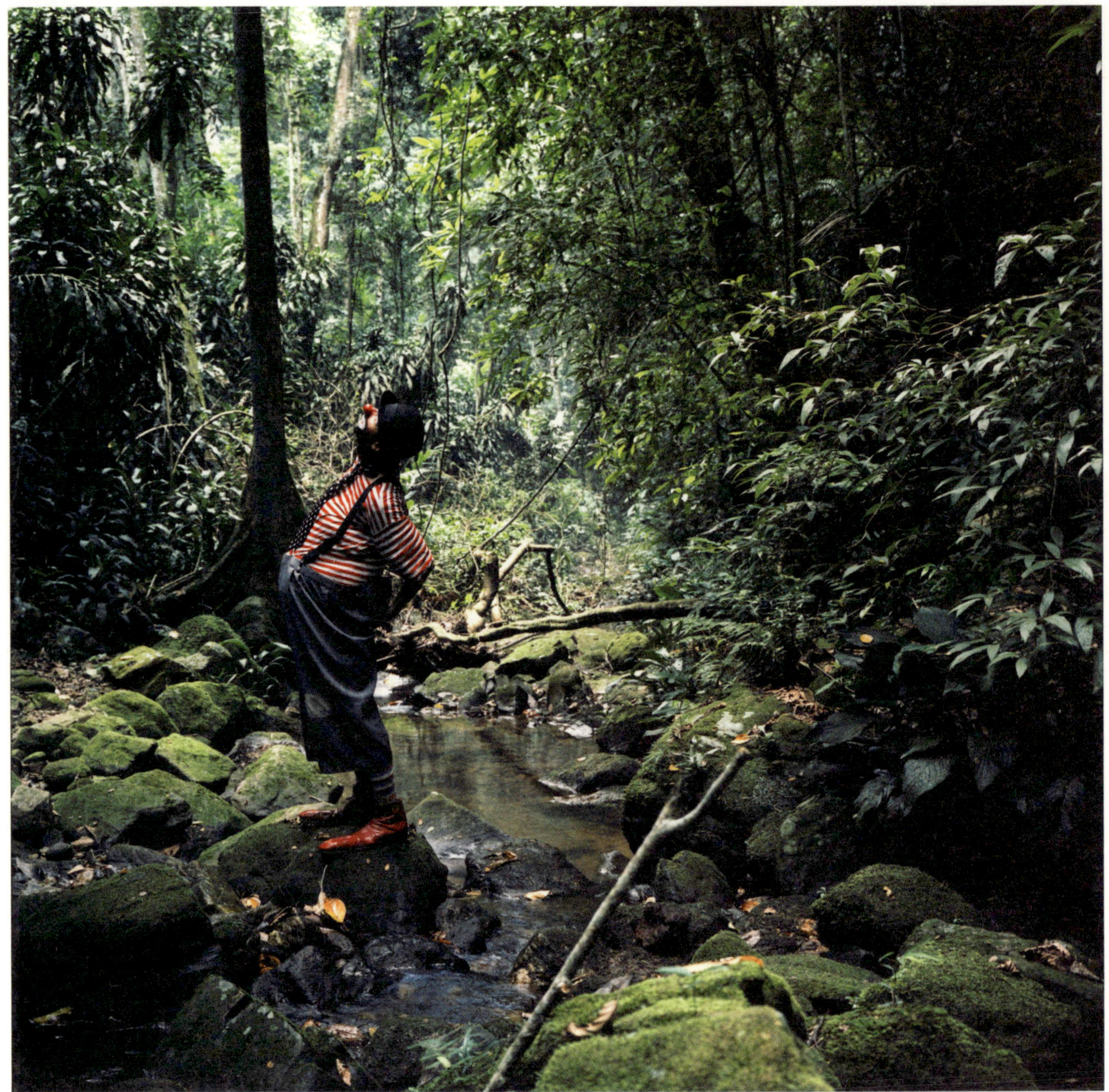

63 Julian Rosefeldt, *Clown*, 2005, production still

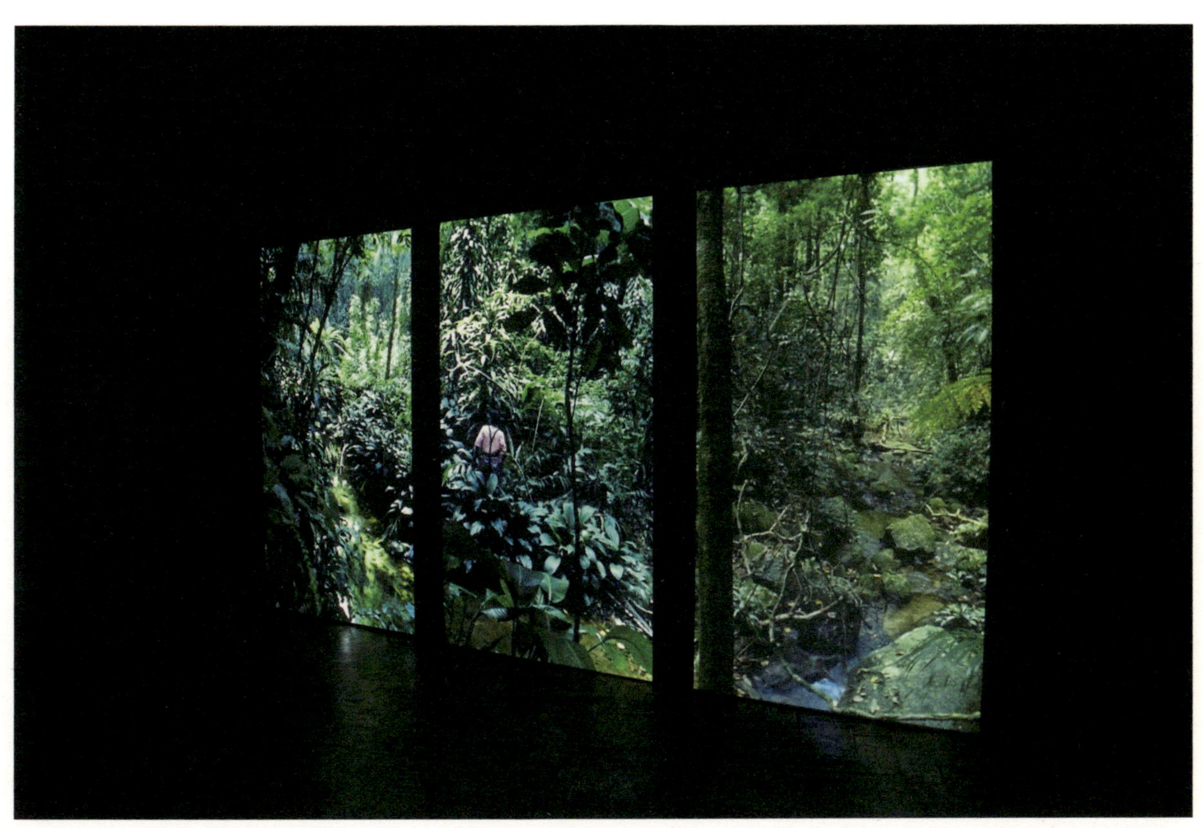

63 Julian Rosefeldt, *Clown*, 2005, installation view: Chapter Gallery, Cardiff

SHIMABUKU

Born in 1969, Kobe, Japan
Lives in Berlin, Germany

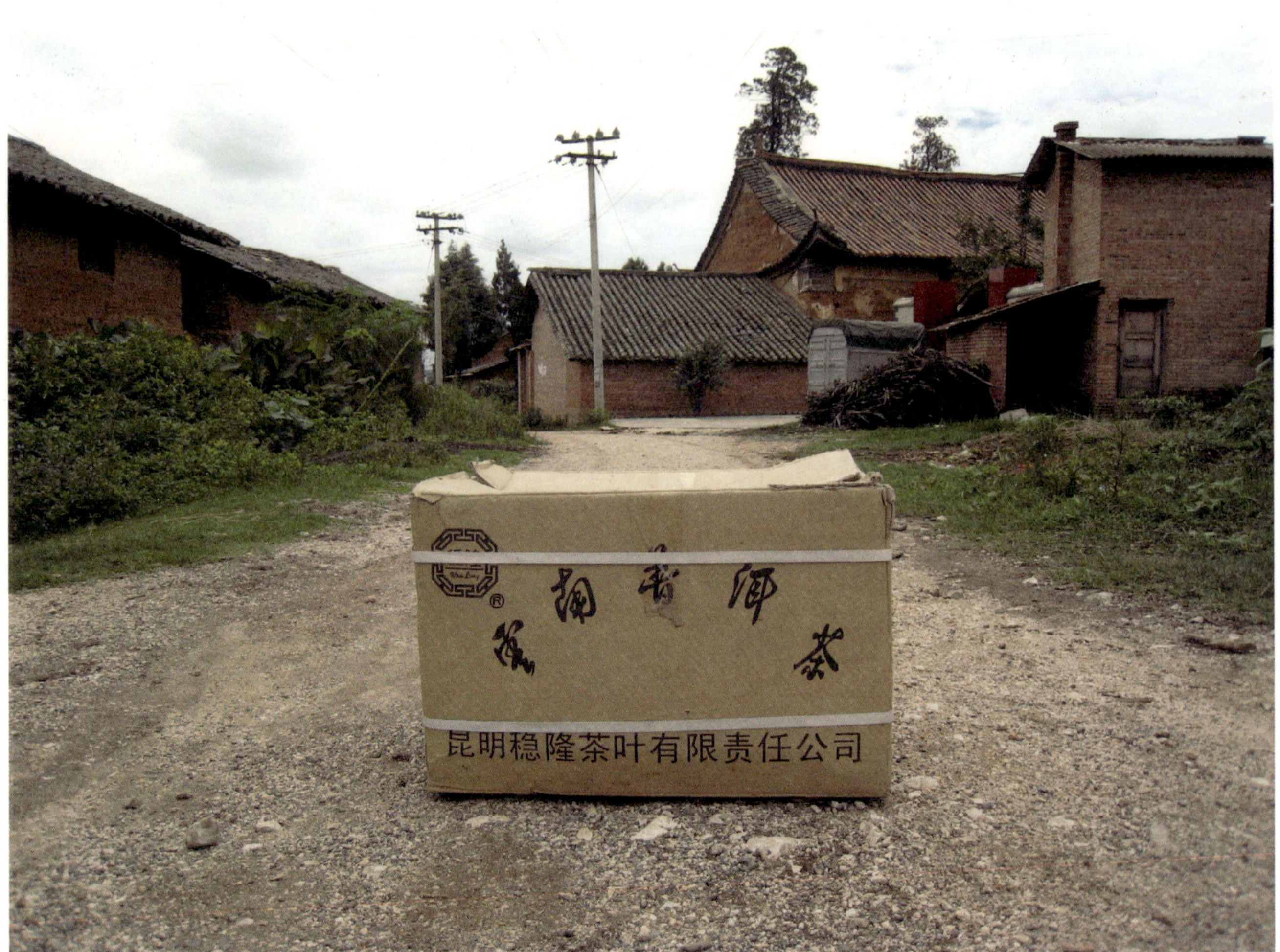

Shimabuku, *Born as a Box (Chinese Version)*, 2007

Shimabuku loves travelling, but for him it is always the journey rather than the arrival that matters. His performances, videos, photographs and installations are often inspired by chance encounters or discoveries made during his expeditions. Sometimes he includes others in his travels, such as the live octopus which he took on a 600-mile trip from the Inland Sea to Tokyo and back again, and sometimes he finds that others have hitched a ride on him, like the stone that lodged itself in his shoe: once discovered, Shimabuku became as attached to it as it was to him.

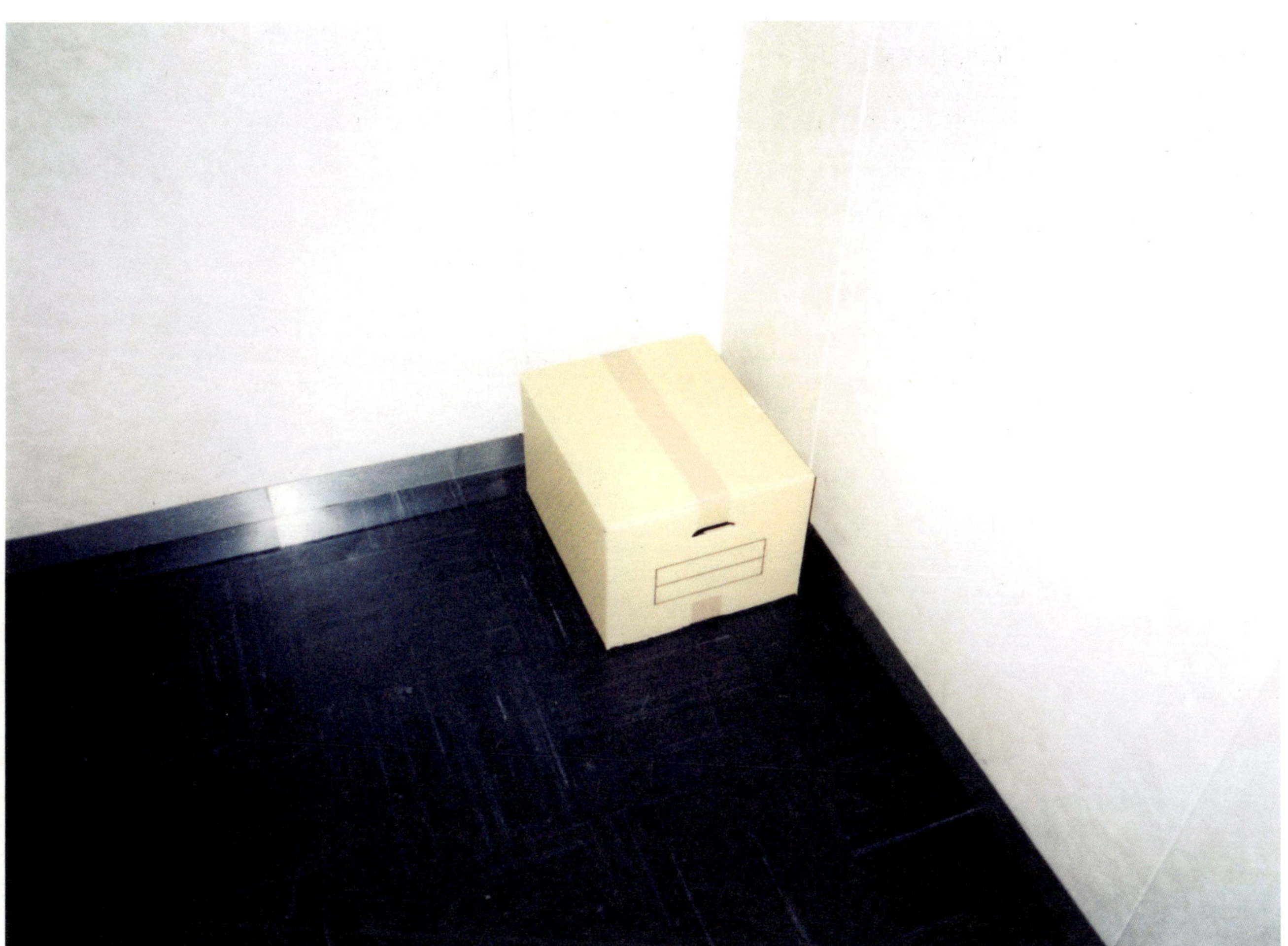

Shimabuku, *Born as a Box (Japanese Version A)*, 2001/04

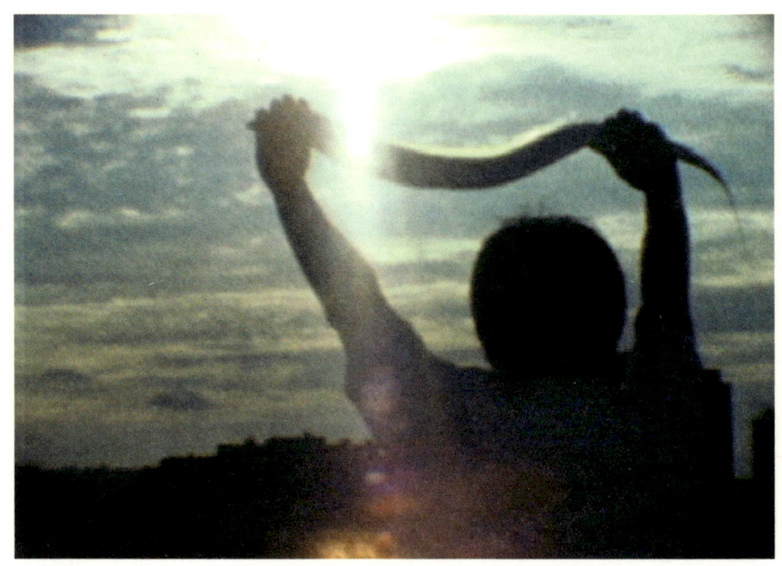

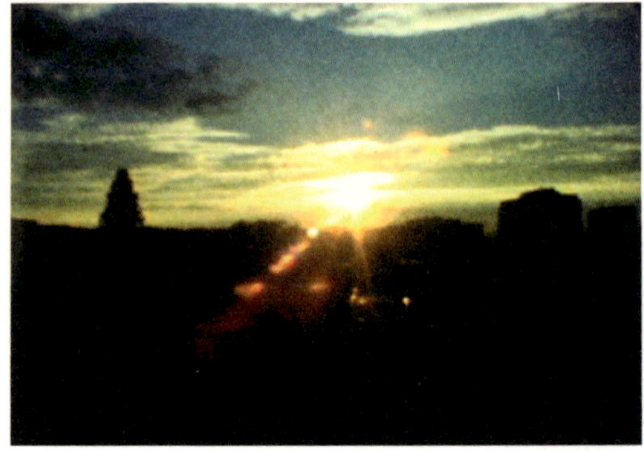

The cardboard container that comes to life in *Born as a Box* also enjoys travelling; one of an international family of boxes (there are different Italian, Japanese and Chinese versions), it speaks to us, and in a philosophical monologue reveals that 'Life as a box is not bad, my friends ... I can go many places. It is a lot of fun.' Rain and rough handling can be problems, but there are the compensations of neat packing. The carton concludes, 'I am happy to be born as a box, I think...' Shimabuku says, 'Art must be magic, very cheap but very good ... In Japan, people are rich but not happy, so I need to show them [what to do]. I'm showing [them] how to become happy with little money.'

Sunrise at Mt. Artsonje documents a dawn performance on the roof of a museum in Seoul, South Korea. Thin, shiny cutlass fish were held up to the sun and used as a heliograph – a mirror to reflect sunlight to a distant observer – and in this way Shimabuku hoped to communicate with unknown beings.

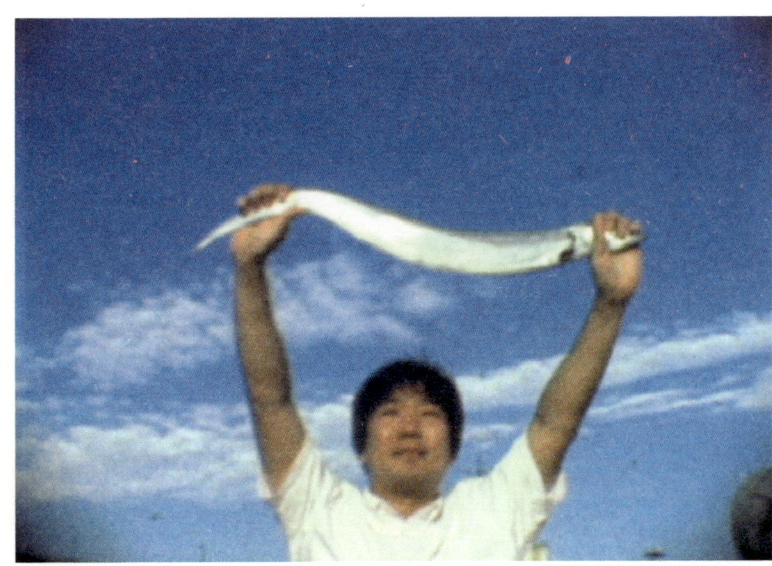

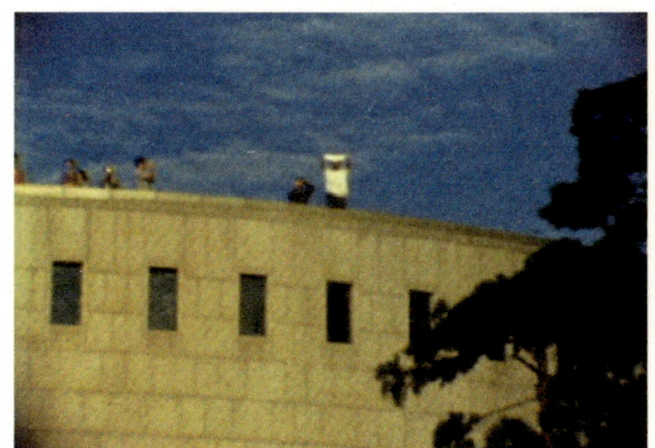

ABOVE AND LEFT Shimabuku, *Sunrise at Mt. Artsonje*, 2007, stills

DAVID SHRIGLEY

Born in 1968, Macclesfield, UK
Lives and works in Glasgow, UK

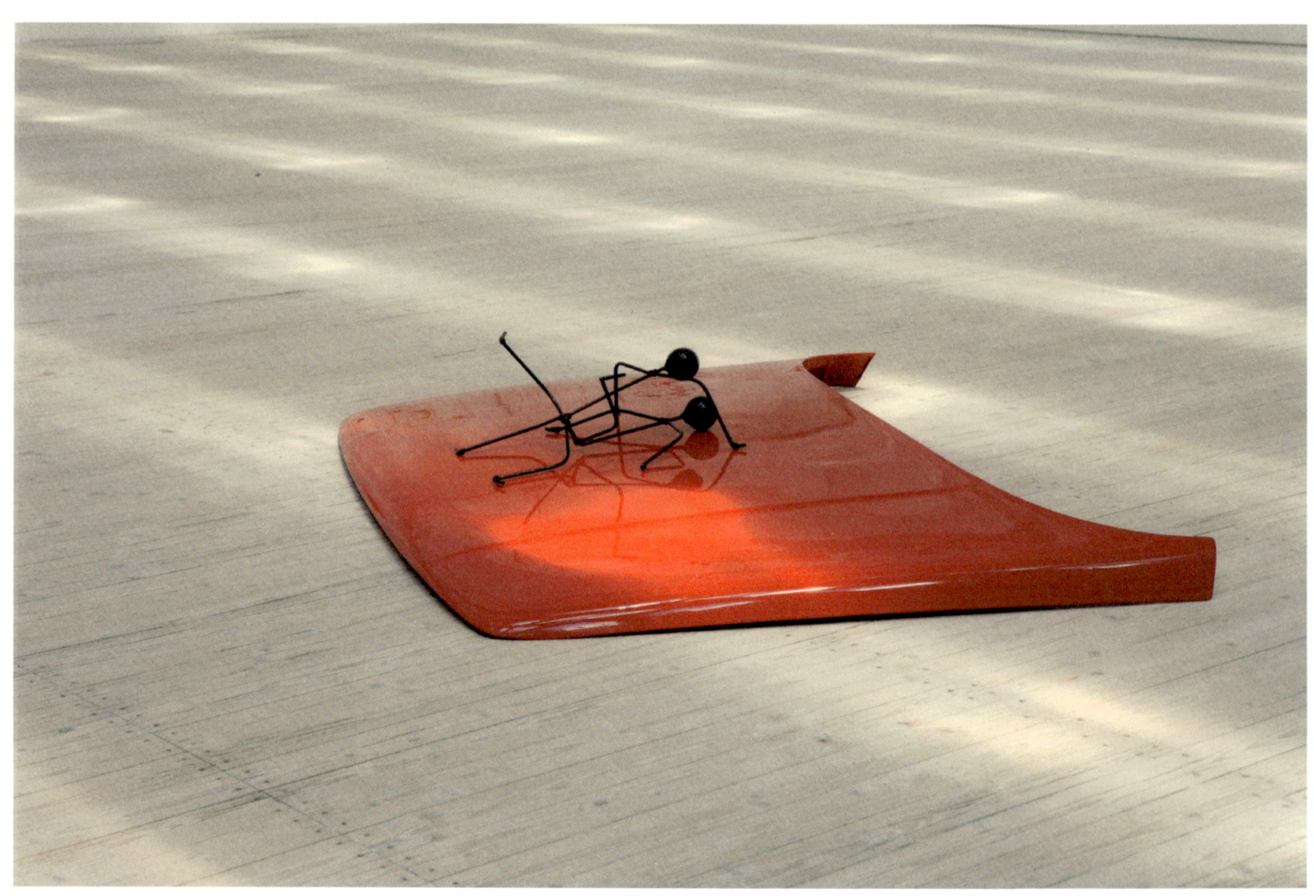

David Shrigley, *Untitled (Stick figures having sex on car hood)*, 2007, installation view

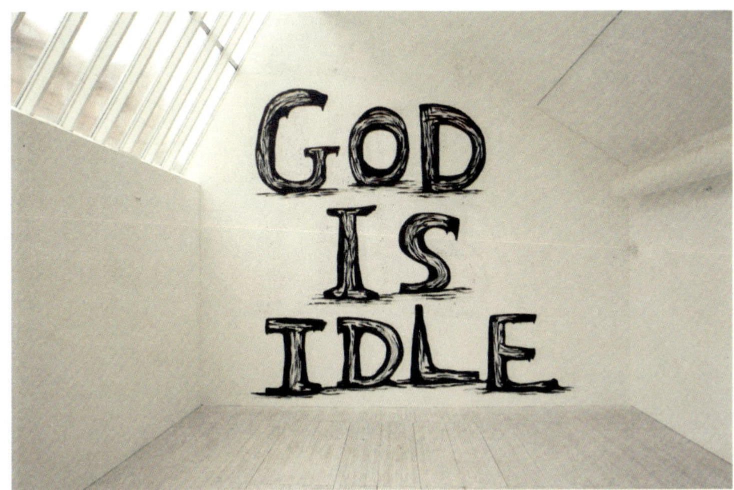

David Shrigley, *God Is Idle*, 2007, installation view

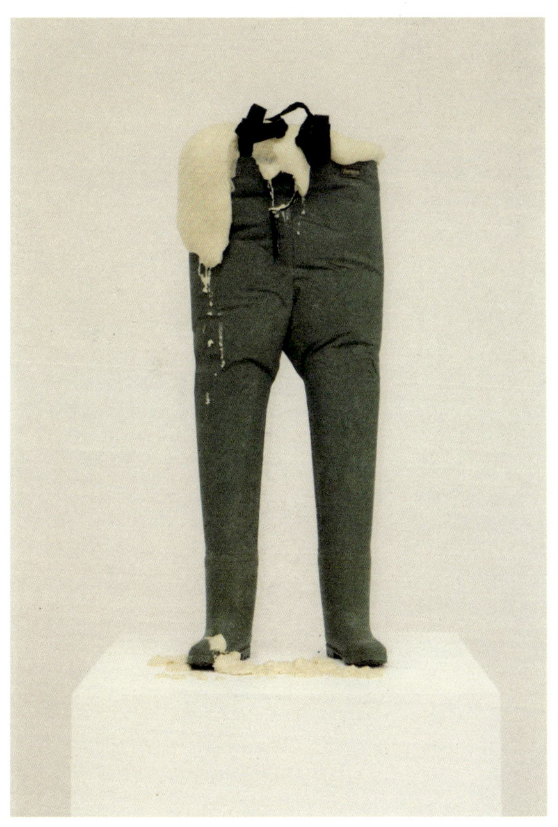

David Shrigley, *Cheers*, 2007, installation view

According to the blurb on the back of his book, *Ants Have Sex in Your Beer* (2007), David Shrigley – who elsewhere describes himself as 'a nasty person with a sense of humour' – is 'an elderly gentleman with white hair and one eye'. It may however be true that, as the same back-cover text maintains, the source material for his artwork comes to him in dreams.

Shrigley is known to countless fans for the quirky vignettes with goofy drawings and maladjusted aphorisms that have appeared in newspapers and magazines such as *The Guardian* and Japanese *Esquire*. But his extraordinarily prolific and oddball humour extends to works in other media, including sculpture, photography and animated videos, and his dark mutterings have been recorded on an audio CD entitled *Shrigley Forced to Speak with Others* (2006).

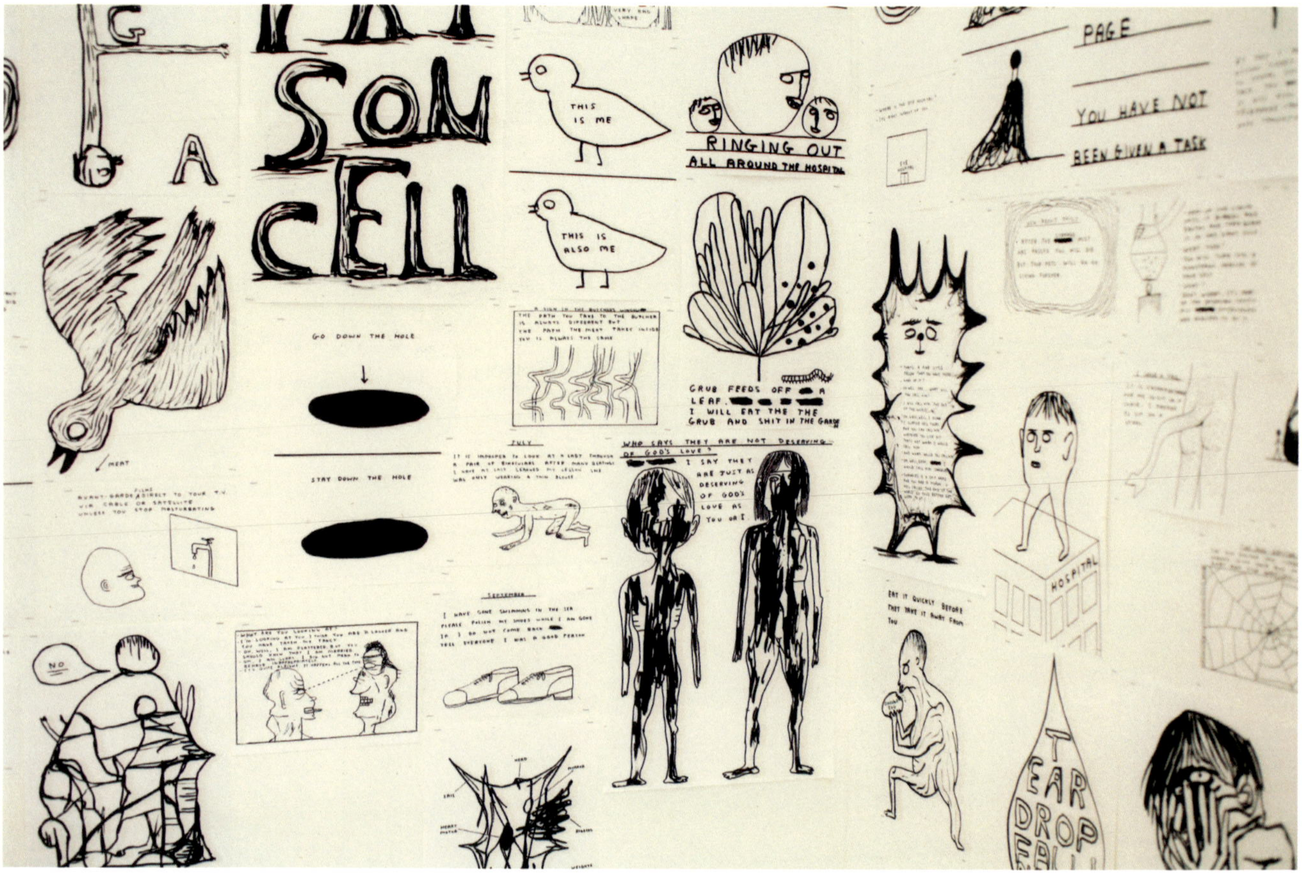

David Shrigley, *Selected drawings*, 2004–07, installation view

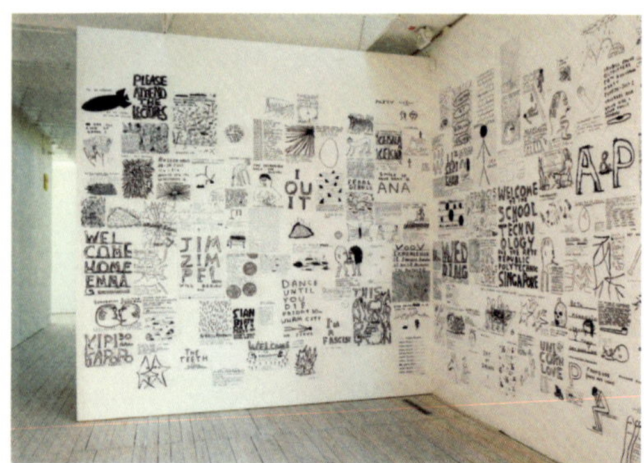

David Shrigley, *Poster Project*, 2006, installation view

Insisting that 'I'm not really so interested in telling jokes as such; most of the time I'm trying to be serious,' Shrigley admits: 'For me everything has to have some kind of humour to it because that's the way life is. It's funny, and it's sad and bad at the same time.' In his images and texts, he tells his stories in the sparest possible way, leaving space for the audience to form the rest of the narrative themselves. Although his work thumbs its nose at political correctness, Shrigley makes it clear that 'There are certain lines which I just would not cross. But then again, as an artist, I am also playing a part. The narrator in my work is somebody other than me. It's some crazed person who either over- or under-moralizes everything.'

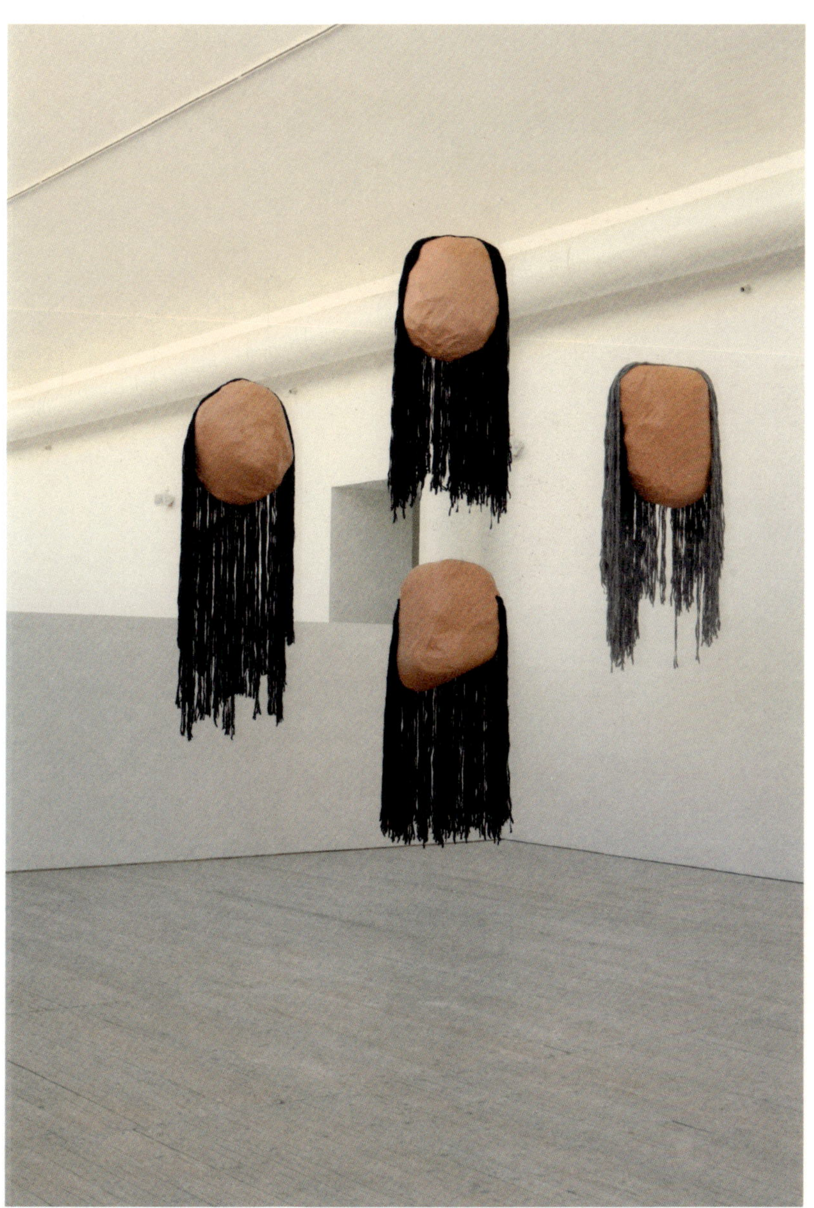

David Shrigley, *Rock Band*, 2007, installation view

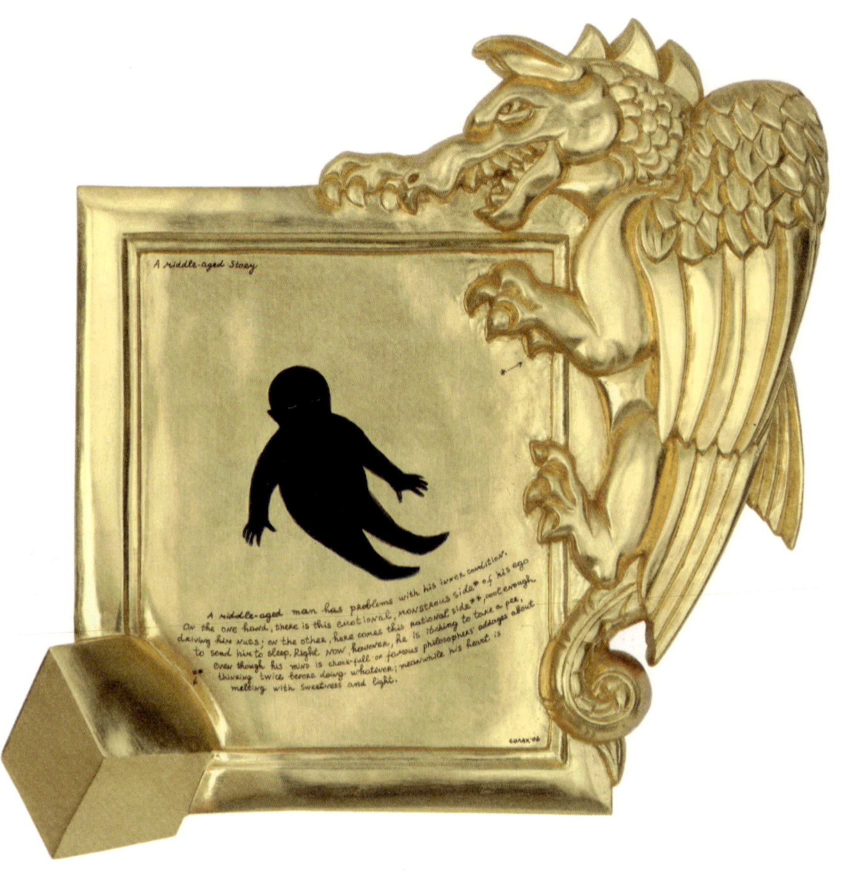

Nedko Solakov, *A Middle Age Story*, 2006

NEDKO SOLAKOV

Born in 1957, Cherven Briag, Bulgaria
Lives in Sofia, Bulgaria

As a student in Bulgaria during the communist regime, Nedko Solakov was trained as a painter of social-realist murals. Now, he tells stories; in hand-made books, drawings and videos; through sculpture and found objects; and by writing texts on walls. In his ongoing *Wallpaper* project, in which tiny figures and messages are hidden amongst the foliage of old-fashioned floral wallpaper, you have to search for his miniscule interventions; bending and stretching and pressing your nose against the wall to see and read them. Looking becomes an energetic treasure-hunt. 'I want to talk to all kinds of people,' Solakov confides.

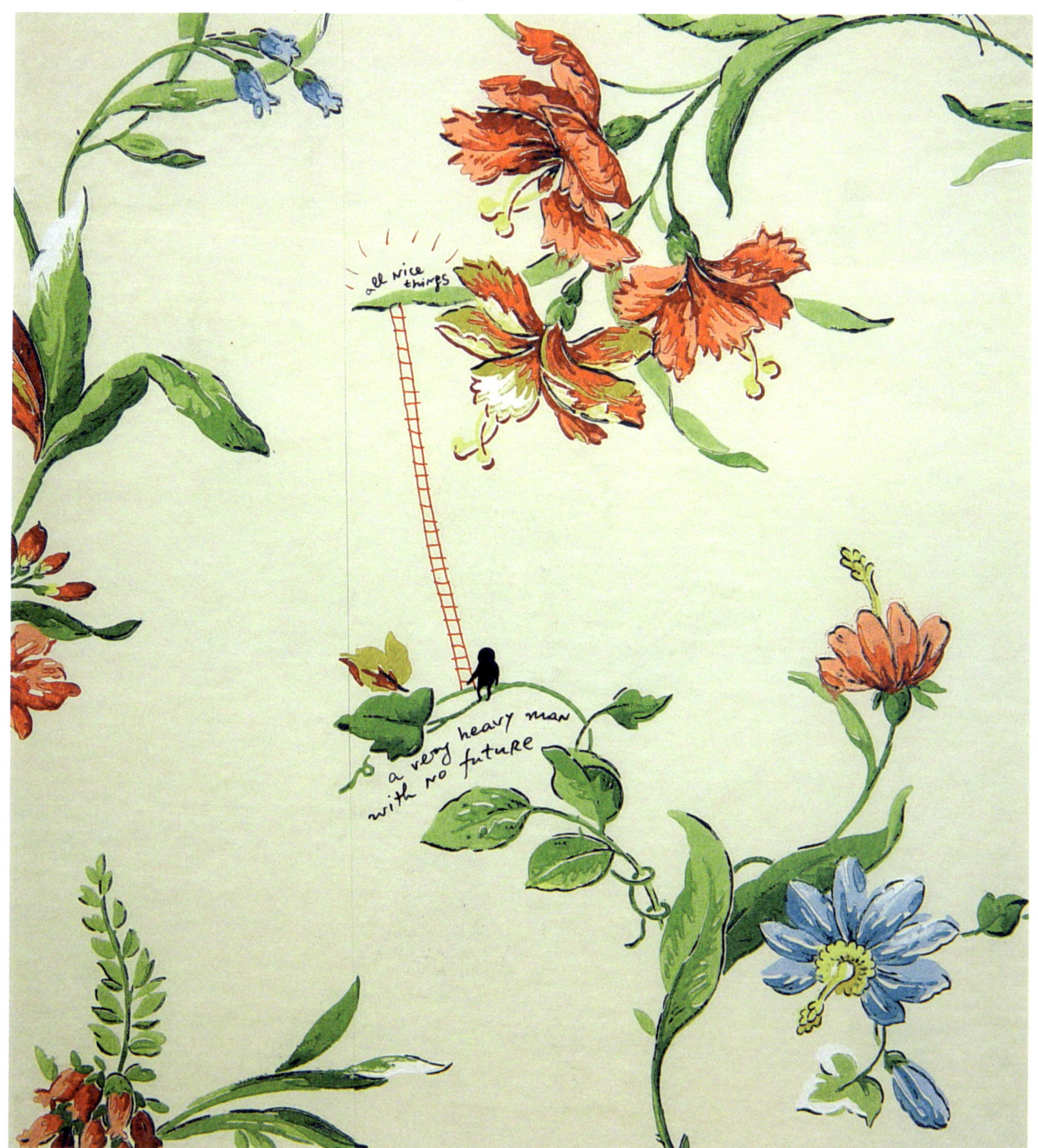

Nedko Solakov, *Wallpaper*, 1993, from *A 12 1/3 (and even more) Year Survey* retrospective exhibition, O.K Centrum für Gegenwartskunst, Linz, Austria, 2004

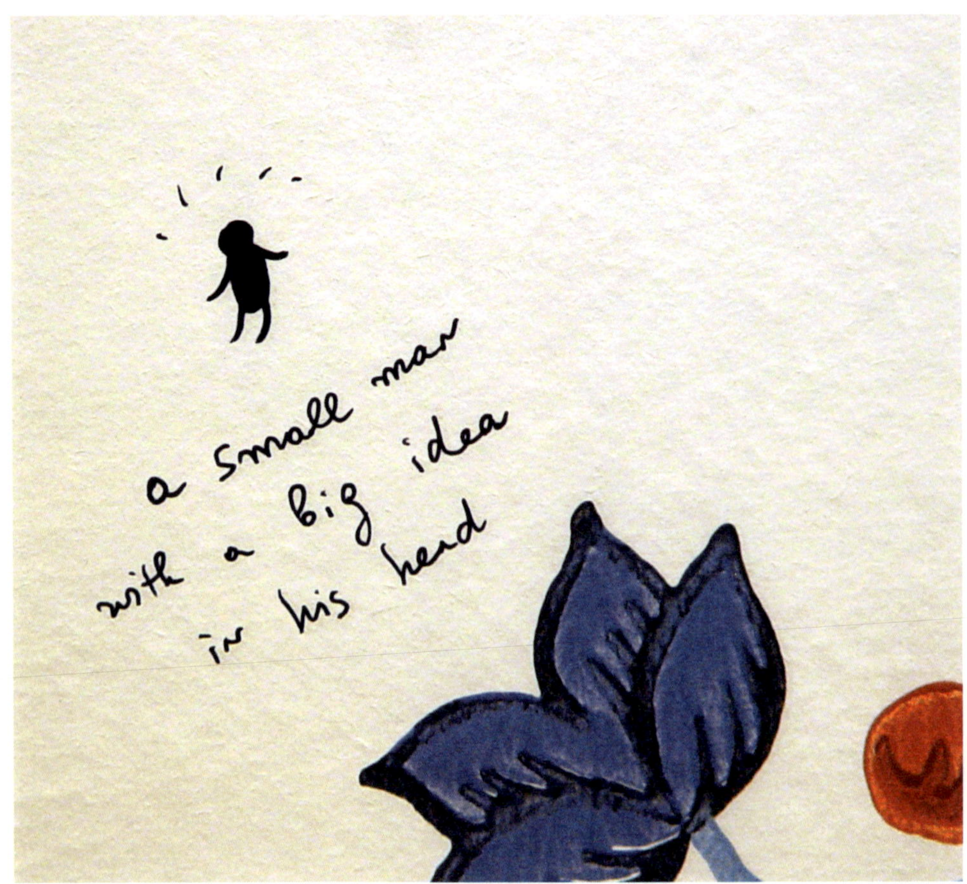

Nedko Solakov, *Wallpaper*, 1993, from *A 12 1/3 (and even more) Year Survey* retrospective exhibition, Rooseum Center for Contemporary Art, Malmö, Sweden, 2004

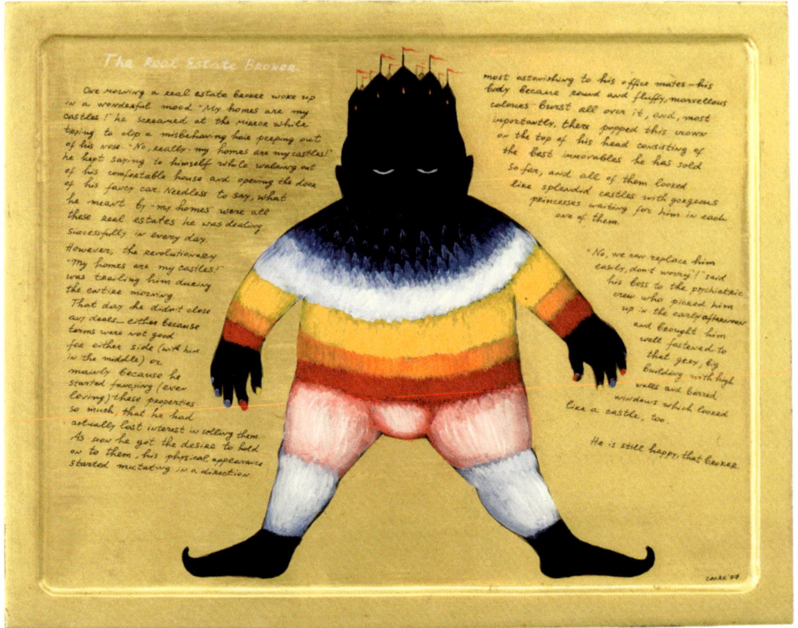

Nedko Solakov, *The Real Estate Broker*, 2007

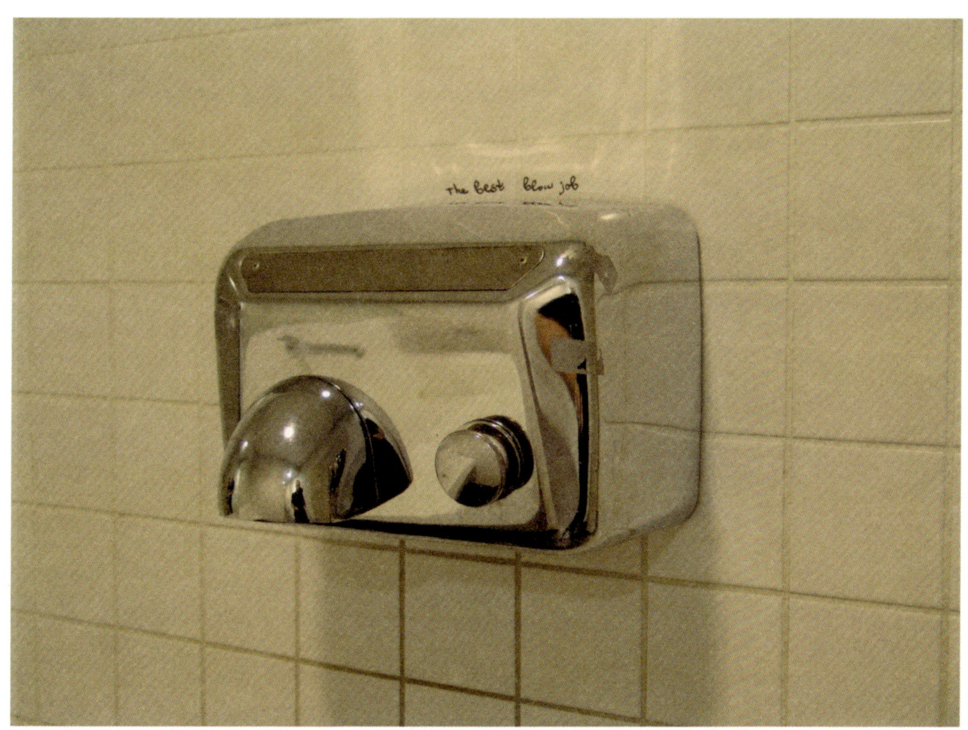

Nedko Solakov, *Toilettes*, 2006, detail, from *Broken Lines/Printemps du septembre* exhibition, Toulouse, France, 2006

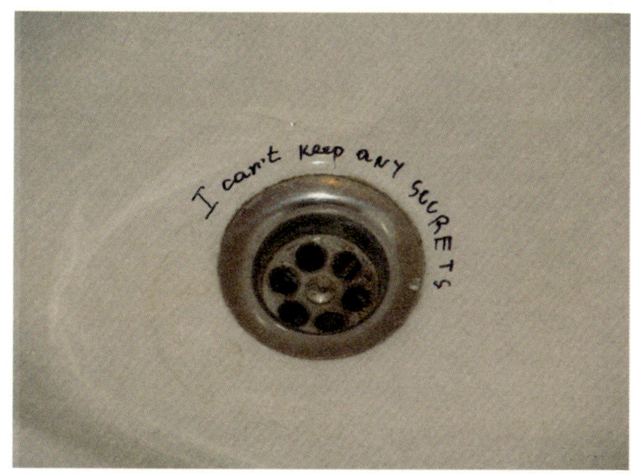

Nedko Solakov, *Bad*, 2006, detail, from *Homework* exhibition, Gagosian Gallery Berlin, Germany (as part of the 4th Berlin Biennial), 2006

'I want to chatter with them about whatever. It'd be great if they responded. They can respond by crouching, jumping, or simply spending more than five minutes with one of my stories.'

Some of his narratives are told in more straightforward ways, as in the paintings *A Middle Age Story* and *The Real Estate Broker*, which are framed and gilded like profane icons, or in the *Toilettes* series, in which neat graffiti were written around various fixtures in the lavatories of Les Abattoirs, Toulouse's centre for contemporary art.

Doodles (Hayward), are site-specific wall drawings that Solakov is making for the *Laughing in a Foreign Language* exhibition. About similar works he has said: 'These texts are actually stories I relate to people, to a person, even if I have no actual face before me at that precise moment. The relevant challenge with the "walls" is that 99% of these works are painted over and disappear at some point. That keeps me going. Just like a spoken word disappears, these works disappear too.'

BARTHÉLÉMY TOGUO

Born in 1967, M'Balmayo, Cameroon
Lives and works in New York, USA; Paris, France; and Bandjoun, Cameroon

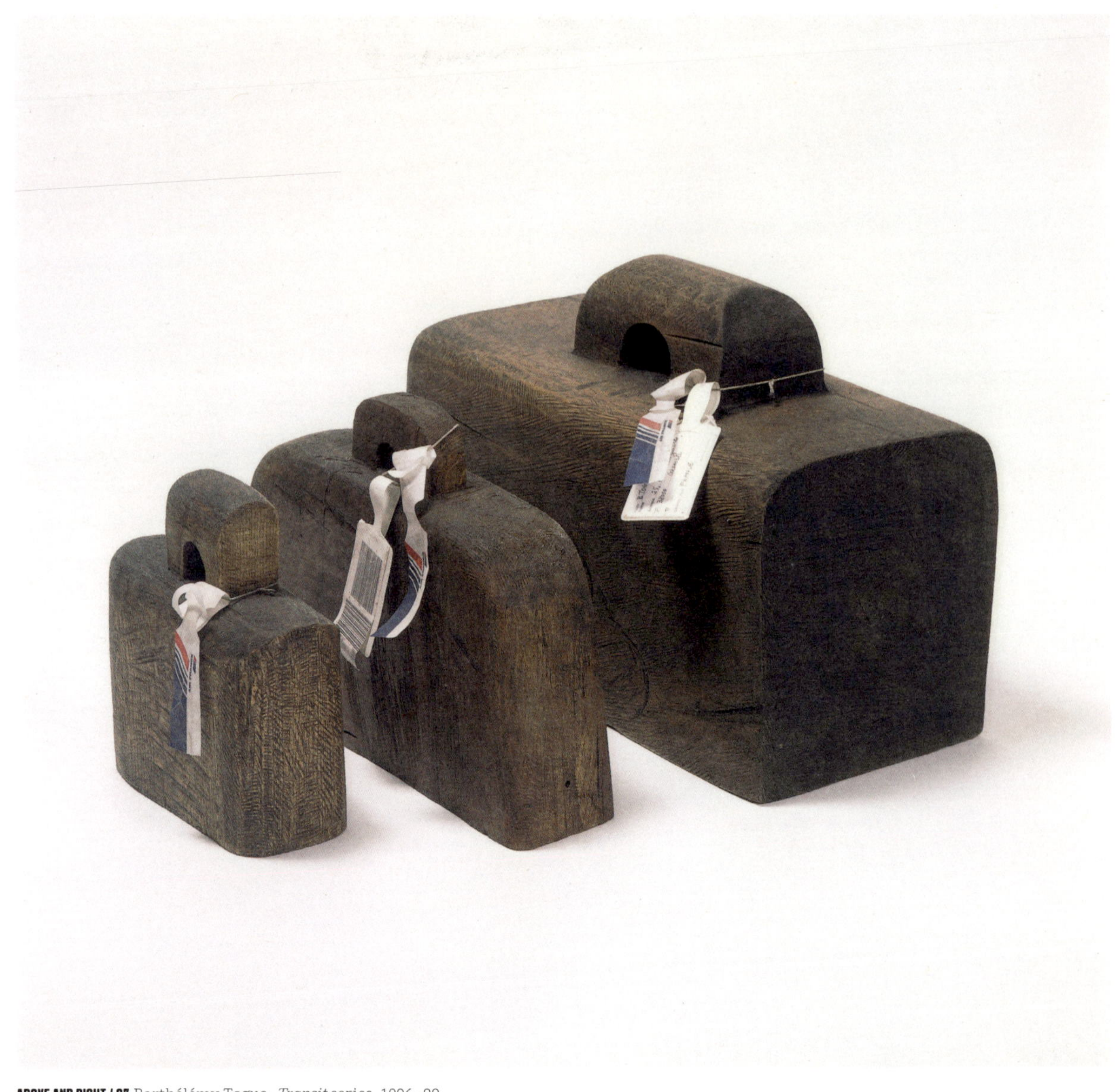

ABOVE AND RIGHT / 67 Barthélémy Toguo, *Transit* series, 1996–99

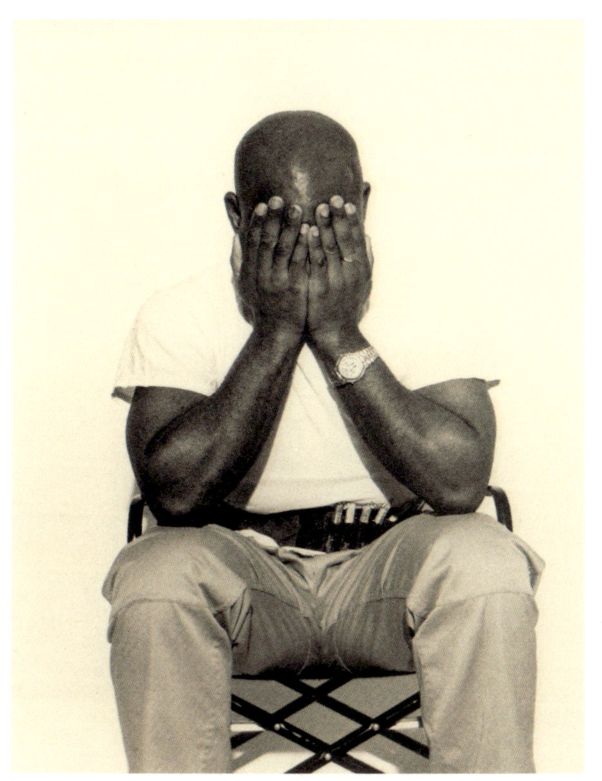

Barthélémy Toguo's work encompasses painting, drawing, printmaking, sculpture, video and performance and often refers to the problems of crossing borders and negotiating political and social boundaries. In the *Transit* series, which dates from the late 1990s, each of the eight prints and its accompanying text tells the story of a 'performance' from Toguo's travels in Europe and Africa. Exasperated by the way in which he was treated by customs officers and border police, he embarked on a sequence of innocent provocations. *Transit 1* features a set of solid wooden suitcases which caused consternation among airport security when it was discovered that they could not be opened and proved impenetrable by X-ray and laser. *Transit 2* documents Toguo's despair as he is prevented from boarding a plane because he is wearing an ammunition belt loaded with Carambars – those sticks of toffee beloved by French children. In *Transit 6*, Toguo challenged class prejudice and snobbery by attempting to take his seat in a first-class train carriage dressed as a road sweeper.

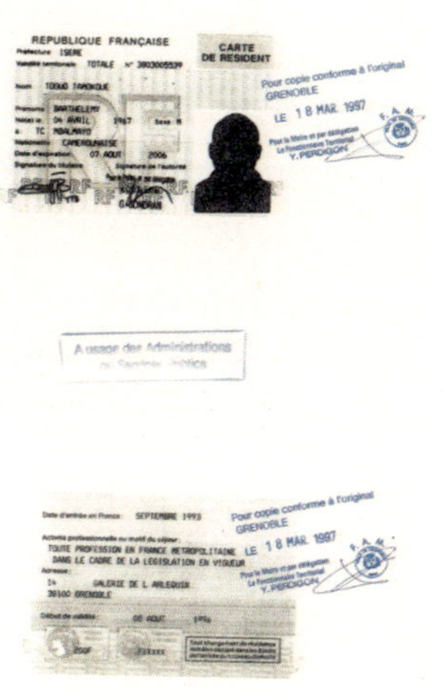

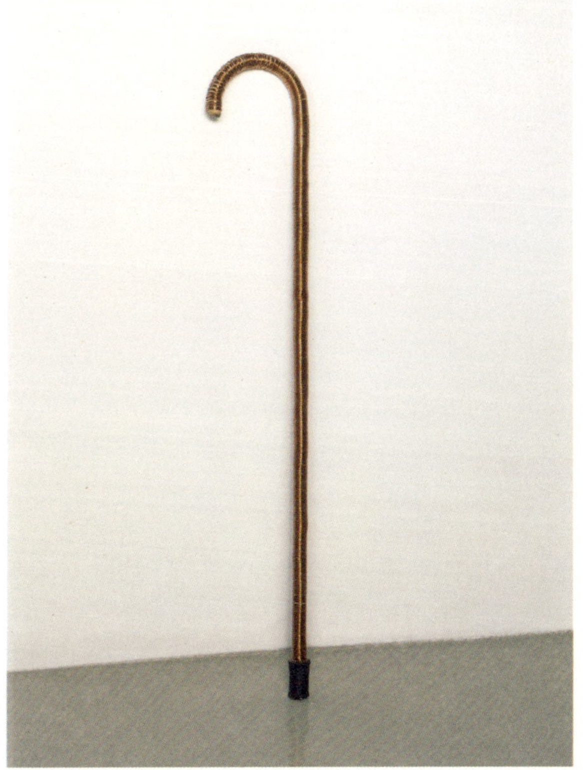

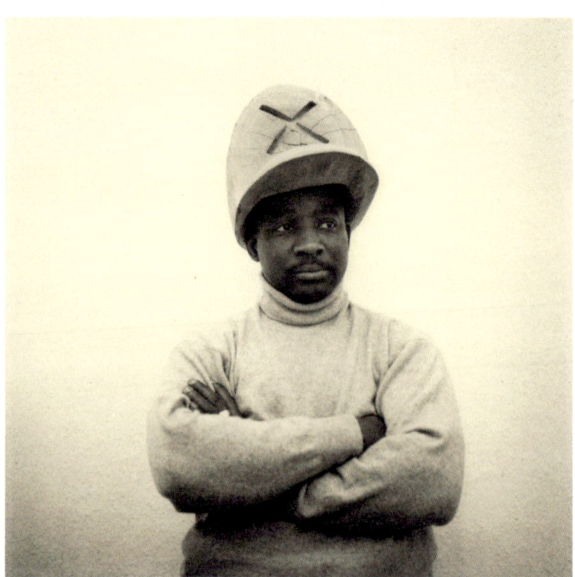

ABOVE AND RIGHT / 67 Barthélémy Toguo, *Transit* series, 1996–99

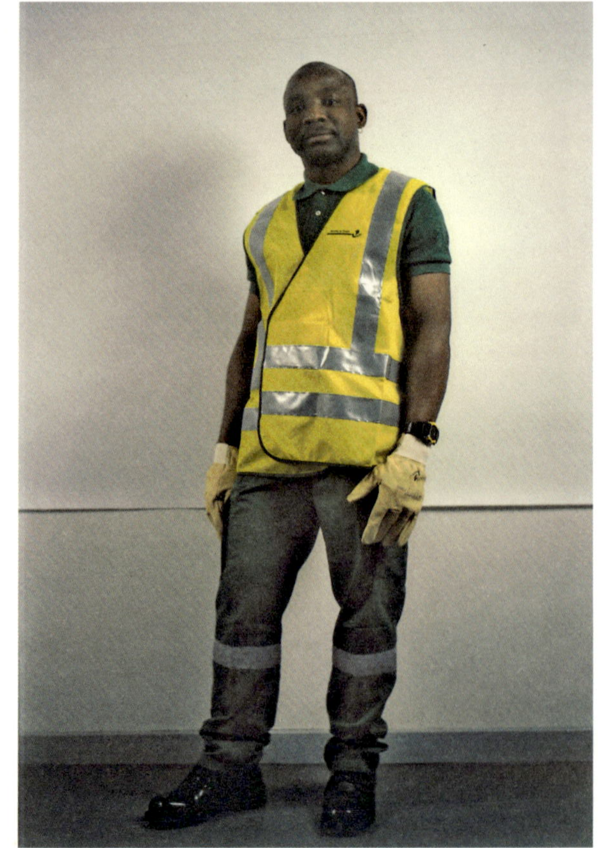

'We are all in a permanent state of "transit",' Toguo points out. 'This concept is universal for the 20th- and 21st-century man, and whether a man is white, black or yellow is of little importance. He is in any case a being who is potentially "exiled", borne along by the driving force that is travel and which is going to make him move. We leave one place for another ... while bringing along with us during these different journeys our culture, which runs up against the other. Of course, this coming together can be either beautiful or difficult.'

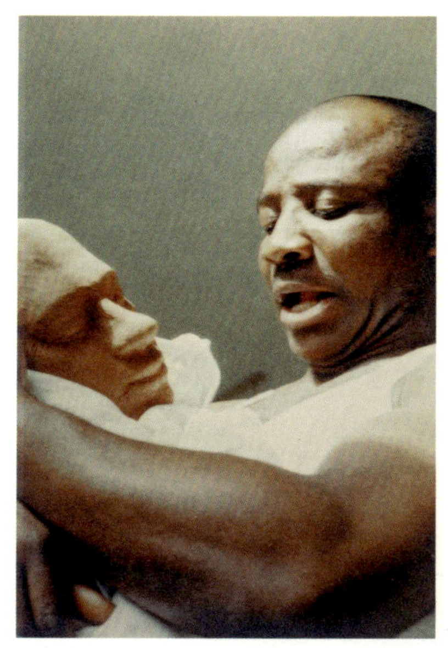

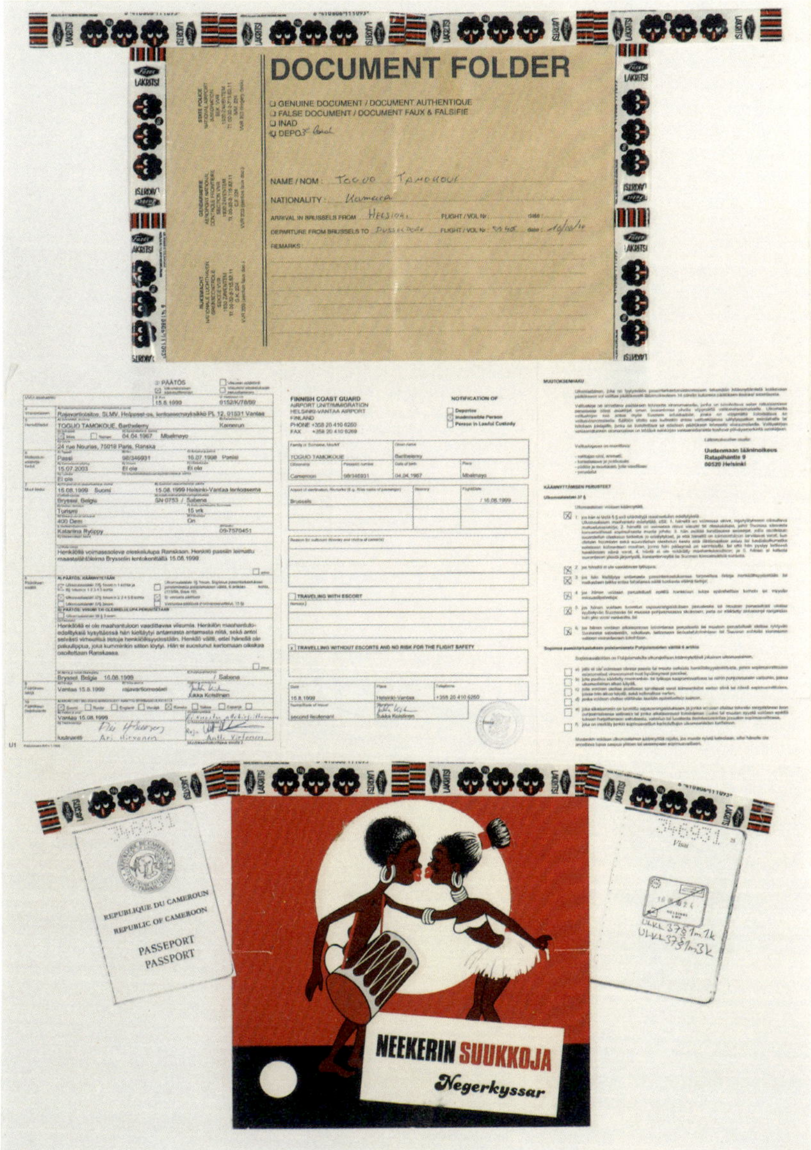

DOCUMENT FOLDER

- GENUINE DOCUMENT / DOCUMENT AUTHENTIQUE
- FALSE DOCUMENT / DOCUMENT FAUX & FALSIFIE
- INAD
- DEPOT

NAME / NOM :

NATIONALITY :

ARRIVAL IN BRUSSELS FROM … FLIGHT / VOL Nr : … date :

DEPARTURE FROM BRUSSELS TO … FLIGHT / VOL Nr : … date :

REMARKS :

FINNISH COAST GUARD

NOTIFICATION OF

REPUBLIQUE DU CAMEROUN
REPUBLIC OF CAMEROON
PASSEPORT
PASSPORT

NEEKERIN SUUKKOJA

Negerkyssar

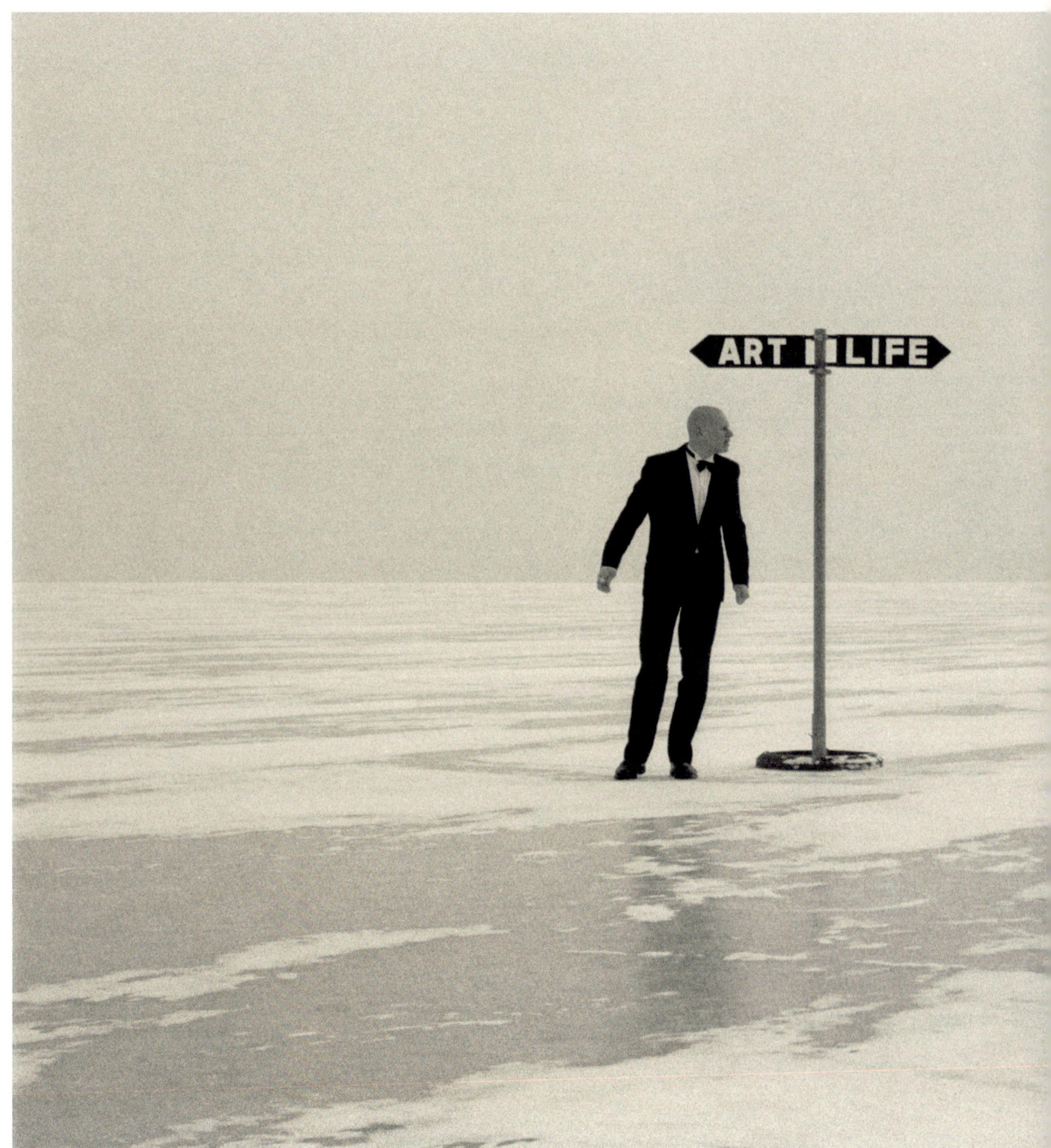

68 Roi Vaara, *Artist's Dilemma*, 1997, production still

ROI VAARA

Born in 1953, Moss, Norway
Lives and works in Helsinki, Finland

Roi Vaara is a performance artist whose works address social, political and ecological issues, and have also often challenged the traditions and conventions of museums and art galleries. In one performance, which toured to three museums, he took the place of a sculpture, packing himself into a crate used for transporting works of art, and exhibited the crate (with himself inside it) at each of the venues.

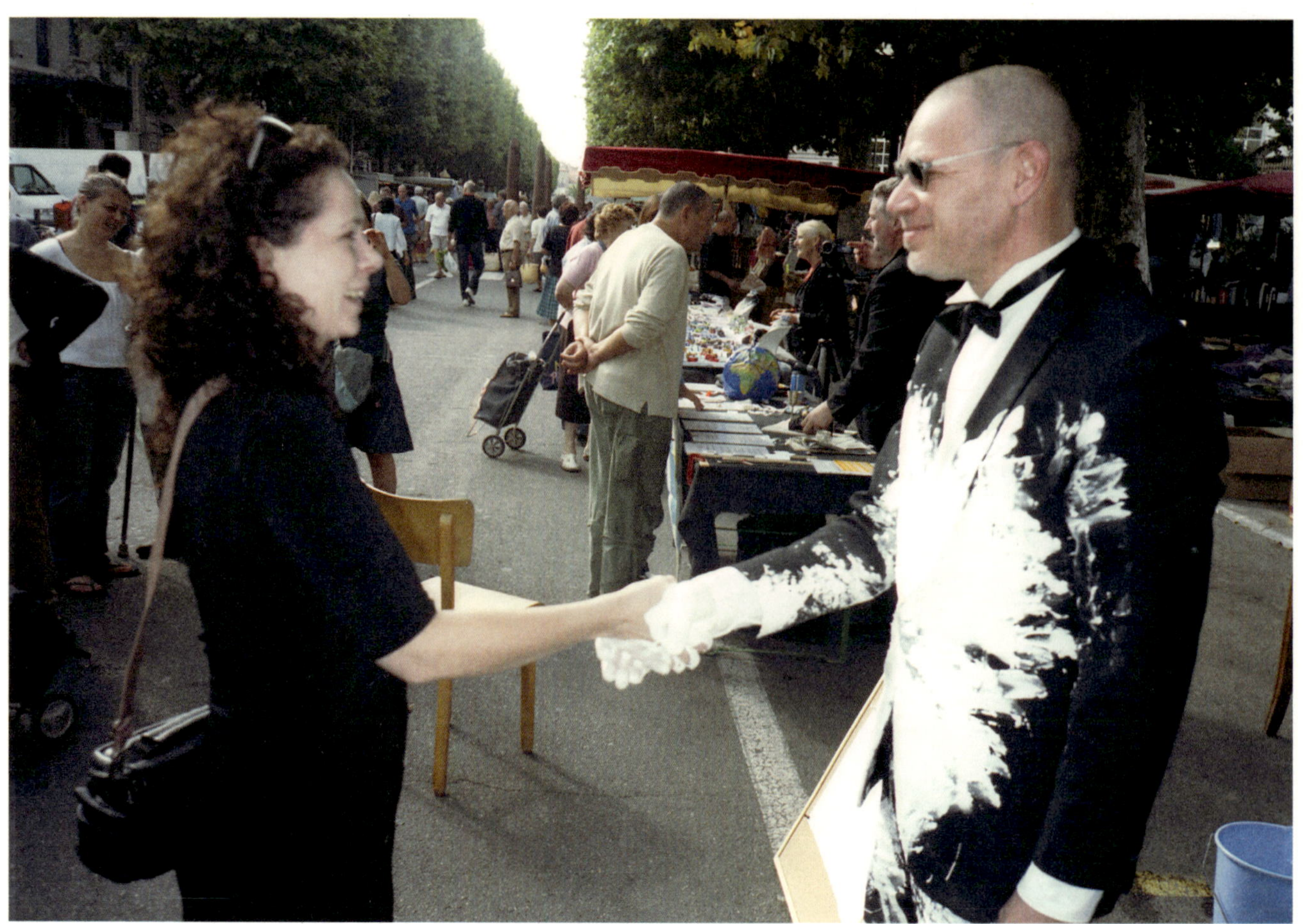

Roi Vaara, *Wet Paint Handshakes*, 2006, performance at Infr'Action, Festival International d'Art Performance, Sète, France, 2006 (see cat. 69)

Most of Vaara's performances are made for a specific place and audience, but occasionally he creates performances for the camera. This was the case with *Artist's Dilemma*, which was shot from a stationary camera in a single, unedited take. The location is the frozen sea east of Helsinki and the film was made in temperatures of minus 30° centigrade. In the middle of nowhere, wearing an elegant 'penguin' suit, the artist dithers and slithers around a signpost pointing in one direction to Art and, in the other, to Life. Which way should he go? And, should he ever decide, can he reach his destination?

For this exhibition, Vaara has made a new version of *Wet Paint Handshakes*, a work that evolved out of a performance in which his right hand was covered in gold leaf, leaving specks of gold on every hand he shook. When he offered golden handshakes to passers-by in the street, he was met with suspicion and so extended wet paint handshakes instead. 'To my astonishment,' he says, 'it became a sort of hit. This time I will experiment with that in a museum context. See what happens then.'

MARTIN WALDE

Born in 1957, Innsbruck, Austria
Lives and works in Vienna, Austria

Martin Walde creates installations that become situations in which the viewer is an active participant. 'Putting a work on display, no matter what, is a strategy,' he explains. 'I experience my work, I don't create it; it just evolves. Visitors interfere and change it even though they remain passive, i.e. don't do anything at all.'

In *The Key Spirit*, we enter the territory of an unsettling dream – and a curator's nightmare. It presents an ongoing shaggy-dog story, which began in 1977 when Walde sent instructions for an installation to a curator in Holland:

October 1997 (to Theo Taegeler, curator at W139, Amsterdam)
Dear T., you have to look for an old door that has been in use for a long time. A door that is not needed any more. When you have found a door, put it somewhere where there has never been a door. Then take the key and put it into the keyhole inside, so when one opens the door one will find the key inside. And when one locks the door, nobody can follow. That is all; that is the story.

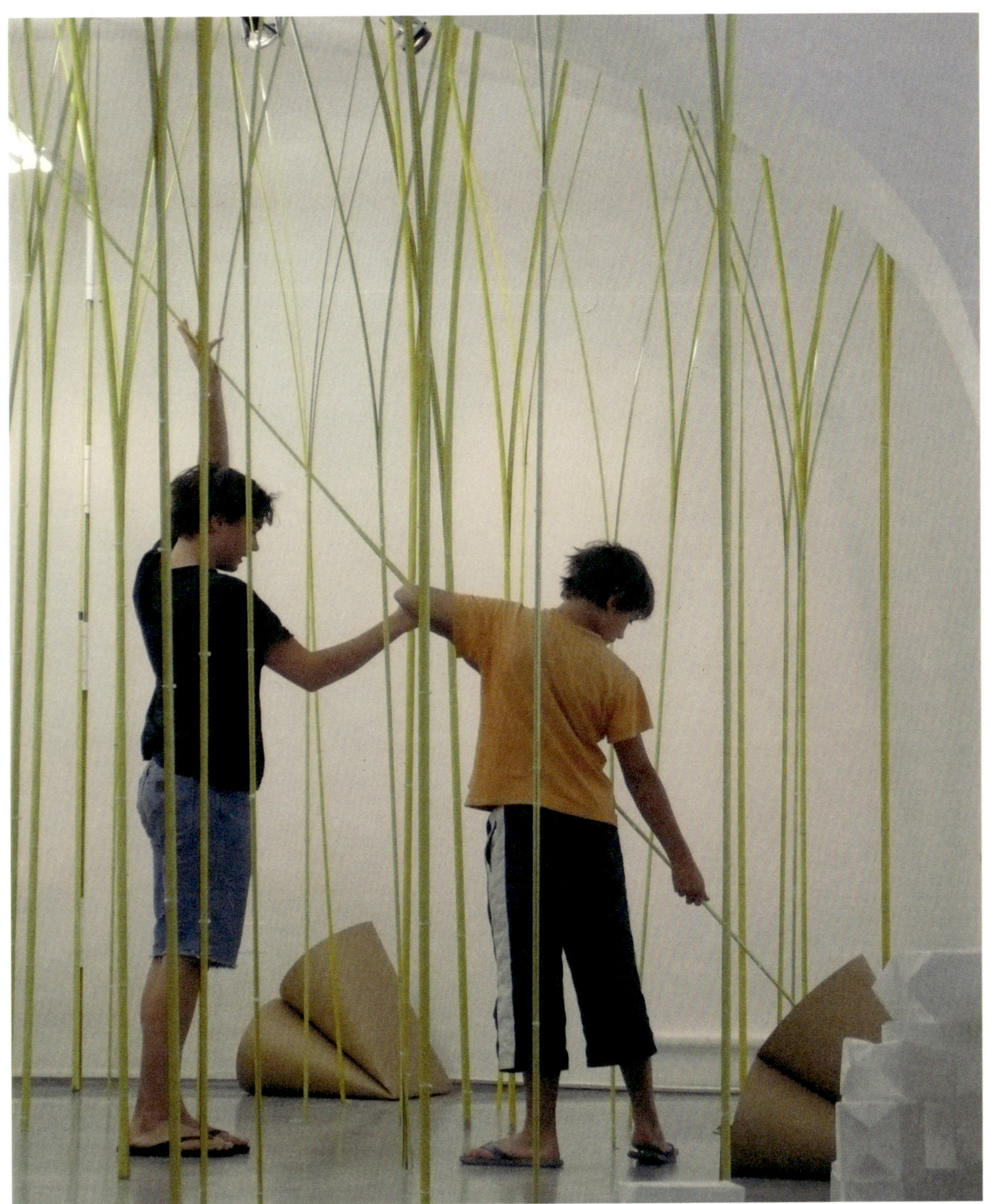

Martin Walde, *battle angel*, 1995/2007

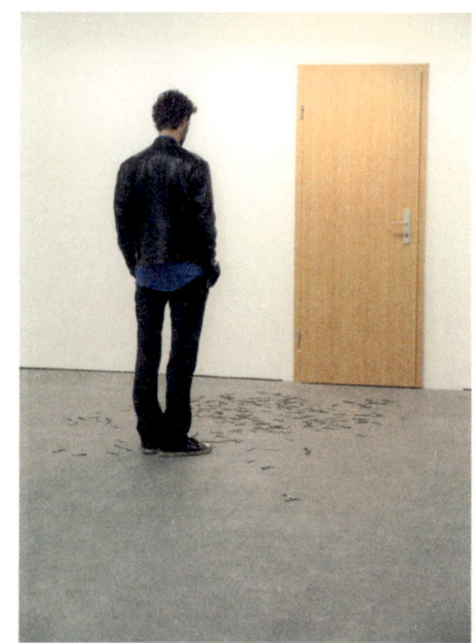

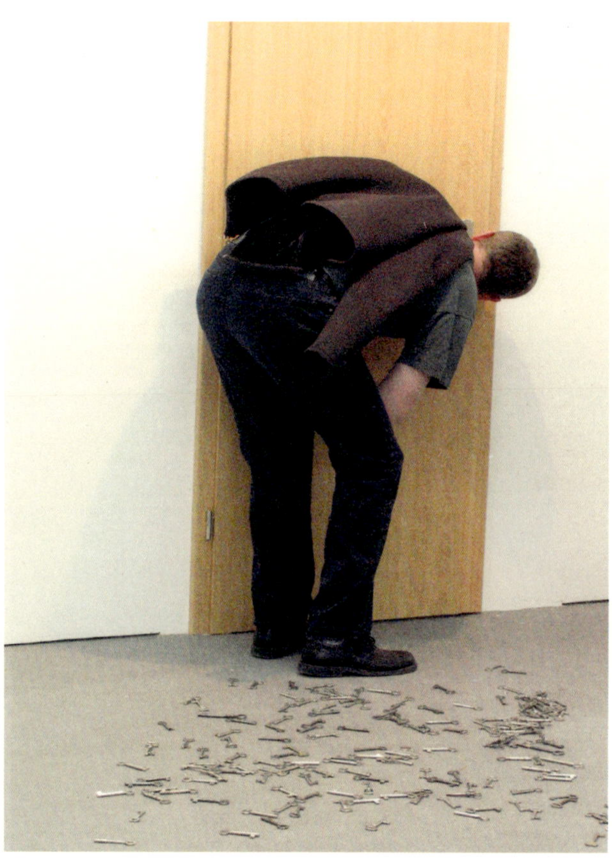

Martin Walde, *The Key Spirit*, 2006, interactive installation: *Humming*, Kunsthaus Baselland, Muttenz / Basel, Switzerland (see cat. 70)

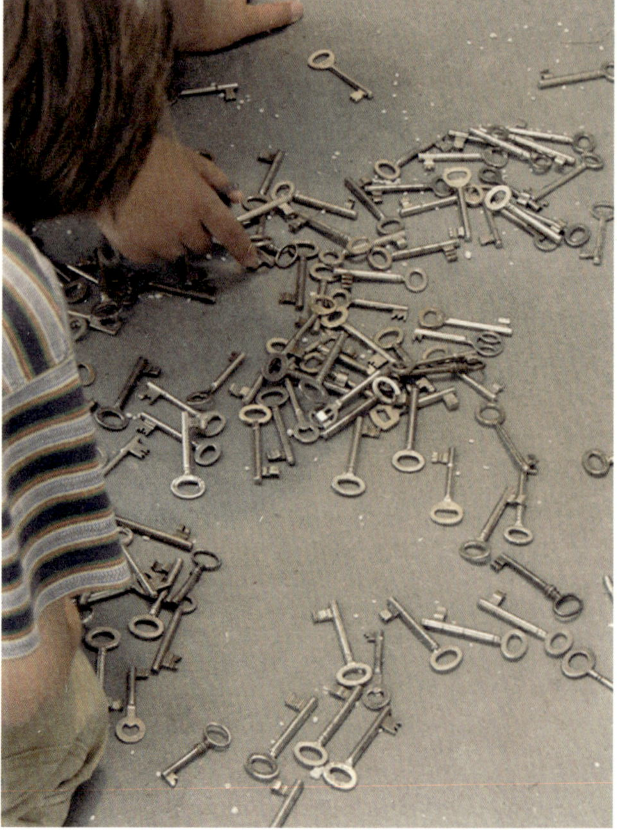

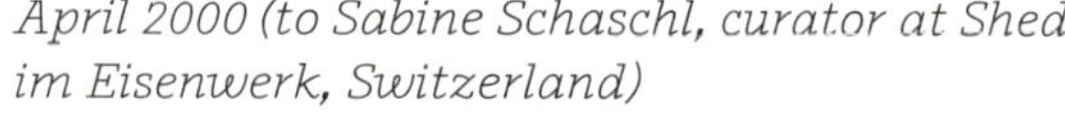

April 2000 (to Sabine Schaschl, curator at Shed im Eisenwerk, Switzerland)

Dear S., you have to look for an old door......... that is the story.

Dear M., I have found a door, it is not an old door, but it is not needed any more.

Dear S., just take that door, but behind that door there should be another door.
And behind that door.....

Dear M., I have only one door. It is a kind of office door. But behind that door there could be bright blue light and one could lock oneself up in this blue brightness.........

November 2005 (to Sabine Schaschl, curator at Kunsthaus Baselland, Switzerland)

Dear S., take a door and put it somewhere where there has never been a door before. And behind that door a cat is meowing. The door is locked. Many keys are lying on the ground in front of the door.

Dear M., I found a door, it is a new door. I put it somewhere where there has never been a door before. And behind that door, what will be behind that door?

November 2007 (to Mami Kataoka, curator at The Hayward, London)

Dear M., look for an old door and put it somewhere where has never been a door before. The door is locked. Many keys are lying on the ground in front of the door. We can hear the sound of a meowing cat from somewhere behind that door. When you find the right key to open the door, you will find another door behind that door. And behind that door a cat is meowing.......

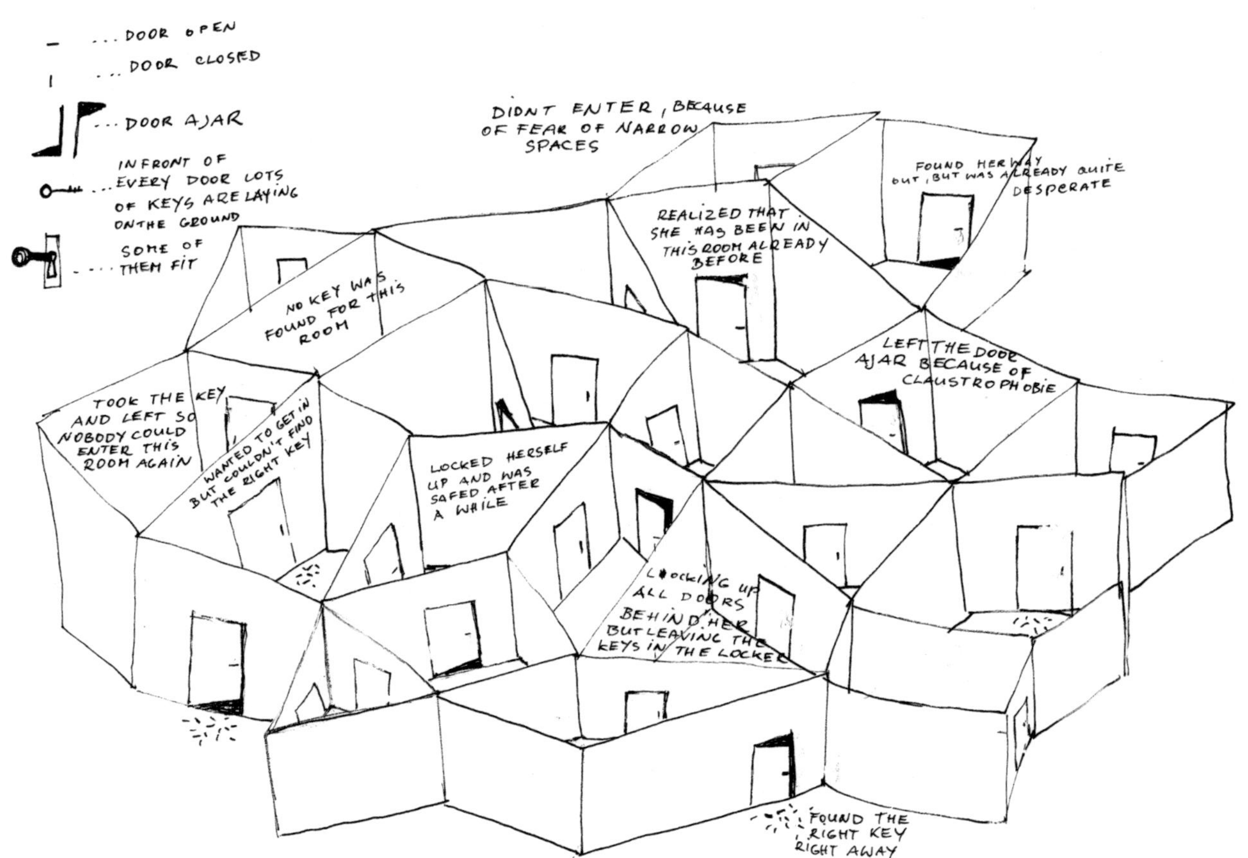

Martin Walde, *There is a door behind the door...*, 2006

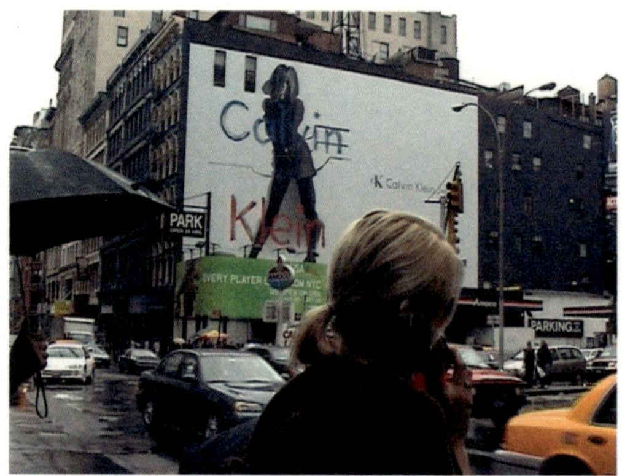

71 Jun Yang, *Camouflage – LOOK like them – TALK like them*, 2002/03, still

JUN YANG

Born in 1975, Tientsin, China
Lives and works in Vienna, Austria

Jun Yang, who was four years old when his family emigrated from China to Vienna, makes videos and installations focusing on cultural and personal identity and the effects of migration and relocation. Filmed in the wake of 9/11, *Camouflage – LOOK like them – TALK like them* reflects the conditions of everyday life in the West for migrants – legal and illegal – in a climate of paranoia. Migrant X was smuggled from China into Austria, where he is designated a person of 'suspicious appearance and behaviour'. The story of X's failed attempts to blend in with the crowd – and his eventual imprisonment as an illegal immigrant – is told against a background of newspaper headlines reporting extraordinary police measures, false alarms and wrongful arrests. As advice to others in the same predicament, Yang describes the camouflage tactics necessary in order to survive. Though the tale is not remotely funny, its *reductio ad adsurdissimum* points to the ridiculous situation where we will all have to look and behave exactly alike in order to be above suspicion.

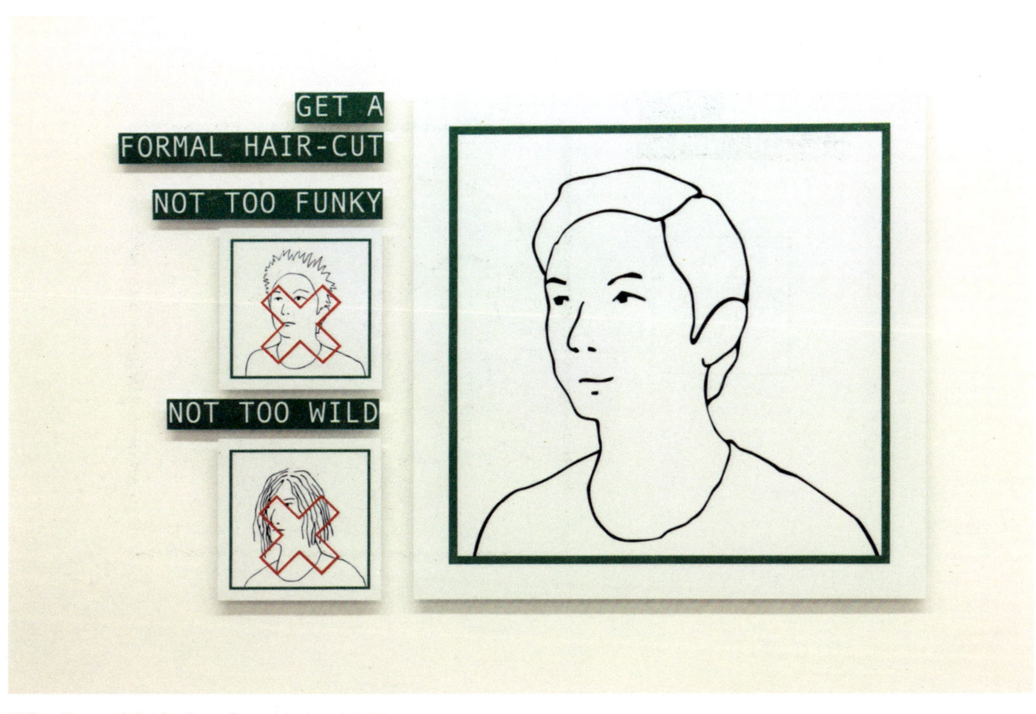

76 Jun Yang, *X-Guide: Get a formal hair-cut*, 2004

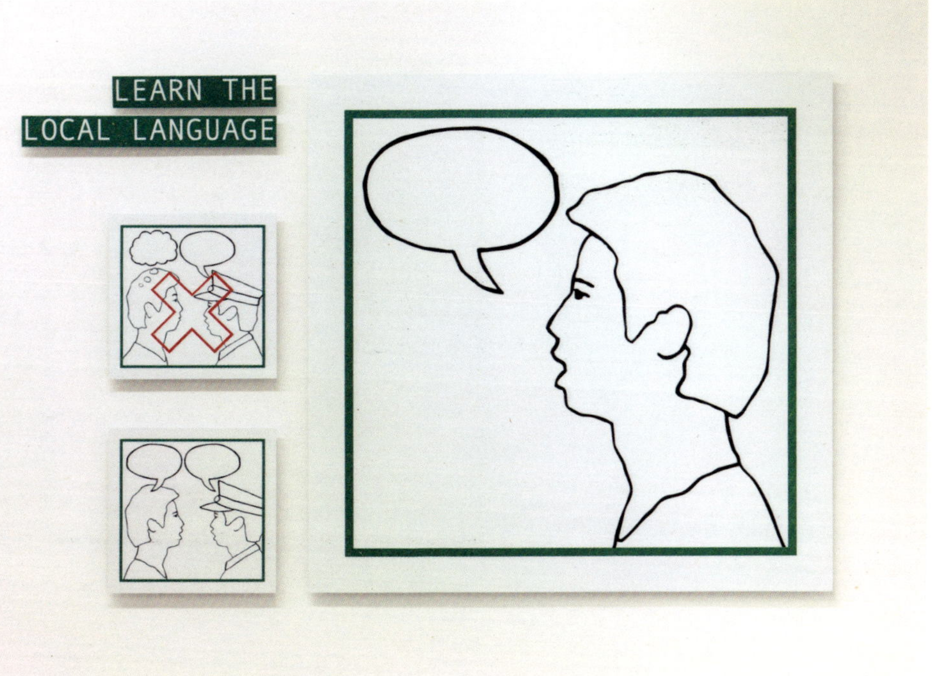

78 Jun Yang, *X-Guide: Learn the local language*, 2004

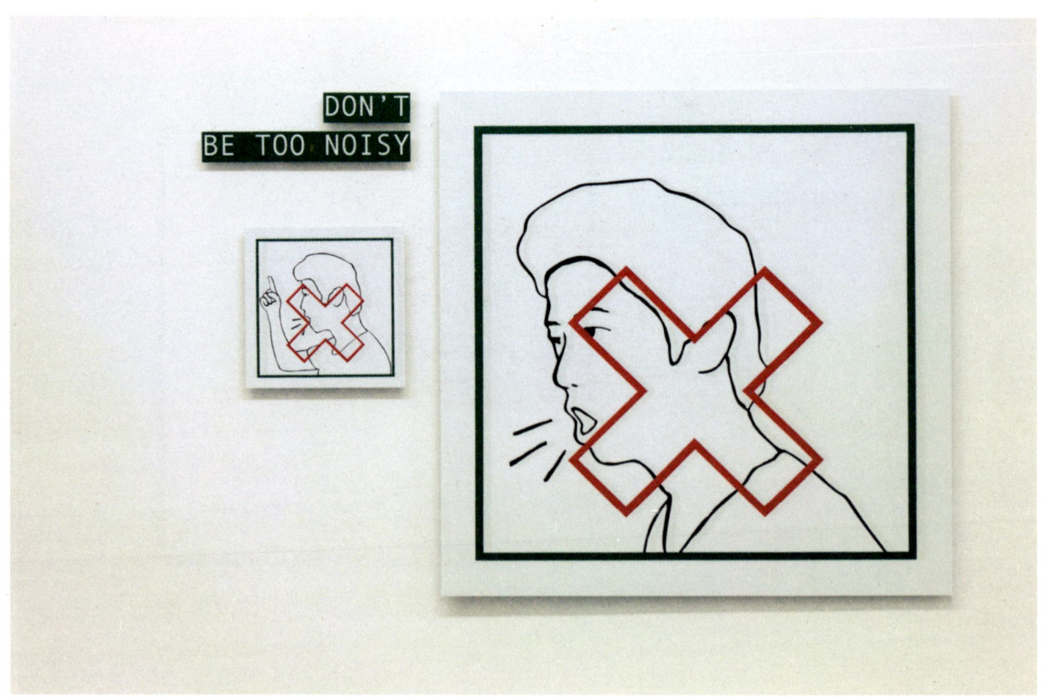

72 Jun Yang, *X-Guide: Don't be too noisy*, 2004

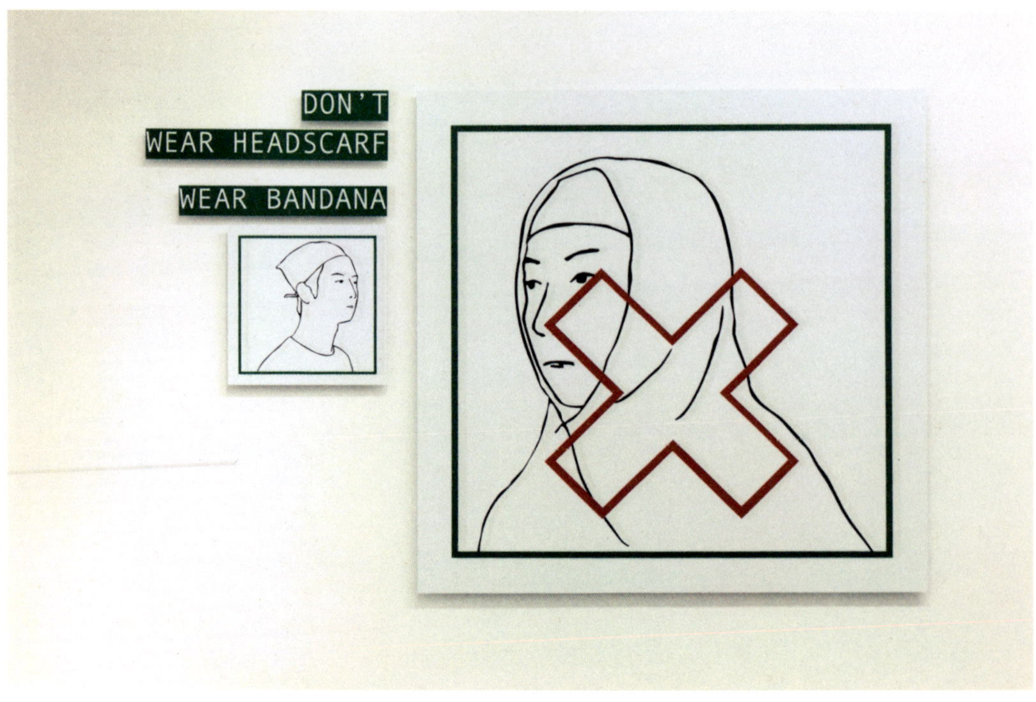

75 Jun Yang, *X-Guide: Don't wear headscarf*, 2004

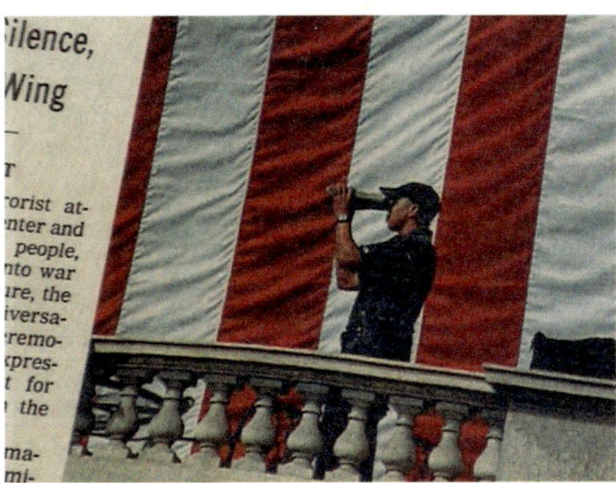

71 Jun Yang, *Camouflage – LOOK like them – TALK like them*, 2002/03, still

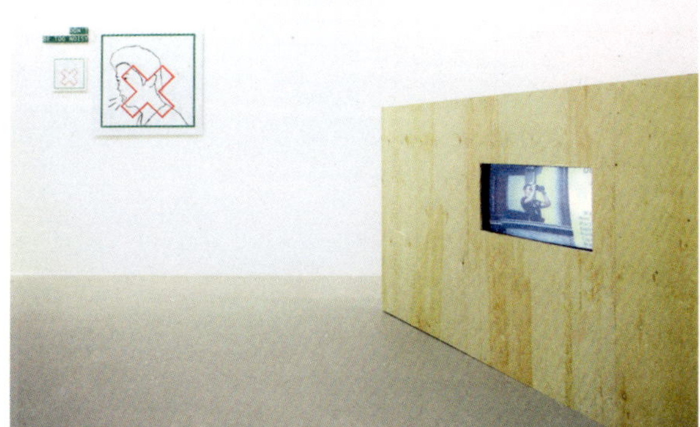

Jun Yang, *X-Guide: Don't be too noisy*, 2004, and *Camouflage – LOOK like them – TALK like them*, 2002/03, installation view: *Daheim in der Fremde-Fremd in der Heimat*, Städtische Galerie Nordhorn, Germany (see cat. 72 and 71)

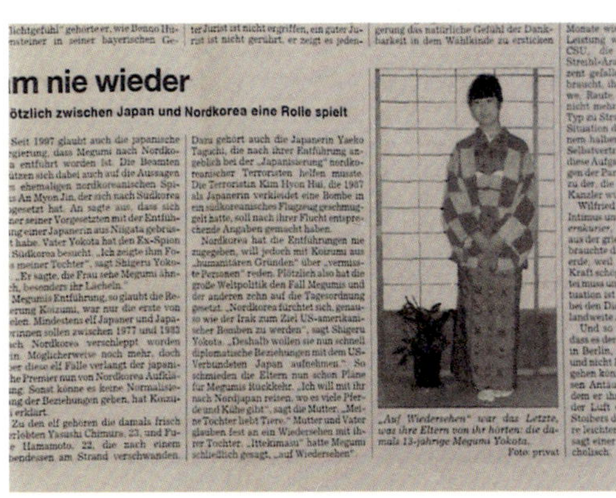

m nie wieder

ötzlich zwischen Japan und Nordkorea eine Rolle spielt

Dazu gehört auch die Japanerin Yaeko Taguchi, die nach ihrer Entführung angeblich bei der „Japanisierung" nordkoreanischer Terroristen helfen musste. Die Terroristin Kim Hyon Hui, die 1987 als Japanerin verkleidet eine Bombe in ein südkoreanisches Flugzeug geschmuggelt hatte, soll nach ihrer Flucht entsprechende Angaben gemacht haben.

Nordkorea hat die Entführungen nie zugegeben, will jedoch mit Koizumi aus „humanitären Gründen" über „vermisste Personen" reden. Plötzlich also hat die große Weltpolitik den Fall Megumis und der anderen zehn auf die Tagesordnung gesetzt. „Nordkorea fürchtet sich, genauso wie der Irak zum Ziel US-amerikanischer Bomben zu werden", sagt Shigeru Yokota. „Deshalb wollen sie nun schnell diplomatische Beziehungen mit dem US-Verbündeten Japan aufnehmen." So schmieden die Eltern nun schon Pläne für Megumis Rückkehr. „Ich will mit ihr nach Nordjapan reisen, wo es viele Pferde und Kühe gibt", sagt die Mutter. „Meine Tochter liebt Tiere." Mutter und Vater glauben fest an ein Wiedersehen mit ihrer Tochter. „Ittekimasu" hatte Megumi schließlich gesagt, „auf Wiedersehen".

„Auf Wiedersehen" war das Letzte, was ihre Eltern von ihr hörten: die damals 13-jährige Megumi Yokota.

Foto: privat

71 Jun Yang, *Camouflage – LOOK like them – TALK like them*, 2002/03, still

The *X-Guide* pictograms reinforce the messages of the *Camouflage* video in simple visual language, illustrating appropriate codes of Western behaviour for foreigners. But at the same time there are deeper ironies at play: while designed to enable us to communicate regardless of nationality, race and age, pictograms used as public information symbols are highly culture-specific and can often be misunderstood. Here, in order to make everything absolutely clear, the pictograms are accompanied by captions in English, though English-speakers presumably should not need these pictographic instructions.

LIST OF WORKS

All measurements are in centimetres, height x width x depth. Page references are to illustrations in this book. This list was accurate at the time of publication. There may have been subsequent changes to works in the exhibition.

1 (pp. 28–29)
Makoto Aida
Your Pronunciation is Wrong!, 2000
C-print
29.7 x 45
Mizuma Art Gallery
© the artist and Mizuma Art Gallery, 2008

2 (pp. 26–27)
Makoto Aida
The Video of a Man Calling Himself Bin Laden Staying in Japan, 2005
Video, 8:14 mins
Mizuma Art Gallery
© the artist and Mizuma Art Gallery, 2008

3 (pp. 30–33)
Kutlug Ataman
Turkish Delight, 2006
Single-channel video projection on DVD
Projection approximately 277 cm high, looped
Thyssen-Bornemisza Art Contemporary, Vienna. Courtesy of the artist and Lehmann Maupin Gallery, New York

4 (p. 34)
Azorro
We Like It A Lot, 2001
Video, 7:30 mins
Courtesy Raster Gallery

5 (p. 35)
Azorro
Portrait with a Curator, 2002
Video, 7:37 mins
Courtesy Raster Gallery

6 (pp. 36–39)
Guy Ben-Ner
Wild Boy, 2004
Video, 17 mins
Courtesy the artist

7 (pp. 40–42)
John Bock
Palms, 2007
Video, 59:14 mins
Courtesy Klosterfelde, Berlin; Anton Kern, New York
© 2007 John Bock. All rights reserved
Photo: Jan Windszus

8 (pp. 45–47)
Candice Breitz
Aiwa To Zen, 2003
A short film on DVD, 11:30 mins
Courtesy Jay Jopling / White Cube, London
Catalogue illustrations: (pp. 44, 46)
The Making of *Aiwa To Zen*, 2003.
Photo by Alex Fahl

9 (p. 50)
Olaf Breuning
20 dollar bill, 2007
Digital print mounted on aluminium, edition 6/6
122 x 155
Courtesy the artist & Galerie Nicola von Senger, Zurich & Metro Pictures NY

10 (p. 48)
Olaf Breuning
collage family, 2007
Digital print mounted on aluminium, edition 6/6
122 x 155
Courtesy the artist & Galerie Nicola von Senger, Zurich & Metro Pictures NY

11 (pp. 49, 51)
Olaf Breuning
Home2, 2007
DVD starring Brian Kerstetter, 30 mins
Courtesy the artist & Galerie Nicola von Senger, Zurich & Metro Pictures NY

12
Olaf Breuning
Untitled, 2008
New site-specific installation
Courtesy the artist & Galerie Nicola von Senger, Zurich & Metro Pictures NY

13 (pp. 52, 54–55)
Cao Fei
Hip Hop: Guangzhou, 2003
Video, 3 mins
Courtesy Vitamin Creative Space

14 (p. 56)
Jake and Dinos Chapman
Dinos and Jake's Progress Plate 1, 2007
Reworked and improved etching from William Hogarth's *Rake's Progress*
66.5 x 71
Pierpaolo and Valeria Barzan
© the artists. Courtesy Jay Jopling / White Cube, London
Photo: Todd-White Art Photography

15 (p. 57)
Jake and Dinos Chapman
Dinos and Jake's Progress Plate 2, 2007
Reworked and improved etching from William Hogarth's *Rake's Progress*
66.5 x 71
Courtesy the artists and Jay Jopling / White Cube, London
© the artists. Courtesy Jay Jopling / White Cube, London
Photo: Todd-White Art Photography

16 (p. 58)
Jake and Dinos Chapman
Dinos and Jake's Progress Plate 3, 2007
Reworked and improved etching from William Hogarth's *Rake's Progress*
66.5 x 71
Collection Pontus Bonnier
© the artists. Courtesy Jay Jopling / White Cube, London
Photo: Todd-White Art Photography

17 (p. 58)
Jake and Dinos Chapman
Dinos and Jake's Progress Plate 4, 2007
Reworked and improved etching from William Hogarth's *Rake's Progress*
66.5 x 71
Private collection
© the artists. Courtesy Jay Jopling / White Cube, London
Photo: Todd-White Art Photography

18 (p. 58)
Jake and Dinos Chapman
Dinos and Jake's Progress Plate 5, 2007
Reworked and improved etching from William Hogarth's *Rake's Progress*
66.5 x 71
Nicolo Cardi Collection
© the artists. Courtesy Jay Jopling / White Cube, London
Photo: Todd-White Art Photography

19 (p. 59)
Jake and Dinos Chapman
Dinos and Jake's Progress Plate 6, 2007
Reworked and improved etching from William Hogarth's *Rake's Progress*
66.5 x 71
From the collection of Fusun and Faruk Eczacibasi
© the artists. Courtesy Jay Jopling / White Cube, London
Photo: Todd-White Art Photography

20 (p. 59)
Jake and Dinos Chapman
Dinos and Jake's Progress Plate 7, 2007
Reworked and improved etching from William Hogarth's *Rake's Progress*
66.5 x 71
Courtesy the artists and Jay Jopling / White Cube, London
© the artists. Courtesy Jay Jopling / White Cube, London
Photo: Todd-White Art Photography

21 (p. 59)
Jake and Dinos Chapman
Dinos and Jake's Progress Plate 8, 2007
Reworked and improved etching from William Hogarth's *Rake's Progress*
66.5 x 71
Nicolo Cardi Collection
© the artists. Courtesy Jay Jopling / White Cube, London
Photo: Todd-White Art Photography

22 (pp. 60–62)
Marcus Coates
Journey to the Lower World, 2004
Two-screen video projection, 30 mins
Courtesy the artist
Catalogue illustrations: Production stills by Nick David

23 (pp. 64–67)
Harry Dodge and Stanya Kahn
Can't Swallow it, Can't Spit it Out, 2006
Mini DVD transferred to DVD, 26:05 mins
Courtesy the artists and Elizabeth Dee, New York
© Harry Dodge and Stanya Kahn 2006

24 (pp. 70–71)
Doug Fishbone
Everybody Loves a Winner, 2004
Video, edition of 8, 8:30 mins
Courtesy the artist
© the artist 2004

25 (p. 69)
Doug Fishbone
Towards a Common Understanding, 2005
Video, edition of 8, 12:30 mins
Courtesy the artist
© the artist 2005

26
Doug Fishbone
Joke Master Jr 2, 2007
Mixed media. Device with pre-recorded jokes
13 x 8 x 2.5
Courtesy the artist, with special thanks to Alexei Blinov and Jackie Martling
Catalogue illustration: (p. 68) *Joke Master Jr*, 2006. © the artist 2006

27 (p. 75)
Ghazel
Peace & Love, 2001
Me series
Digital print
75 x 51.2
Courtesy the artist
© ghazel 2001

28 (p. 75)
Ghazel
Valentine's Day, 2001
Me series
Digital print
75 x 51.2
Courtesy the artist
© ghazel 2001

29 (p. 74)
Ghazel
Keep the Balance, 2004
Me series
Digital print
75 x 51.2
Courtesy the artist
© ghazel 2004

30 (p. 74)
Ghazel
Olé, 2004
Me series
Digital print
75 x 51.2
Courtesy the artist
© ghazel 2004

31 (p. 73)
Ghazel
Wanted, 2007
2 digital posters
162 x 114.5 each
Courtesy the artist
Catalogue illustration: (p. 72) *Wanted*, 2006, installation view, detail, 2 posters reproduced for JC Decaux Citylights in the central business district of Sydney during the Biennale of Sydney, 2006.
© ghazel 2006. Photo by Greg Weight

32 (p. 76)
Gimhongsok
The Bremen Town Musicians, 2006–07
Foam rubber, fabric
183 x 300 x 200
Courtesy the artist
© the artist 2006

33 (p. 81)
Matthew Griffin
Spare Girlfriend, 2004
C-print
60 x 49.5
Courtesy the artist and Uplands Gallery, Melbourne
© the artist 2008, courtesy Uplands Gallery, Melbourne

34 (p. 83)
Matthew Griffin
Free Burzum, 2005
C-print
101.5 x 76.3
Courtesy the artist and Uplands Gallery, Melbourne
© the artist 2008, courtesy Uplands Gallery Melbourne

35 (p. 83)
Matthew Griffin
Infinity Hombre, 2005
C-print
101.5 x 76.3
Courtesy the artist and Uplands Gallery Melbourne
© the artist 2008, courtesy Uplands Gallery Melbourne

36
Matthew Griffin
Infinity Hombre (Dude), 2005
C-print
101.5 x 76.3
Courtesy the artist and Uplands Gallery, Melbourne

37 (p. 83)
Matthew Griffin
I've Peaked, 2005
C-print
62 x 50
Courtesy the artist and Uplands Gallery, Melbourne
© the artist 2008, courtesy Uplands Gallery Melbourne

38 (p. 82)
Matthew Griffin
I'm Waiting, 2007
C-print
75 x 50
Courtesy the artist and Uplands Gallery, Melbourne
© the artist 2008, courtesy Uplands Gallery Melbourne

39 (p. 80)
Matthew Griffin
Knowing Me Knowing You, 2007
C-print
45 x 62
Courtesy the artist and Uplands Gallery, Melbourne
© the artist 2008, courtesy Uplands Gallery Melbourne

40
Matthew Griffin
Not Quite Right Hand, 2007
C-print
75 x 50
Courtesy the artist and Uplands Gallery Melbourne

41
Matthew Griffin
Too Much Libido, Not Enough Future, 2007
C-print
75 x 50
Courtesy the artist and Uplands Gallery, Melbourne

42
Matthew Griffin
Untitled, 2008
New site-specific wall drawing
Courtesy the artist and Uplands Gallery, Melbourne

43
Nina Jan Beier and Marie Jan Lund
The Play me series (Clap in Time), 2006
Video, 5 mins
Courtesy the artists

44
Nina Jan Beier and Marie Jan Lund
The Play me series (Hide Behind the Trees), 2006
Video, 5:20 mins
Courtesy the artists

45
Nina Jan Beier and Marie Jan Lund
The Play me series (Jump in Time), 2006
Video, 30 secs
Courtesy the artists

46
Nina Jan Beier and Marie Jan Lund
The Play me series (Stay Underneath the Surface), 2007
Video, 16 secs
Courtesy the artists

47 (p. 87)
Nina Jan Beier and Marie Jan Lund
Les Sabots, 2007
16mm film transferred to HD, 5 mins
Courtesy the artists

48
Nina Jan Beier and Marie Jan Lund
One on One (The Curtain), 2007
Used curtains, thread, metal
300 x 200
Courtesy the artists

49 (p. 85)
Nina Jan Beier and Marie Jan Lund
One on One (The Maraca), 2007
Used maracas, glue, varnish
36 x 8 x 8
Courtesy the artists
Photo: Nina Jan Beier and Marie Jan Lund

50
Nina Jan Beier and Marie Jan Lund
The Dedication (For Elizabeth Bishop – For Robert Lowell), 2007
Second-hand books (Elizabeth Bishop, *The Complete Poems*, containing the poem 'The Armadillo' dedicated to Robert Lowell; and Robert Lowell, *Life Studies*, containing the poem 'Skunk Hour' dedicated to Elizabeth Bishop), glue
22 x 24 x 20
Courtesy the artists

51 (p. 90)
Taiyo Kimura
Black Hole, 1995–2005
Radios, earphones, teddy bear
35 x 40 x 35
Courtesy Taiyo Kimura
Photo: Takashi Watanabe

52 (p. 90)
Taiyo Kimura
Untitled (performance photo 1996), 1996–2007
C-print
45 x 55 approximately
Courtesy Taiyo Kimura

53 (pp. 88–89)
Taiyo Kimura
Typical Japanese-English, 2005
Performance video, 5 mins, laundry, clothes basket, screen, DVD
29 x 56 x 40
Courtesy Taiyo Kimura
Catalogue illustration: installation view, photo by Mie Morimoto

54 (p. 91)
Taiyo Kimura
Untitle me (stool for guard), 2007
Mixed media, clothes, CD player, speaker
50 x 40 x 49
Courtesy Taiyo Kimura

55 (p. 94)
Peter Land
Hi I'm new around here, so please don't rob me, mug me or kill me. Could you please direct me to a cheap hotel? (New York), 1996
C-print, edition of 5
152 x 100
Galleri Nicolai Wallner

56 (p. 93)
Peter Land
Hello – I don't speak your language very well, so please when you talk to me speak slowly and clearly and please don't use any slang, Thank You. (Chicago), 1998
C-print, edition of 5
152 x 100
Galleri Nicolai Wallner

57 (pp. 96–99)
Janne Lehtinen
Sacred Bird, 1998–2004
8 Lambda prints
101 x 137
Courtesy the artist

58 (pp. 101, 103)
Kalup Linzy
Conversations wit de Churen III: Da Young and Da Mess, 2005
DVD, colour, sound, 17:30 mins
Courtesy the artist and Taxter & Spengemann, New York

59 (pp. 100, 102)
Kalup Linzy
Conversations wit de Churen IV: Play wit de Churen, 2005
DVD, colour, sound, 15:49 mins
Courtesy the artist and Taxter & Spengemann, New York

60 (pp. 101–102)
Kalup Linzy
Conversations wit de Churen V: As da Art World Might Turn, 2006
DVD, colour, sound, 11:16 mins
Courtesy the artist and Taxter & Spengemann, New York

61 (p. 104)
Yoshua Okon
Staphylococcus, 2004
Lightjet prints and metal structures
420 x 450
Courtesy the artist and The Project, New York
© the artist 2004

62 (p. 108)
Ugo Rondinone
ZERO, 2006
Artificially-aged leather, artificial nail
100 x 60 x 25
Collection of Amalia Dayan and Adam Lindemann
© the artist 2006, courtesy Sadie Coles HQ, London

63 (pp. 113–115)
Julian Rosefeldt
Clown, 2005
3-screen film installation, Super16mm transferred onto DVD, Loop 11 mins
The artist, courtesy Arndt & Partner Berlin / Zurich and Max Wigram
Catalogue illustrations: (pp. 113–114) production stills © the artist 2005, courtesy Arndt & Partner Berlin / Zurich and Max Wigram Gallery London; (p. 115) installation view at Chapter Gallery, Cardiff © the artist 2005, courtesy Arndt & Partner Berlin / Zurich and Max Wigram Gallery London. Photo: Mark Arkless

64
Shimabuku
Born as a Box (New Version), 2001–08
Cardboard box, CD player, speaker, CD
60 x 40 x 60 approximately
Collection of the artist

65
David Shrigley
Site-specific installation with drawings, 2008
Inkjet prints
Courtesy the artist

66
Nedko Solakov
Doodles (Hayward), 2008
Felt-tip pen on wall and various supports
Dimensions variable
Courtesy the artist

67 (pp. 128–131)
Barthélémy Toguo
Transit series, 1996–99
8 photographs
100 x 75 each
Bandjoun Station, Cameroon
Courtesy Galerie Anne de Villepoix, Paris & Barthélémy Toguo, Bandjoun Station, Cameroon

68 (pp. 132–133)
Roi Vaara
Artist's Dilemma, 1997
Performance for video, Finland, 1997, 2:23 mins
Courtesy the artist
Photo: © Naranja 2008

69
Roi Vaara
Wet Paint Handshakes, 2008
Performance, tuxedo, video
Courtesy the artist
Catalogue illustration: (p. 134) *Wet Paint Handshakes*, 2006, performance at Infr'Action, Festival International d'Art Performance, Sête, France, 2006. Photo by Willem Wilhelmus

70 (p. 138)
Martin Walde
The Key Spirit, 1997–2008
2 doors, keys, sound recording of cat meowing
Dimensions variable
Courtesy the artist
Catalogue illustrations: *The Key Spirit*, 2006, interactive installation, *Humming*, Kunsthaus Baselland, Muttenz / Basel, Switzerland. Photos by Julia Schulz and Viktor Kolibàl

71 (pp. 140, 143)
Jun Yang
Camouflage – LOOK like them – TALK like them, 2002/03
Video, 16:33 mins
Courtesy Galerie Martin Jande, Vienna
© the artist, 2008. Courtesy Galerie Martin Janda, Vienna
Catologue illustration: (p. 143) installation view, *Daheim in der Fremde-Fremd in der Heimat*, Städtische Galerie Nordhorn, Germany. Photo: Helmut Claus / © Städtische Galerie Nordhorn

72 (p. 142)
Jun Yang
X-Guide: Don't be too noisy, 2004
Aluminium panel, vinyl letters
116 x 160 approximately
Courtesy Galerie Martin Janda, Vienna
© the artist, 2008. Courtesy Galerie Martin Janda, Vienna
Catologue illustration: (p. 143) installation view, *Daheim in der Fremde-Fremd in der Heimat*, Städtische Galerie Nordhorn, Germany. Photo: Helmut Claus / © Städtische Galerie Nordhorn

73
Jun Yang
X-Guide: Don't blow the nose, 2004
Aluminium panel, vinyl letters
116 x 160 approximately
Courtesy Galerie Martin Janda, Vienna

74
Jun Yang
X-Guide: Don't spit on the ground, 2004
Aluminium panel, vinyl letters
116 x 160 approximately
Courtesy Galerie Martin Janda, Vienna

75 (p. 142)
Jun Yang
X-Guide: Don't wear headscarf, 2004
Aluminium panel, vinyl letters
116 x 160 approximately
Courtesy Galerie Martin Janda, Vienna
© the artist, 2008. Courtesy Galerie Martin Janda, Vienna

76 (p. 141)
Jun Yang
X-Guide: Get a formal hair-cut, 2004
Aluminium panel, vinyl letters
116 x 160 approximately
Courtesy Galerie Martin Janda, Vienna
© the artist, 2008. Courtesy Galerie Martin Janda, Vienna

77
Jun Yang
X-Guide: Get a shave, 2004
Aluminium panel, vinyl letters
116 x 160 approximately
Courtesy Galerie Martin Janda, Vienna

78 (p. 141)
Jun Yang
X-Guide: Learn the local language, 2004
Aluminium panel, vinyl letters
116 x 160 approximately
Courtesy Galerie Martin Janda, Vienna
© the artist, 2008. Courtesy Galerie Martin Janda, Vienna

LIST OF COMPARATIVE ILLUSTRATIONS

p. 43
John Bock
Dandy, 2006 (stills)
Video, 58:55 mins
Courtesy Klosterfelde, Berlin; Anton Kern, New York
© 2006 John Bock. All rights reserved
Photo: Jan Windszus
Co-produced by Foundation EDF and Printemps de Septembre

p. 53
Cao Fei
Hip Hop: Fukuoka, 2005 (still)
Video, 8 mins
Courtesy Vitamin Creative Space

p. 53
Cao Fei
Hip Hop: New York, 2006 (still)
Video, 6 mins
Courtesy Vitamin Creative Space

p. 59
William Hogarth
A Rake's Progress, plate 8, 1735, 'improved' in 1763
Etching and engraving
Photo: © Tate, London, 2008

p. 63
Marcus Coates
Radio Shaman, 2006 (stills)
High definition video
Courtesy the artist

p. 77
Gimhongsok
The Bremen Town Musicians – Donkey, 2006 (installation view: 6th Gwangju Biennale, 2006)
Foam rubber, fabric, text
227 x 78 x 67 cm
Courtesy the artist
© the artist 2006

pp. 78–79
Gimhongsok
This is Coyote, 2006 (installation view)
Foam rubber, resin, fabric, plywood
145 x 69 x 140 cm
Walker Art Center, Minneapolis
© the artist 2006

p. 84
Nina Jan Beier and Marie Jan Lund
The Play me series (Hang on for as long as you all can), 2006
Lambda print
76.2 x 76.2 cm
Courtesy the artist

p. 86
Nina Jan Beier and Marie Jan Lund
The Play me series (Look in the window until someone looks back at you), 2006
Lambda print
50.8 x 50.8 cm
Courtesy the artist

pp. 106–107
Yoshua Okon
Office Ceiling Tile, 2002 (installation view and detail: Daimler Chrysler, Mexico City, 2002)
Duratrans, drop ceiling
Courtesy the artist

p. 109
Ugo Rondinone
if there were anywhere but desert. 0, 2001 (installation view at Galerie Almine Rech, Paris, 2001)
Fibreglass, paint, clothing, glitter
Courtesy Galerie Eva Presenhuber, Zurich
© Ugo Rondinone, courtesy Galerie Eva Presenhuber, Zurich; Galerie Almine Rech, Paris; Private Collection Paris

pp. 110–111
Ugo Rondinone
I don't live here anymore, 1997
3 of 5 parts, C-prints mounted on perspex
50 x 100 cm
Courtesy Galerie Eva Presenhuber, Zurich
© Ugo Rondinone, courtesy the artist; Galerie Eva Presenhuber, Zurich; Sadie Coles HQ, London

p. 116
Shimabuku
Born as a Box (Chinese Version), 2007
Cardboard box, CD player, speaker, CD, 4:30 mins
Courtesy the artist

p. 117
Shimabuku
Born as a Box (Japanese Version A), 2001/04
Cardboard box, CD player, speaker, CD, 2:20 mins
© the artist & Wilkinson Gallery 2008

pp. 118–119
Shimabuku
Sunrise at Mt. Artsonje, 2007 (stills)
Super 8 transferred to DVD, 3:30 mins
Courtesy the artist
© the artist 2007, collaboration with SAMUSO, Seoul

p. 120
David Shrigley
Untitled (Stick figures having sex on car hood), 2007 (installation view)
Metal figures and car hood
31 x 157 x 115 cm
Courtesy Stephen Friedman Gallery
Photo: Helene Toresdotter

p. 121
David Shrigley
God Is Idle, 2007 (installation view)
Wall painting
Dimensions variable
Courtesy Stephen Friedman Gallery
Photo: Helene Toresdotter

p. 121
David Shrigley
Cheers, 2007 (installation view)
Waders with foam
142 x 55 x 40 cm
Courtesy Stephen Friedman Gallery
Photo: Helene Toresdotter

p. 122
David Shrigley
Selected drawings, 2004–07 (installation view)
Inkjet prints on paper
Dimensions variable
Courtesy Stephen Friedman Gallery
Photo: Helene Toresdotter

p. 122
David Shrigley
Poster Project, 2006 (installation view)
Injet prints on paper
Dimensions variable
Courtesy Stephen Friedman Gallery
Photo: Helene Toresdotter

p. 123
David Shrigley
Rock Band, 2007 (installation view)
Wire mesh, papiermaché,
wool and paint
90 x 62 x 62 (each head); 190 x 65 x 65
cm (each head with hair)
Courtesy Stephen Friedman Gallery
Photo: Helene Toresdotter

p. 124
Nedko Solakov
A Middle Age Story, 2006
Acrylic and black drawing ink
on gilt carved lime wood
61 x 60 x 8 cm
Courtesy of the artist / Arndt & Partner
Berlin/Zurich
© the artist 2008, courtesy of Collection
of Barbara and Aaron Levine, USA
Photo: Bernd Borchardt

p. 125
Nedko Solakov
Wallpaper, 1993, from *A 12 1/3*
(and even more) Year Survey
retrospective exhibition, O.K
Centrum für Gegenwartskunst,
Linz, Austria, 2004
Mixed media on local industrial
wallpaper, dimensions variable
Courtesy of the artist and Casino
Luxembourg – Forum d'art
contemporain, Luxembourg; Rooseum
Center for Contemporary Art, Malmö;
O.K Centrum für Gegenwartskunst, Linz
Photo: Nedko Solakov

p. 126
Nedko Solakov
Wallpaper, 1993, from *A 12 1/3*
(and even more) Year Survey
retrospective exhibition, Rooseum
Center for Contemporary Art,
Malmö, Sweden, 2004
Mixed media on local industrial
wallpaper, dimensions variable
Courtesy of the artist and Casino
Luxembourg – Forum d'art
contemporain, Luxembourg; Rooseum
Center for Contemporary Art, Malmö;
O.K Centrum für Gegenwartskunst, Linz
Photo: Nedko Solakov

p. 126
Nedko Solakov
The Real Estate Broker, 2007
Acrylic and black drawing ink on gilt
carved lime wood
40 x 50 x 4 cm
Courtesy of the artist / Arndt & Partner
Berlin/Zurich
© the artist 2008, courtesy Private
Collection, Netherlands
Photo: Bernd Borchardt, Berlin

p. 127
Nedko Solakov
Toilettes, 2006, detail, from *Broken*
Lines/Printemps du septembre
exhibition, Toulouse, France, 2006
Felt-tip pen, handwritten texts
on various surfaces of the toilets
of Les Abattoirs Museum
Courtesy of the artist / Arndt & Partner
Berlin/Zurich
Photo: Nedko Solakov

p. 127
Nedko Solakov
Bad, 2006, detail, from *Homework*
exhibition, Gagosian Gallery Berlin,
Germany (as part of the 4th Berlin
Biennial), 2006
Felt-tip pen, handwritten texts
on various surfaces
Courtesy of the artist / Arndt & Partner
Berlin/Zurich
Photo: Nedko Solakov

p. 137
Martin Walde
battle angel, 1995/2007
Rollmeter
Dimensions variable
Courtesy the artist
© Martin Walde
Photo: Martin Walde

p. 139
Martin Walde
There is a door behind the door..., 2006
Storyboard
Courtesy the artist
© Martin Walde